Hill 488

Ray Hildreth
and
Charles W. Sasser

POCKET BOOKS
New York   London   Toronto   Sydney

An *Original* Publication of POCKET BOOKS

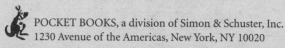 POCKET BOOKS, a division of Simon & Schuster, Inc.
1230 Avenue of the Americas, New York, NY 10020

ISBN 13: 978-0-7434-6643-1
ISBN 10:   0-7434-6643-8

First Pocket Books printing October 2003

10   9   8

POCKET and colophon are registered trademarks of
Simon & Schuster, Inc.

Front cover photo by Robert Ellison, "Under Fire—Images from
Vietnam" *www.pieceuniquegallery.com*; back cover photo
courtesy of the author

Manufactured in the United States of America

For information regarding special discounts for bulk purchases,
please contact Simon & Schuster Special Sales at 1-800-456-6798
or business@simonandschuster.com.

This book is dedicated to the brave men
of Hill 488, and to all the other men
who have fought for their own hills.

CHARLES W. SASSER

This book is dedicated to the memories of my
fallen comrades in arms. Also, my thanks to
Mike Von Merveldt for planting the seed
that eventually grew into this book.

RAY HILDRETH

My Soul, there is a country
Far beyond the stars,
Where stands a winged sentry
All skillful in the wars.

HENRY VAUGHAN

Authors' Note

This is a personal narrative of the events leading up to and occurring during the time period 13–16 June 1966 on Hill 488 in South Vietnam during the war. Actual names are used throughout the book except in those instances where names could not be recalled or where public identification would serve no useful purpose. Dialogue and scenes have by necessity been re-created in various instances. Where this occurs, we have tried to match personalities with the situation and action while maintaining factual content. The recounting of some events may not correspond precisely with the memories of all individuals concerned. (For example, there are large discrepancies in time periods, even among official records. Times used in this book are what most of those on the hill recall.)

Much time has passed since the events in this book occurred. Time has a tendency to erode memory in some areas and selectively enhance it in others. People may see the same events from different perspectives. Where errors in recollection occur, the authors accept full responsibility and ask to be forgiven.

The authors also apologize to anyone who may have been omitted, neglected, or slighted in the preparation of this book. While some interpretational mistakes are bound to have occurred, we are certain that the content of this book is true to the reality, spirit, and incredible courage of the brave men who fought and died on Nui Vu Hill that terrifying night of 15–16 June 1966, Republic of South Vietnam.

Introduction

In the East Room of the White House on 21 August 1967, Gunnery Sergeant Jimmie Earl Howard stood proudly at attention while President Lyndon B. Johnson placed the blue-starred Congressional Medal of Honor around his neck. He was the sixth U.S. Marine to win the nation's highest award for valor during the Vietnam war.

President Johnson praised Howard as a "professional Marine" who was typical of the men who "endure the savage heat of battle abroad so that their countrymen may walk in peace here at home."

With tears in his eyes, the grizzled Marine with short-cropped, prematurely graying hair stepped to the microphone to accept the honor and to give credit to the fifteen Marines and two Navy corpsmen who, with him, defended Hill 488 against an estimated 400 to 450 well-disciplined North Vietnamese Army regulars and Viet Cong Main Force guerrillas throughout a terror-filled night in June 1966. He began to speak in a hesitant voice.

"I don't know how to speak, gentlemen," he said, "but I want to say in all sincerity . . ." His voice wavered and broke. He finally waved a hand at the survivors of that unbelievable night of horror and courage who were all present for the ceremony. ". . . That's the guys who did it right there."

The medal belonged as much to them, he said, as to himself. He took the President by the hand and personally introduced him to each man who lived through that most improbable battle of modern warfare.

The defense of Hill 488, also called Nui Vu Hill, was certainly about individual courage. Men like Howard endured the bitter winter at Valley Forge, stormed the Normandy beaches, fought alongside John F. Kennedy in the Pacific. They faced aggression on the frozen hills of Korea and manned lonely fire bases in Vietnam.

But Hill 488 was also something more than individual courage. If the action had centered around only the one man, it might have been considered a unique incident of exceptional bravery by an exceptional man. As it turned out, however, *Uncommon Valor Was a Common Virtue* that surmounted the courage of any single individual. That phrase is inscribed on the U.S. Marine Corps War Memorial in Arlington, Virginia, spoken by Admiral Chester Nimitz to describe the heroism of those who fought on Iwo Jima during World War II. It is a maxim that certainly applies to the members of Howard's platoon.

First Platoon of Charlie Company, First Reconnaissance Battalion, First Marine Division, became the most highly decorated unit of its size in the entire history of the United States military. Decorations included: the Medal of Honor; four Navy Crosses, the nation's second highest award for valor; thirteen Silver Stars, the third highest valor awards; and eighteen Purple Hearts. Every man on the hill was either killed or wounded.

Few would have noticed anything unique or particularly special about First Platoon before the night of 15–16 June 1966. The men of the platoon were a sampling from places all over the nation—New York, California, Tennessee, New Mexico, Kansas, Texas, Oklahoma. . . . Even though they had been selected and trained for reconnaissance and four were trained snipers, they were in most respects typical American young men, most of whom were recently still in high school. They were an average lot, country and city boys, who underwent the seemingly magical training process by which green recruits become United States Marines.

Perhaps this training was their great strength. It allowed them to rise above normal expectations to fight one of the truly great stands in all of history. As one Marine officer stated after studying the After Action reports, "This was an Alamo—with survivors."

Those who survived—those few, those brave, those Marines—owe it to both individual and group courage. Those who lived and those who died were true American heroes. This is the story of the exceptional men who made their valiant stand on the Hill, recorded so history may never forget that such Americans exist.

Charles W. Sasser

Foreword

When many Americans think about Vietnam, visions of negative headlines such as "My Lai Massacre," "Pot Smoking Marines," "Baby Killers," "War Protests," "AWOL Soldier Seeks Sanctuary," and "Draft Dodgers" come to their minds. I would like for these people to realize that many Vietnam veterans never used illegal drugs and did not intentionally kill innocent civilians.

Most of us who served in Vietnam prior to 1968, in my opinion, went there with a different attitude. We never questioned whether, morally or politically, we should have been in Vietnam. We never talked about it. We were told and believed that we were helping a country to stave off communism and upholding the ideals of our way of life and government. What we wondered about most was why we (the American fighting men) were not allowed to conduct the type of campaigns that would ultimately win the war. Maybe, in retrospect, we should not have been involved in the Vietnam conflict, but those of us who served there did not have the luxury of that choice. We were there as representatives of the people of the United States of America, sent by our elected officials of the United States government to uphold American ideology and we certainly did not deserve the type of treatment and negligence that we received upon our return.

I think that many Americans, now, recognize that the Vietnam veteran made sacrifices on their behalf and more often I hear sincere words of "Thank you." Others, it seems, do not know how to express themselves or do not want to admit their part in this tragedy, so they just "sweep it under the carpet."

In the Marine Corps, we have a saying, "Semper fi," from the Latin words *Semper Fideles*, which mean "always faithful." I would liken this saying to most Vietnam veterans who were honoring their oath of allegiance, to be faithful, to the United States of America.

Ray Hildreth

Preface

If you were in the common crotch, a grunt U.S. Marine, you went where you were told, did what you were told, and tried in the process to keep your butt from getting shot off. The brass back at Division or somewhere higher up moved your colored pin from place to place on the map and you simply followed it. You rarely saw the "Big Picture." What you saw of the war was what there was of it in your immediate vicinity.

Right now, what we saw of it—PFC James McKinney and I, Lance Corporal Raymond Hildreth—wasn't much. What we saw of anything wasn't much. McKinney and I hunkered shoulder to shoulder on the eastern slope of Hill 488. It was so dark that if I scratched my nuts I had to ask James if they were mine or his I was scratching. Vietnam defined the word *dark*.

Breezes rustled surreptitiously through the wheatlike grass fields that covered the hill, making little whispering sighs like predators passing in the night.

"Daylight belongs to us," Lance Corporal Osorio explained when I first arrived in-country. "The dark belongs to *them*."

As far as McKinney and I were concerned, we could have

been on another planet twenty-five *million* miles away from Chu Lai instead of a mere twenty-five. Darkness hid danger while at the same time providing a false security that it also hid you *from* danger.

"Ray?" McKinney whispered, nudging me.

"Yeah. I'm awake." Sergeant Howard had placed the platoon on fifty percent alert at dusk, which meant one of us could sleep.

"Reckon there's still a world out there?"

McKinney was a bit of a pessimist.

"The world is what you can see, James."

"It's a small world, Ray. I can't even see my feet."

He edged closer. Our knees touched. Touching another human being provided a great deal of comfort when you were two nineteen-year-olds in the dark a long way from home and surrounded by people who wanted to kill you. We talked for a while, whispering about home and family and girls and cars. After awhile, McKinney pulled a poncho over his head so the glow wouldn't be seen while he smoked a cigarette. He yawned and nestled down under his poncho, saying he was going to catch a few Z's.

"Wake me in a couple of hours and I'll let you grab some rack time," he said.

He was soon breathing deep and regular. I repositioned my M-14 across my legs. Corporal Jerald Thompson, Squad Leader, slipped down the hillside and dropped on one knee next to us. We were about twenty meters off the crest of the hill where Sergeant Howard had established his command post behind a boulder about the size of a VW with the top chopped off. The rest of the platoon, also in pairs, formed a three-sixty degree perimeter around the top of the hill.

Thompson hissed, "You guys awake?"

"Yeah," I said.

McKinney stirred and leaned against me in his sleep, like a little brother. It had been a long day.

"Sergeant Howard has put us on one hundred percent alert. Hildreth, move over to your right about twenty meters."

"What's up?" Something cold and slimy stirred inside my guts.

"There's been lots of movement," Thompson whispered. "One of the other Recons had to be pulled out. If we have to bug out, Hildreth, you're point man. Lead us down that draw in front and then around to the right. Got it?"

"Yeah."

He followed to check my new position. I settled down in the tall grass with my rifle, pack and ammo belt.

"Remember to fire underneath the muzzle flashes," he said before he moved on to pass the word.

A shiver skittered up my spine and prickled the short hairs on my neck. Folks back in Oklahoma said you got a shiver like that whenever someone walked over your future grave.

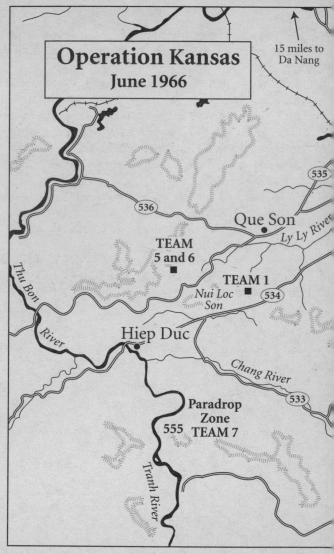

Team 2, Sergeant Howard's recon team, was inserted on Nui Vu Hill on 13 June at the beginning of Operation Kansas. This map shows the locations of the other reconnaissance teams of the First Recon

NORTH VIETNAM

Map area

SOUTH VIETNAM

South China Sea

Thang Binh

Truong Giang River

29

TEAM 4

TEAM 3

TEAM 2

1

586

Tam Ky

Tien Phuoc Special Forces Camp

| 0 | | 10 miles |
| 0 | | 10 kilometers |

Battalion and the locations of their insertions. Sergeant Howard's First Platoon received artillery support from the Tien Phuoc Special Forces camp approximately five miles to the south.

Part I

Accursed be he that first invented war.

MARLOWE

1

My dad was fifty years old and working on his second wife when I was born. I had two brothers and a half-sister, but they were so much older that it was like I was an only child. Mom died when I was fifteen, which left Dad and me bacheloring it together in the rough neighborhoods of North Tulsa, Oklahoma. He was an old man by the time I reached high school. He hadn't the energy to ride herd on a rebellious teenager. I started running with a bad crowd at Rogers High School. Some might have said *I* was the bad crowd. Whichever, the cops picked me up for burglarizing a vending machine two months before graduation. That was in March 1965. A couple of other guys and I were popping Laundromat soap boxes and rifling the machines for coins.

I was seventeen and therefore no longer a juvenile, according to Oklahoma law. I went to the big boy's jail at the County Courthouse downtown. Talk about a hollow feeling when that steel door clanged behind my punk ass. I shook all over. It reminded me that I wasn't that stud I thought I was.

Dad left me behind bars for four days to think things over before he showed up to get me out. I did a lot of thinking too. Here I was four months from being out on my own, from being an independent adult, and I was already on my way to prison.

"You're heading down a bad road, son," he said.

"Yes, sir."

"So what are you going to do about it?"

"Go in the Marines—if they'll still have me."

Like I said, I had been doing a lot of thinking. I had wanted to be a Marine as far back as I could recall. My infatuation with the Marine Corps began after I watched an old Wallace Beery movie set during World War II. Marines were the fightingest, baddest warriors on land or sea anywhere in the world. It took a *real man* to wear the Marine Corps uniform.

"What are you going to do when you get out of school?" friends asked.

"Join the Marine Corps," I automatically responded.

Well, it was time to put up or shut up. Dad nodded in that slow way of his. The Marines were honest and honorable, and they knew how to jerk the kink out of a bad boy's tail.

"Dad?"

Dad walked away. He left me in jail one more day just for good measure. My half-brother Homer, a retired Tulsa police detective, talked him into getting me out. By the time he made my bail, I could hardly wait to run down to the nearest recruiting station. I had embarrassed my dad and embarrassed myself, but surely I could redeem myself in the Marines.

I received a deferred sentence and probation on the condition that I enlist in the Marines, if they would have me. I signed up on the delayed entry program along with a couple of high school buddies, Gary Montouri and Stephen Barnhart, which meant we were allowed to graduate from high school before shipping out to boot camp. That day I raised my hand and swore loyalty and obedience to God, country, and the Marine Corps, not necessarily in that order, and promised to rain fire and brimstone upon all enemies happened to be only two weeks after the buildup of troops began in Vietnam with the landing of the Ninth Marine Expeditionary Brigade at Da Nang on 9 March 1965.

Still, at that time, Vietnam was little more than a once-a-week footnote on *NBC News.* Vietnam was a long way off. Most people, including me, couldn't have picked it out on a map. I was little aware of how the situation was rapidly eroding and becoming a *real* war.

Things changed even more from March to July, the month I actually packed my bags and left for Oklahoma City to catch my first airplane ride to the United States Marine Corps Recruit Training Depot in San Diego, California. Viet Cong sappers crept onto the air base at Da Nang and destroyed three aircraft and wounded three Marines. Three Marines were killed and four wounded in a firefight at Duong Son. Lieutenant Frank S. Reasoner became the first Marine in South Vietnam to win the Congressional Medal of Honor, posthumously.

Walter Cronkite, "the most trusted man in America," was now talking about the war every night on the news. Friends asked me if I weren't afraid of going. Nah. There were already enough Marines in Vietnam to handle the job without adding me to the number. I could wear the good-looking uniform and have the name without the game. Besides, when you were a strapping eighteen-year-old kid a couple of inches under six feet tall and full of yourself, you thought you were going to live forever.

What I couldn't know at the time was that 1965, the year I completed Marine Corps training, would be a year of bloody fighting in the highlands between Chu Lai and Ban Me Thout—and that I would be personally involved in the strategy of attrition announced by General William Westmoreland, Commander, U.S. Military Assistance Command,

Vietnam (MACV). That strategy, simply put, stated that we would kill more of them than they killed of us.

"We'll just go on bleeding them until Hanoi wakes up to the fact that they have bled their country to the point of national disaster for generations," he said.

That was the beginning of the practice of counting dead bodies, the all-important "body count," to keep track of how well we were doing.

My half-brother Homer saw it coming. He was a lot older than me, and a veteran of World War II as well as a retired cop. He came back from the war as a colonel with a chest full of medals.

"Don't try to be a hero," he counseled when I came home for boot camp leave. "Don't take any chances. Don't think. Act on your instincts. Expect the unexpected and always be on the alert."

It didn't take a rocket scientist to understand that the aim of Marine Corps boot camp was to emotionally strip us of our individualities and mold us back into a single functioning combat unit. A mean, lean, green fighting machine. Generations of scraggly, undisciplined youth from across the country had undergone that traumatic metamorphosis from civilian to warrior the Marine way. It started the moment the bus from the airport pulled into the Receiving Depot in San Diego and that hard hunk of mean in the drill instructor hat let you know immediately who was in charge and that you had better jump through your ass to please him.

"All right, ladies," he growled in a way that you *knew* his bite was worse than his bark. "You puke maggot pussies shut your meat traps and listen. Get off my bus and get off it now. You got five seconds, or your ass is mine."

I was off in three flat.

"That was slow, that was sloppy, your breath stinks, and you don't love Jesus. You goofy-looking maggots are gonna have to do better than that. Get with the program, pussies. Get on those yellow footsteps. Don't speak unless you're spoken to. The first word out of your mouth is 'sir,' and the last word out of your mouth is 'sir.' Is that understood, ladies?"

It was a clusterfuck of responses. The DI liaison went bugfuck, red in the face. "*What?*"

I had never heard someone so proficient in the art of profanity.

"What part of that didn't you cunts understand? Let's hear it again, the right way. Is that understood, ladies?"

"Sir, yes, sir." More or less in unison.

"I can't hear you . . ."

Bellowing it out. "Sir, yes, sir!"

"You fucking dickheads will *never* be Marines."

I was in total shock for the first five days. Scared to hell. Every DI—you called them *drill instructors* to their faces, as they said DI stood for *damned idiot,* which they weren't— looked capable of taking on Man Mountain Dean and whipping his ass in the ring. I didn't sleep at all the first night. DI's yelled at us constantly. They expected us to obey and react instantly.

"You pussies gonna sleep all day?" It was still the middle of the night. "Get your asses out of them fart sacks . . ."

"You're getting your haircuts. Don't speak. If you got a mole or something, point to it, but keep your mouths shut . . ."

"Boot! What was that? Were you talking about my mother? I love my mother. Get down. *Get down!* Give me twenty pushups and every time your chest hits the ground I want to hear it . . ."

First, they tore you down. Then they built you back up. The Marine way.

All through basic training, DI's underplayed and understated the actual war element of the drills while stressing the mechanics of it. For all that Vietnam loomed over our shaved heads like a prophetic specter, for all that our eyes popped suddenly open at night looking into the ghost world of times to come, none of us actually *believed* we would go.

One afternoon on the firing range, a DI brought in a photo clipping from a newspaper. It showed a dead U.S. Marine lying on his back clutching a bloodstained bayonet across his chest. The picture made its silent way through the ranks. Everyone stared at it and swallowed. This dead guy wasn't much older than any of us, if at all. The war that seemed so far away suddenly became a lot closer. Something queasy stirred in the pit of my stomach, seriously disturbing my sense of immortality.

"If you guys don't pay attention in boot camp," the DI said, "this guy could be any of you."

I paid attention, but I paid *more* attention after that. My forte was the ability to shoot a rifle. I had been on the rifle team at Rogers High School. The recruit who fired the highest score received an automatic promotion to PFC, private first class. I fired expert, a 224, but I missed getting the promotion by one point. The score was high enough, however, as I found out later, to qualify me to attend Marine sniper school.

After twelve weeks of basic, Recruit Training Platoon 345 graduated fit, tanned, tough, and full of ourselves. Automatically, we were no longer "boots," "shitheads," "maggots," or "pussies."

"Today, you are *United States Marines*."

Jesus, I stood tall, addressed like that for the first time. *Semper fi* and all that. Hey, I could eat the enemy for breakfast and still devour a platter of eggs, bacon, and SOS prepared by other by-God *United States Marines*. Dad was going to be proud of me. I looked forward to going on boot leave and strutting my stuff around Rogers High in my uniform. Watch out, girls.

The commander summoned a formation to read off our next duty assignments. He called us off alphabetically, followed by the duty station. I couldn't help noticing that about every other man was being sent to the Third Marine Replacement Company. *Replacement* for whom?

The alphabet reached me. "Hildreth, Raymond Stanley: Third Replacement."

Afterward, the commander explained. "For those of you assigned to the Replacement Company, that's a stop-off point in Okinawa. Congratulations. It means you're going to Vietnam."

2

Vietnam? The war no longer seemed quite so unreal. Still, when you were eighteen years old, about the only reference point you could hang *war* on was *Sands of Iwo Jima* or *To Hell and Back.* The substance of war was a slippery concept to grasp. I thought about it and understood the words, but the reality occupied a much more incomprehensible elevation. After all, this time last year I was going to high school football games at Skelly Stadium and chasing cheerleaders on the Restless Ribbon.

The concept continued to become more tangible, however. Following ITR, Infantry Training Regiment, a kind of advanced boot camp, and a thirty-day leave, those of us with pending orders to the Third Replacement Company were assigned to Camp Pendleton's Staging Battalion. Staging, as in *staging for war.*

A full Vietnamese village, complete with thatched-roof mud huts, pig pens, bamboo fences, and narrow booby-trapped trails through jungle growth expelled any lingering doubts I might have harbored about my not being needed personally for the war effort. For a week we trained hard in jungle warfare, booby traps, small unit actions, escape and evasion, survival, and underwent orientation about the country and the people and why the United States was involved.

I learned to respect and fear the enemy before I ever saw him. The Viet Cong, or VC, we were assured, were formidable infantry opponents. Vietnam bred fighters, women and children as well as men. After all, generations of Vietnamese had cut their first teeth on war. Fathers, uncles, older brothers, grandfathers, and great grandfathers, had fought the Japanese, the French, Saigon's troops, and now the Americans. For a thousand years before that, they had fought the Chinese, Cambodians, Thais, and anyone else who attempted to invade their rich lands. Generations past remembered little but wars interspersed with brief periods of peace.

Small kids started out in on-the-job war training by spying on the enemy, carrying supplies, setting out booby traps, caring for the wounded, and burying the dead. Older brothers and sisters barely into their teens were trained in the basic skills of guerrilla warfare. They joined the local guerrilla units to protect the home turf and assist any Main Force VC working the area. When they were older, they became replacements for the Main Force.

Everybody was potentially the enemy. The pretty girl waving from the side of the road might shoot you in the back of the head if she got the chance, or detonate a mine to blow up a dozen Marines. The old *papasan* tilling his field often went out nights to set booby traps. Kids begging for "chop-chop" or offering to sell "boom-boom" with their sisters or mothers acted as scouts and sometimes tossed grenades into a truck full of Americans. Lesson being: Trust no one.

The VC had no scruples. There was no such thing in Vietnam as the Geneva convention. A favorite VC trick was to open fire at a U.S. unit from a village in order to get the Americans to fire back and kill civilians. It was an effective way to build animosity against the Americans and convert even more VC. When such forms of persuasion failed, the communists were not above using terror, torturing and executing those villagers who refused to cooperate. And heaven help any Marine captured by the VC. His death would be prolonged and tormented.

"We've recovered bodies where all the skin has been ripped off," an instructor said.

Jesus! What kind of monsters were they?

The VC Main Force units were the biggest concern. They were organized and trained by either Chinese "advisors" or instructors from the North Vietnamese Army. They were also as well equipped as the NVA, with AK assault rifles, RPDs, 50-caliber and BAR machine guns, rocket-propelled grenades (RPGs), recoilless rifles, grenades, and mortars.

Because of superior American firepower, airborne surveillance capabilities and helicopter mobility, the enemy operated primarily at night, under cover of darkness. His favorite tactic was to attack U.S. units with lightninglike infantry assault supported by rockets and mortar barrages, then shag into hiding once the sun rose.

"Men," the instructors said, "this is a guerrilla war unlike any the United States has ever been engaged in. We have to be as tough, as smart, and as ruthless as our enemy in order to survive and conquer."

War moved a little closer when we shipped out to Okinawa to attach ourselves to the Third Replacement Company and await further transfer to the war zone. I felt a sense of anticipation at embarking upon some great adventure. At the same time, a gnawing but ill-defined unease crept into the pit of my stomach.

Since it took time for the Green Machine to ingest, digest, and excrete, we hung around for a couple of weeks doing PT, some training, and pulling a lot of shit details. There was another Marine outfit awaiting transportation to Vietnam. I watched it with awe and some envy. No shit details for these guys. Marine Reconnaissance consisted of young, tough, bronzed warriors with an attitude. A gung ho bunch of killers. Hoo-ya! And all that. They were always out running and training. They seemed eager to get into combat.

> *Everywhere we go-o . . .*
> *People want to know-o . . .*
> *Who we are-r . . .*
> *So we tell them*
> *We are Recon*
> *Mighty, mighty Recon.*

One morning after we replacements completed the daily dozens and a two-mile run, a sergeant came down and read a bulletin to the formation. Volunteers were needed to attend a newly formed sniper school. Applicants must have fired expert on the rifle range and would be required to first pass the Marine Reconnaissance Indoctrination Program. Upon completion of the sniper course, all shooters would be assigned to Marine Recon. Hoo-ya. Those guys.

I hardly thought about it. My hand seemed to fly up on its own. Something romantic about the idea of sniping attracted me. Plus, I could *shoot* a rifle. It also meant a delay in my going to Vietnam.

Don't be a hero. Homer had warned me.

3

In combat, the aim was to survive and to kill before you were killed. The weapon most dreaded on any battlefield was the lone sharpshooter, whose single rifle crack almost invariably meant death for the enemy. As U.S. Marine Corps General George O. Van Orden wrote in 1940: "(The sniper) is the gadfly of a great war. He must harass the foe. . . . He must hammer relentlessly upon the nerves of the rank and file of the opposing forces until his rifle crack, joining with others of his kind, becomes a menace more to be feared than the shrieking shells from cannon or the explosive hail from the mortars. His bullets must come from *nowhere. . . .*"

A look at statistics showed that it was damned hard to kill an enemy soldier on the battlefield. During WWII, Allies fired an average of 25,000 bullets for each enemy soldier they killed. The ratio of bullets to KIA (killed in action) kept climbing. UN troops in Korea expended 50,000 rounds for every dead enemy. That ratio in Vietnam was approaching 200,000 rounds for every body count.

Machine gunners, artillery, and aircraft killed VC, but the cost was something like $4,000 for every kill. It cost Uncle Sam's snipers twenty-seven cents, the price of an

M-14 round, to zero out one. As snipers became more common in Vietnam, they were using an average of 1.3 rounds per kill. Say, thirty cents average for a VC death. It was called cost efficiency.

Vietnam, with its lack of combat lines, its fluid battlefields, and an enemy that often operated singly or in small units, presented itself as the ideal setting for classic sniper warfare. However, sniping, for all its effectiveness, had always been looked upon as somehow underhanded and unfair. Although the United States had used snipers in all its wars dating back to its Revolutionary War and before, it quickly ridded itself of any sniper programs at the end of each conflict. As a result, there were few trained snipers at the beginning of the Vietnam involvement.

The VC soldier considered himself relatively safe at 600 yards or more. There were instances of VC walking in plain sight at distances of 700 to 1,000 yards while they directed mortar fire on American positions. In the jungles and hamlets of the countryside, communists felt free to move about at will, confident they could spot U.S. patrols first and either avoid them or lure them into ambushes for their own marksmen.

So desperate was the need for qualified U.S. snipers to counteract the enemy in this new kind of war that when the Marines became the first U.S. forces in Vietnam to establish authentic sniper schools in midwinter 1965, sniper classes were only three days long. With time, however, these "shooting classes" would become true schools teaching not only marksmanship but also stalking, land navigation, hides, shooting influences, and the other skills of the sniper's trade.

In 1966, about the time I reached Okinawa to report to the Third Marine Replacement Company, Major General Herman Nickerson Jr., who would assume command of the First Marine Division in October, was already thinking about snipers. He found the perfect man to form and train them in Captain Jim Land, who at that time commanded the Third Force Service Regiment Ordnance Company in Okinawa. Captain Land was already influential in training snipers for Vietnam when I arrived there.

As General Nickerson would say to him later that year, "Captain Land, I have an assignment for you. I want you to organize a sniper unit within the First Division. Captain Bob Russell in the Third Division started training snipers last year. I want *mine* to be the best in the Marine Corps. I want them killing VC, and I don't care how they do it...."

Land had been studying and teaching the lost art and science of the sniper's craft since 1959. A marksman himself, he held Distinguished Division medals and had been captain of the Pacific Division shoot team. He and Sergeant Carlos Hathcock, who later in Vietnam became the most successful sniper in American history, shot together for the Marine Corps team at the National Matches at Camp Perry. Hathcock went on to win the 1965 Wimbledon Cup for the best long-range rifle shot.

Of course, being eighteen years old and a green boot, I knew little about the background of this new and deadly trade for which I had volunteered. Nor did I know that the two-week sniper course put on in Okinawa by, I assumed, Land's Ordnance Company was only one of a number of such programs cropping up both in Vietnam and in rear areas. Trained as riflemen, scouts, and hunters, snipers were beginning to blanket themselves across Vietnam.

But first I had to complete RIP, the Recon Indoctrination Program. I was in good shape, and I was gung ho. It was more of the same from basic training, ITR, and the Staging Battalion. Swimming in and out of the surf on beach reconnaissance, boat training, jungle patrols, immediate action drills, land navigation, ambushes... I was Common Grunt in the process of becoming *Super* Grunt.

In RIP, five of us began hanging together, became tight.

Private First Class B.E. Moore was a skinny bullshit artist from Texas, with dark hair cut high 'n tight, like the rest of us, and a rather large nose.

"We are going to kick some Vietnamese ass and come back with a whole pot full of medals," he vowed.

"Maybe so," PFC Bill Norman acquiesced, "but for one I intend to watch my own ass and stay out of trouble when I can."

"That makes two of us," I seconded. "You cover mine and I'll cover yours."

Norman and I had got acquainted one evening in the barracks while I was bent over a chess board strategizing against another Recon trainee. Norman stopped to watch.

"You're not bad, Hildreth," he said. "I'm taking a portable set with me. We can play on the boat when we ship over."

"Sounds great."

Norman was about my height, five-ten or so, slender with light brown hair burred short. He was born in Illinois but had moved out to Arizona where he grew up steeped in the Old West of Zane Grey. He even walked with the easy swaggering gait of a cowboy.

The fourth member of the tight little group was PFC Joseph Kosoglow, a Yankee from Pennsylvania with dark brown hair and a bit more nose than even Moore. He liked to laugh. He laughed loudly and often through a nasal eastern accent. Moore joked that everybody ought to own a Yankee.

Then there was PFC James McKinney, a quiet Cajun boy from Louisiana with a southern bayou accent and the perpetually surprised air of someone who hadn't been long out of the swamps. McKinney became our tag-along, treated as kind of a kid brother by the rest of us. He was skinny, dark-tanned, and more than a bit of a pessimist. He amazed and pleased us all when he made it through RIP. The kid had a tough inner core.

Together, we were cookie cutouts off a Marine recruiting poster—lean, a bit taller than the average kid off the block, more aggressive than the ordinary Joe. We were, after all, *Marine Recon.*

McKinney went straight to the First Reconnaissance Battalion and prepared to ship to Vietnam while the other four of us in the group reported for sniper training.

"Nothing strikes terror into the enemy and demoralizes him like an unexpected bullet that can come with deadly accuracy from nowhere, at any time," instructors drilled into us. "There'll be two of you on each sniper team. You'll go out into enemy country for four or five days at a time where you'll hunt targets of opportunity and waste them."

McKinney licked his lips and looked anxious when he learned how we would be working. "Jeez! Just *two* of you?"

I had to admit it also seemed rather daunting to me.

"Out there by yourselves? What if you get in trouble?"

Kosoglow brushed it off. "We just won't get in trouble."

McKinney still looked anxious.

The sniper school was still in its infancy, an ad hoc affair at best. More of a "shooting school" than the true sniper training it would later become under Captain Land and Sergeant Hathcock. The 7.62mm M-14 main battle rifle with which we trained didn't even have a scope, although we were promised 30.06 Remington Model 70s upon completion of the course.

Each day, it was the same routine. Stalking and shooting at ranges of up to one thousand yards. At the end of two weeks, we were fine marksmen, no doubt, but in reality nothing more than super grunts modified by a few additional shooting skills. The promised Model 70s failed to materialize. So did the Winchester Model 40s that were supposed to be a substitute. Instead, we ended up being issued M-1D Garand rifles left over from World War II, each equipped with an inexpensive 2X scope likely lifted off a commercial shelf. We got them on the last day of sniper training. We sighted them in, fired for familiarization, and cleaned them just in time to clamber aboard ship with the First Reconnaissance Battalion replacements to ship out for Vietnam.

4

U.S.S. *Whitfield County,* a World War II LST (landing ship, tank) that doubled as a troop transport, left Okinawa on 20 March 1966 packed with young fodder bound for the killing fields of Vietnam. Our destination, I learned, was a place called Chu Lai in I Corps where we would link up with the rest of the First Marine Division. From the time I enlisted a year ago until now, Vietnam had gone from a footnote to a steady Walter Cronkite dinner fare of body bags and firefights on TV sets across the U.S. of A. America went to war big-time—and was taking me with her.

Vietnam did not begin like World War II with a Pearl Harbor or like Korea with a communist invasion. The United States slipped gradually into war through the thin crust of quicksand, one step at a time. Successive presidents beginning with Harry Truman believed communists were trying to take over the globe domino-style. China went communist in 1949. Communist revolts rocked Malaya and the Philippines during the 1940s and 1950s. North Korea invaded noncommunist South Korea in 1950.

The Viet Minh, backed by North Vietnam and the international communist movement, defeated French colonial forces at Dien Bien Phu in 1954. U.S. Marines became involved in the war soon thereafter, in 1955, by aiding in the evacuation of 300,000 refugees from North Vietnam. Like Truman, President Dwight D. Eisenhower believed it was America's duty to stop the dominoes from falling. Vietnam was the mountain he and the next three Presidents—Kennedy, Johnson, and Nixon—chose to defend.

By 1956, U.S. Marine drill instructors were training South Vietnamese recruits. U.S. Army Special Forces were "advising" Viet units. Navy SEALs arrived in-country in 1962. The war's first real impact on America, however, came with the landing of the Ninth Marine Expeditionary Brigade at Da Nang in March 1965. Two battalions of Marines, about 3,500 men, began serving as security troops for the Da Nang air base. Secretary of State Dean Rusk said the Marines would shoot back if fired upon. Although the Gulf of Tonkin Resolution of August 1964 gave President Johnson full authority to repel attacks against U.S. forces, this was the first time ground forces in Vietnam were openly authorized to engage the enemy.

When Marines landed at Da Nang, a single 3,000-yard runway on the golden beaches of the South China Sea cut between bunkers left by the Japanese in 1945 and old blockhouses abandoned by the French. The adjoining city of Da Nang was Vietnam's second largest city and boasted a population of 200,000, including refugees. It was one of the few secure areas in the north of South Vietnam. The land out in the countryside belonged to the Viet Cong. ARVN troops—Army of the Republic of Vietnam—rarely ventured outside a few outpost garrisons of bamboo stakes and mud walls.

At first, Marines stuck to patrolling the air base perimeter, only gradually venturing into the highlands west of Da Nang. The first Marines to die were killed there by "friendly fire" when a three-man patrol got lost, separated, and mistakenly fired upon each other. Two were killed.

President Johnson continued a steady commitment of troops. By January 1966, U.S. forces in Vietnam totaled 184,000, of which 38,000 were Marines committed to the northernmost provinces. The American air base at Da Nang was rapidly becoming one of the three busiest airports in the world.

For planning and strategic purposes, South Vietnam was broken down geographically into what were called Corps Tactical Zones. Four of them. I Corps, the northernmost of these, consisted of 10,000 square miles starting in the Annamite Mountains and spreading north to the DMZ with North Vietnam. I Corps, pronounced "eye," was the U.S. Marines' TAOR, tactical area of responsibility.

It was perfect guerrilla country. The enemy infested it like fleas on a stray dog. Rich rice land provided the VC with food. The coastline afforded easy resupply of weapons and war materiel by sea. A dense population allowed the VC in their anonymous black pajamas to "swim like fish among the people," as Mao Tse-Tung put it.

U.S. Marines manned three coastal enclaves in I Corps, for which they were responsible, along with the adjacent TAORs. Da Nang, centrally located in Quang Nam Province, was the largest. The headquarters of III MAF (Marine Amphibious Force), Third Marine Division headquarters, and First Marine Aircraft Wing were all located there. Two regiments—the Third and the Ninth, each consisting of three maneuver battalions—operated out of Da Nang, supported by the artillery of the Twelfth Marines.

Ten kilometers south of the ancient city of Hue lay the smallest Marine enclave at Phu Bai in Thua Thien Province. Small units of Marines were stationed there primarily as security for the small air base.

The third enclave at Chu Lai near Hoi An came into existence on 7 May 1965 when the Third Marine Amphibious Regiment came ashore on a barren beach seventy kilome-

ters south of Da Nang to secure it for the construction of a
new airbase to relieve the growing congestion at Da Nang.
The base was named after a Marine general named Krulak,
Chu Lai being his name in Chinese characters. The airfield
went into operation on 1 June 1965 with the arrival of four
A-4 Skyhawks from Cubi Point in the Philippines. By January 1966, two battalions of the First Marine Division were
committed to Chu Lai. Two regiments of the First—the
Fourth and the Seventh—arrived shortly thereafter, with
supporting artillery.

The division was responsible for the two southernmost
provinces of I Corps, Quang Tin and Quang Ngai, a TAOR
that covered more than 300 square kilometers with a
known population of 100,000 people. What was unknown
was how much the population was expanded by enemy soldiers. American and ARVN troops at Da Nang and Chu Lai
actually controlled only their own base area and the nearby
cities. Outside these areas, small outpost district headquarters existed in a hostile sea of VC and NVA forces.

In late 1965, VC overran the small ARVN garrison hold-
ing Hiep Duc in Quang Tin Province. Hiep Duc, located
at the western end of the Hiep Duc Valley (also known as
the Que Son Valley), was the district capital and one of
the most strategic areas between Da Nang and Chu Lai.
General Lewis W. Walt, commander of III MAF (Third
Marine Amphibious Force), launched Operation *Harvest
Moon*. Skirmishes in the valley throughout November and
December claimed 45 Marines killed and 218 wounded.
First Lieutenant Harvey C. Barnum received a Medal of
Honor for exceptional courage at Ky Phu.

Marines undertook a near-constant pattern of patrolling
the Hiep Duc Valley in advance of search-and-destroy operations. During the first three months of 1966, Marines
conducted a number of operations in the TAOR. Operations *Double Eagle I* and *Double Eagle II* resulted in

24 Marines killed and 156 wounded. Seventeen were killed and 120 wounded in the Da Nang TAOR. Another seventeen were killed east of Phu Bai. In early March, only two weeks before U.S.S. *Whitfield County* set sail, Operation *Utah* lost 98 Marines killed and 278 wounded.

The Marines might be kicking ass, but they were also suffering.

The Hiep Duc Valley and the Que Son area would remain bitterly contested throughout the rest of the Vietnam War. I didn't realize it at the time, knowing little of the overall strategy (I was, after all, a low-ranking grunt), but fate was drawing me toward my destination as inexorably as a magnet attracts steel shavings.

What with all the combat training I had undergone, beginning with boot camp and ending with sniper school, it took me nearly a year to get ready to go to Vietnam. It took five days to actually get there from Okinawa. It was hot and miserable below decks of the U.S.S. *Whitfield County*. Hundreds of raw-green leathernecks bound for the First Division crammed ourselves into steamy bays like spoiled sardines in a tin can. We played cards, chess, listened to music on Armed Forces radio—"Help" by the Beatles and "I Can't Help Myself" by the Four Tops—and talked a lot of macho bullshit about Vietnam to hide our true apprehensions.

Several roll calls were held each day to keep track of the troops. I didn't know where the officers expected us to go on a boat that was less than 350 feet long in the middle of the Pacific. Norman managed to get himself into trouble when he curled up in a six-by (two and a half ton truck) to watch a live fire exercise by the ship's big guns and missed roll call. As punishment, he had to scrape paint in the bilges with the swabbies for an afternoon.

An LST was slow, flat-bottomed, ungainly, and rough-riding. Flat cargo decks took up most of the ship from the far-forward superstructure to the fantail. The boats had played major roles in some of the bloodiest battles of the twentieth century. Troops and equipment carried aboard them established beachheads in World War II during the Allied invasions of Sicily, Salerno, and Normandy in Europe; and in the Philippines, Iwo Jima, and Okinawa in the Pacific theater. Many saw action at Inchon during the Korean War.

The idea for the ships is said to have come from British Prime Minister Winston Churchill after the battle of Dunkirk in 1940, when British troops were forced to leave behind tons of equipment because they had no vessels capable of approaching the shore closely enough to retrieve it. The United States, at the request of the British government, designed a ship—the LST—that could take on water ballast for stability at sea and discharge it to produce a shallow-draft ship capable of a beach landing.

Rumor had it that we on-board Marines bound for Vietnam were going to make a combat beach assault once we reached our destination. In my imagination I saw another Salerno or Iwo Jima with Marines storming ashore under heavy enemy fire. The thought was both exciting and scary.

Because of the sweltering below-decks heat, some of us escaped by sleeping topside on the fantail. I lay sleepless under the Pacific stars with the ship's wake making a silver path in the moonlight, my throat raw from the diesel stench, and counted off the days until we reached Vietnam. McKinney and Kosoglow curled up on their ponchos nearby.

"Ray?" McKinney said. "What do you reckon it's gonna be like?"

The Cajun accent sounded strained, uncertain, the way I sometimes felt but would never admit to. McKinney was more open, more revealing.

"I don't know," I admitted.

"Are you afraid, Ray?"

I didn't answer him.

"I am," he said. "Sometimes. Jeez . . ."

On the fifth afternoon, shouts started at the bow of the ship and echoed all the way to the stern and below decks.

"Vietnam! I can see Vietnam!"

Eager, excited, scared shitless, we scrambled to catch a first glimpse of this dreadful land about which we had heard and thought so much during the past months of training. Moore, Norman, Kosoglow, McKinney, and I crowded the rail and strained to see details. We watched speechless as a finger of shit-brown land on the horizon emerged from the low haze of early afternoon and drew nearer and nearer. Everything we had to say about it had already been said. Now the reality of Vietnam came within view.

The South China Sea appeared oily as it rose and fell without breaking its crest. There was a slight tinge of tan to the blue-green water as the ship neared shore. A dead fish floated next to an abandoned dugout sampan with a hole in it. A sailing junk with a dried blood–colored sail made its way north along the coast. From the land blew a wave of heat saturated with strange odors.

"It smells like human shit," Moore finally decided.

"Vietnam is the asshole of the world," Norman said.

Kosoglow laughed his loud, nasal laugh. "If it's the asshole and we're going there, what does that make us?"

McKinney looked more tense than usual, but tried to hide it.

I thought there should be a musical overscore, "The Shores of Montezuma," some fanfare to welcome the troops. Instead, there was only an eerie hush, broken by someone's portable radio tuned to the Armed Forces station. Playing Nancy Sinatra's "These Boots (Are Made For Walking)."

. . . and they're gonna walk right over you.

Two silver specks high in the distant sky caught my eye. I watched, mesmerized, as they quickly materialized into a pair of Marine A-4 Skyhawk fighter jets. Wasplike, rocket-laden wings catching the glint of the sun. They swept down and roared low overhead, buzzing the ship so that our battle blouse utilities flapped in the jet wash. I felt like cheering.

Somebody was watching over us.

5

U.S.S. *Whitfield County* landed on hostile shores on 25 March 1966. New meat lined the rails as the LST approached the beach as though intent on ramming it. I smelled cooking fires, dead fish, rot, and human shit. Beyond that expanse of shimmering water were the enemy, the gooks, Charlie, Viet Cong, or VC as they were being called. LBJ said they were commies trying to take over the world and needed their asses kicked. The Marines could do some ass kicking.

It was hot. The sun itself was a burden. It sucked moisture out through the pores of my skin until I felt like a fish left to dry on the sand. Hot. My heavy pack rode in a darkness of sweat on my back as we were ordered into full combat gear for the beach assault. Web gear, pouches, full 782 packs, weapons, and ammo. Someone once observed that a Marine was nothing more than a life-support system for his rifle; my M-1D sniper rifle, with scope, was doing fine.

Lieutenants and Captains jumped through their asses. "Ladies, get your fuckin' asses in gear. We are going to war, Marines, not to some old hen's tea party. Make goddamn sure you are locked and loaded when the boat hits the beach and the gate drops. Make goddamn sure."

The decks of the *Whitfield County* came alive with gray-green utility uniforms. They echoed with the clank of rifles and bayonets, E-tools and Ka-bars. Vibrated with the shouts of platoon sergeants and young officers. In the excitement I half expected to be confronted on the beach by masses of enemy soldiers screaming for blood.

"Now hear this . . . Now hear this . . ."

Nothing happened aboard ship unless the PA systems announced it first.

"Hear this . . . Prepare for disembarkation . . ."

Engines drummed in reverse at the last moment, braking the ship's forward movement. It shuddered in the water and its wake washed ashore as noisy waves. I caught a glimpse of the faces of my friends—Norman and Moore, Kosoglow and McKinney. Sweat poured out from under their patrol caps—Recon never wore helmets; we were super troops. I decided they were feeling the same things I was. We were a bit awed by the proposal of combat, but we were also young and somewhat thrilled at the prospect of adventure and a chance to do our duty as by-God Marines.

We had a Noble Cause. Growing up beneath the dark cloud of the Cold War and the threat of communist expansion and the Bomb, we were finally getting a chance to strike back. Travel and adventure. Go to foreign lands, meet new and exciting people—and kill them.

"I thought we were supposed to have artillery or airplanes or something to soften up the beach before we landed," McKinney worried.

Kosoglow scoffed. "We're *Marines*. We don't need that shit."

"Prepare to disembark . . ." the PA roared.

Still no fire from the beach. The gooks must be waiting to open up on us when we stormed onto the sand.

The boat hit with a jolt that jammed us against each other. The bow doors opened and the ramp lowered directly onto the beach. I glimpsed a white-sand strip backed by palm trees and sand dunes. Almost like a postcard from Miami Beach. *Wish you were here . . .*

"Hit the beach! Go, go, go, go, go . . . ! Goddamnit, go!"

Caught up in the excitement, I charged off the ramp. I stopped on the sand, sweating in the oven turned to *Broil,* breathing hard. Puzzled Marines stopped and looked around to catch their bearings. Instead of a fierce enemy with machine guns and mortars, I saw a bunch of six-by trucks parked waiting back of the high tide line. Bored drivers watched with amusement.

"Welcome to Vietnam, jarheads," an officer shouted. "Kill something for God, country, and the U.S. Marine Corps."

It wasn't a combat assault; it was all a training exercise. We had landed on the Marine base itself at Chu Lai. Non-coms began droving us like cattle. "Move it, girls. We don't want the war to be over by the time we get there."

Chu Lai at this point of time was a very young base, nothing like the more orderly garrison it became later with various-sized Quonsets and trailer houses in rows. I hadn't quite known what to expect, so how could I be disappointed? Still, this *slum* of OD-green tents and mountains of *stuff* all jumbled and piled and stacked and transforming the environment almost overwhelmed my senses. Before now, the military had always seemed so *orderly,* so *organized.*

The Chu Lai Subsector Five Defense Area, which included First Recon Battalion's home, stretched along a picturesque beach that had everything except bikinis and wrinkled old tourists in baggy trunks. Wooden hastily constructed watchtowers rose on spindly legs at various points. Back of the beach rose the knotty sand mounds that made up the oceanside country before it merged into the rice fields, jungle, and highlands of the interior. It was a huge base encompassing the airfield. I couldn't see the perimeter. Later, I took a look and discovered to my chagrin that the only thing that kept *us* inside secure against *them* outside was a boundary of sand-bagged bunkers and isolated watch towers. No fences, no moats, no . . . *nothing*. Just fields of fire cleared to prevent the enemy from sneaking up and cutting our throats. How anyone could muster the energy to sneak *anywhere* to cut *anyone's* throat in this heat seemed impossible.

What impressed me most was the activity. Everywhere I looked, bare-chested Marines and Navy Seabees scurried about like army ants reconstructing the landscape. Armored vehicle Amtracs growled around like big steel green dung beetles with bellyaches. Helicopters capered as agile as grasshoppers—wicked-looking UH-1 "Hueys" bristling with rocket pods and machine guns, lumbering Sikorsky H-34 troop transport choppers bringing in troops or taking them out. A-4 Skyhawks shrieked in and out of the landing strip. All for the war effort.

I saw my first Vietnamese. I was amazed that Vietnam civilians, hired labor, worked all over the base and seemed to have free run. I thought you couldn't trust any of them, although these looked innocent enough. Skinny little people, the women hardly more than four-and-a-half feet tall. Even the shortest Marine towered over the tallest Vietnamese man and outweighed him by at least forty or fifty pounds.

"*That's* who we're fighting, these little bitty fuckers!" Moore exclaimed.

"*Mean* little bitty fuckers," Kosoglow amended. He looked around and laughed. "Hey, fellas," he called out to the bored truck drivers. "Which way's the war?"

One of them pointed inland. "It ain't far. It'll find you."

We five friends were separated immediately. Moore and I were assigned to work parties, while Kosoglow, Norman, and McKinney disappeared somewhere into the green machine. For the next week, the skinny Texan with the big nose and I labored like Chinese coolies staking down tents, building outdoor community comfort stations—*shitters*, burning shit from already-established shitters, pulling KP, cleaning stuff, stacking stuff, rearranging stuff, riding shotgun for trucks hauling stuff . . . Settling in.

Moore accepted it more philosophically than I. I chafed at the bit. This was some fucked-up way to fight a war. I was a trained Recon *sniper*, for God's sake, and here I came all this way to burn shit and stack stuff.

Finally, at the end of the week, Battalion Sergeant Major Turner called off our names at morning formation: "Hildreth. Moore. Gather up your shit and report to Charlie Company."

Staggering underneath the weight of seabags, weapons, bedding, and personal gear, Moore and I made our way through the tents and sand knobs to where C Company of the Recon Battalion had its headquarters in a GP-large tent. Field desks, file cabinets, chalk boards, maps, radios, tech manual libraries, and other equipment needed for managing a CP, command post, cluttered the interior of the tent. Maybe World War II Marines traveled on beans and bullets; it seemed the modern Corps traveled on paperwork.

One map was marked all over with different-colored grease pencils, a different color apparently representing particular units or particular activities. I had always heard you never wanted your outfit marked in black, which meant you ceased to exist. That was what I heard.

Next to the map stood a tri-legged chalk board upon which a clerk paper shuffler kept a running body count of both dead enemy troops and dead friendly troops. We were winning the war if the enemy dich board reflected a higher body count than did the friendly column. *Dich* was one of many slang terms applied to the enemy dead.

Charlie Company's commander, Captain Tim Geraghty, was an average-sized, average-looking lifer in his thirties. He greeted Moore and me with, "Welcome aboard, men. We like to think Charlie is the best company in the Recon Battalion."

"Yes, sir."

Moore and I carried our M-1Ds with scopes, which should have clued in the commander that we weren't just ordinary grunts. When he failed to notice, I thought I ought to point it out and establish our status.

"We're snipers, sir."

He looked at us like he didn't know what the hell I was talking about.

"That's good," he said dismissively. "You're assigned to First Platoon. That's Sergeant Jimmie Howard's. It's the first tent on your right as you go out. Do your jobs and we'll get along."

Bewildered by our less-than-stellar reception, Moore and I hefted our gear and lugged it over to the two tents in tandem that quartered the members of First Platoon. According to our sniper instructors on Okinawa, a sniper team of two shooters was supposed to be attached to each platoon. That meant Moore and I must be working with First Platoon. I wondered where Norman and Kosoglow had been assigned. I hoped McKinney ended up in the same outfit with either Norman or me.

Judging from the raucous sounds coming from the front tent, the platoon was at home and engaged in a bout of grabass. Just as we approached, Kosoglow, laughing as always, burst out through the flaps and almost bowled us over. He gave a whoop of surprise.

"You're in First Platoon!" I exclaimed.

"So's Norman."

"*Two* sniper teams in the same platoon?"

Kosoglow shrugged as Norman heard us and came outside. They explained that they had already gone on a mission and had only returned this morning for stand down. Showers and a hot meal. Moore stared at them wide-eyed.

"What was it like?" he asked.

Norman shrugged it off, but Kosoglow assumed the

contrived nonchalance of an old salt. "I saw rougher days on Okinawa during RIP."

"Did you see any gooks? Did you snipe any?" Moore asked.

Norman gave a nervous chuckle that cracked his Arizona cowboy image a bit. "My butt was squeezed around my neck so tight I could hardly breathe," he admitted. "But we didn't see squat."

"If we're snipers," Kosoglow added, "nobody seems to know what to do with us."

That seemed obvious from the fact that four of us were committed to the same platoon.

The two tents together housed about twenty men, depending upon how many were assigned to the platoon at any given time. Five cots lined each side of a walkway of sand and padded earth down the middle of each tent. Next to every cot sat a wooden foot locker, which the occupant of that berth used as a table, nightstand, or whatever else his imagination conjured up. Some men were loudly playing cards on one of the lockers. Others read or came down off the mission with talk. A radio turned to Armed Forces radio played "Eve of Destruction" by Barry McGuire.

In appearance, all these Marines were as similar as cookies off the same sheet. The Marine Corps simply reached out across the United States and pulled people in without the slightest concern for what they were, what they wanted to be, or what they did. Some were brown or blond or black, but all were lean young Americans with the *Semper fi* mentality stamped a little deeper into their souls because they were, by God, *Recon*.

A tall, slender, light-skinned black man with curly, short-cropped hair stood up from his bunk where he was writing a letter. He regarded Moore and me with dark, brooding eyes. I figured him to be a year or so older than me, maybe twenty or so. A lance corporal, he exuded an air of confidence that said he was a take-charge kind of guy without his actually having to say so.

"Who are you guys?" he asked.

"We're your two new snipers," I explained.

"New meat," somebody commented.

"Snipers?" the lance questioned in a chiseled island accent, probably Jamaican. He glanced at our M-1Ds. "You can take those cots here." He indicated three cots that appeared unoccupied.

"Who's the third one for?" Moore asked.

"Marilyn Monroe," the black lance said, and left the tent.

"That's Rick Binns," Kosoglow explained. "He has all his shit in one ditty bag."

That was a supreme compliment.

"You can count on Binns," Norman said.

Moore and I had barely settled in, which primarily entailed emptying the contents of our seabags into foot lockers and tossing our rubber lady air mattresses and sleeping bags on the cots, when the intended occupant of the third empty bunk showed up. McKinney carrying all his gear and weapons stood blinking hesitatingly in the tent entrance, obviously expecting to be greeted by cold strangers. His lean Cajun face broke into a relieved grin when he spotted his old buddies.

"Jeez! I was afraid I'd be over here in this swamp all by my lonesome."

6

If John Wayne wasn't John Wayne, he might have been Staff Sergeant Jimmie Earl Howard. Howard was a John Wayne type of guy, a lean, mean fighting machine. A hard slab of a man with a poker face, hair prematurely graying at age thirty-six, and a direct manner that had got him busted in rank at least twice. He walked into an area and you could almost hear the theme song from *The Sands of Iwo Jima*. You might call some of the other sergeants by their first names, but not him. Sergeant *was* his first name. Binns or one of the other "old-timers" in the platoon occasionally called him "Top Notch," but that was as far as the familiarity went.

Although his reputation preceded him, it failed to do him justice in the flesh. He had already won the Silver Star for valor and three Purple Hearts fighting in the Korean War. He didn't merely enter a place, he took it over, occupied it. The man was an actual *presence*, an imposing, no-nonsense figure, very military, very Marine, very businesslike. At the same time his gruff straightforward manner made officers unsure of themselves look upon him as a rogue or renegade.

He entered the tent by ducking his head and twisting his

shoulders and chest to avoid the top and side flaps. The tent went silent. He was old enough to be father to most every man in the platoon. If Sergeant Howard wasn't *the Word,* he was at least the conveyor of *the Word.*

"All right, lads," he boomed. "Get your swim trunks on."

That was my introduction to the platoon sergeant and, since the outfit was temporarily short an officer, also the acting platoon leader. He was Marine enough to handle both jobs. I stared. The way he entered, I expected enemy at the gates, an attack by the yellow hordes, the end of the world. Instead . . . Get on our *swim trunks?*

Turned out that recreation at the Chu Lai Marine slumville was almost nonexistent aside from movies shown on an outdoor screen in the battalion area. Howard thought swimming in the ocean as a unit, especially after returning from the bush, built esprit de corps, relieved stress, and drained off excess youthful zeal that could get troops in trouble. The outfit that fought together and played together stayed together. Something like that.

The second most respected and mysterious man in the platoon was Lance Corporal Ricardo "Rick" Binns, Second Squad Leader. Although other NCOs in the platoon out-ranked him, Binns assumed the position of second-in-command behind Howard as more or less his natural right. Binns possessed what some people might have called gravitas. He seldom talked about himself and smiled even less. Rumor had it that, of Jamaican ancestry, he came up tough on the mean streets of New York City. He was one of two black men in the platoon, the other being Hawkins, who was a short-timer and about to transfer back to the land of the Big PX. He was light-skinned, indicating some kind of mixture with his African. He never said what and nobody asked, not that it mattered.

Like Howard, Binns took naturally to soldiering and thrived on the adrenaline of patrolling. He had previously been assigned to an MP unit at Da Nang, but requested a transfer to Recon in order to experience some action. Hawkins, Osorio, and the other old salts said he was a cool dude under fire, a man to go to the field with. If he feared anything other than God, he never showed it. The way he looked at you with his dark eyes literally withered you on the vine.

First Platoon was on a transitional stand down to allow the short-timers to out-process and transfer back to the States while we replacements integrated into the outfit and got acquainted. Horsing around in the ocean one afternoon during a swim, I dived and playfully grabbed Binns around his legs to trip him. He kicked up, neither in irritation, anger, nor playfulness. His heel caught me underneath the chin, inflicting a gash that required two stitches to close. He looked down at me with those dark casual eyes and never said a word about the incident, then or later. The look said it all: *You dumb fuck.*

From every corner of the United States the Marines vacuumed a mass of raw, diverse raw material, dumped it into a hopper and molded it into a single system with common goals and values. There was a sameness about us—young, lean, robust, aggressive. At the same time, each man retained his unique personality. Eating together, sleeping together, living together, we quickly came to know each other's quirks, faults, strengths, and weaknesses.

Lance Corporal Ralph Victor, for example, a fireteam leader, proved to be as much the pessimist as McKinney. From Ogden, Utah—a Mormon, I think—he was a dark-skinned, slender kid of nineteen who spoke with a mild, clicking stutter. Like the C&W singer Mel Tillis.

"We're in a war," he explained. "How can you b-b-be anything but a pessimist?"

On the other hand, Lance Corporal John T. Adams, twenty-two, was a martial artist and a bit of a bully. Lean-muscled and slightly short of six feet tall, he seldom missed an opportunity to flex his biceps on the beach or demonstrate his karate moves. He reminded me of the muscle-bound character in the Charles Atlas ads who kicked sand in the face of the skinny little guy until the skinny little guy took the Atlas muscle-building course and kicked sand in *his* face.

Some minor incident occurred on the beach that had nothing to do with kicking sand but nonetheless led to a minor confrontation between Adams and me. He shoved me. I shoved back, even though he probably could have twisted me into a pretzel. I would rather have taken a beating than appear yellow in front of my new platoon.

"Why don't you do something about it?" I foolishly challenged. Like two kids on the playground daring each other.

He sneered. "Yeah? With the power I know I possess, I could hit you in the chest and stop your heart beating."

Maybe so. But he didn't shove me anymore. We established a restive trust that gradually grew into a reserved friendship.

First Platoon consisted of two eight-man squads and a command element composed of the platoon leader, platoon sergeant, radiomen, and medical corpsmen. Lieutenants were in short supply, so most of the time a single sergeant filled both top spots. Each squad was made up of two fireteams of four men and a team leader. Sergeant Howard assigned Moore, McKinney, and me to First Squad. Both the squad leader, Corporal Ronnie G. Knowles, and our fireteam leader, Lance Corporal Osorio, were short-timers and would soon *di di* out of the Nam and back to the World.

Knowles was a broad-shouldered Texan with light brown hair so stiff it resembled small nails driven into his skull. Osorio was a short, dark Puerto Rican with black hair that made the top of his head seem to disappear after nightfall. He eyed our M-1D's and scopes and, like everyone else so far, appeared uncertain about what they meant.

"If I was you guys," he advised, "I would trade in them M-1s for M-14s."

An M-1 was a heavier weapon than the standard M-14 battle rifle. It loaded a clip of only eight rounds compared to a twenty-round magazine for the M-14. Plus, higher-higher authorized Recon units to rig their M-14s with a selector switch for full automatic fire for increased punch, an option unavailable in the M-1.

"But we're supposed to be snipers," I protested.

Osorio shrugged. "Suit yourselves."

Norman and Kosoglow went to Binns's fireteam in Second Squad. Lance Corporal Michael Hucal, also a short-timer, was their fireteam leader, while the fourth man on their team was a Californian named Thomas Powles, twenty, a likeable, funny kid with a mild lisp that drew him his share of good-natured garrison ragging.

"I need somebody from California to come over and thuck my dick," someone might quip.

Powles always fired back with a "Fuck you, man" or "Kith my California ath."

Powles idolized Binns.

The Reconnaissance Battalion was a division asset. Its elements—companies and platoons—were designed as the advance eyes and ears for the First Marine Division and its rifle battalions and companies. We were sent out into VC country in platoon-sized units or smaller to scout for the bad guys. Once we located them, we bugged out and the ground pounders combat assaulted in to, along with artillery and air support, put the old three F's on them: Find 'em, fix 'em, and fuck 'em over. Although Recon inserted heavily armed, just in case, we were not intended to be used in general combat. We were too valuable as a source of intelligence and information to waste needlessly. Knowing that always made me feel better.

Sergeant Howard used the stand down time to up-train the platoon and get the influx of new guys ready for mission. Map reading and compass courses, reconnaissance tactics, SALUTE (Size, Activity, Location, Uniforms, Time, Equipment) reporting, immediate action drills on the beach . . . It wasn't that I was eager to go into combat. Curious, yes, but eager, no. Still, I grew impatient as the uneventful days passed. First, shit details. Now, this. I never expected war to be so much boredom.

"It's not much of a war," Kosoglow commented with a laugh. "But it's the only war we got."

More Marines arrived in Chu Lai every day. We heard two battalions of the Fifth Marine Regiment were coming, while rumors circulated among the troops of a big offensive code-named Operation *Hot Springs.* Typically, McKinney worried that we were all going out to attack the gooks and the gooks would kill us all.

"We always kill more of them than they kill of us," Osorio assured him.

"Hooray for our side!" mock-cheered Navy Hospitalman Third Class Billy D. Holmes, twenty-three. Auburn-haired, freckled-faced Billy D, as he was affectionately called, was assigned to First Platoon as its medical corpsman. He was tall and outspoken and exuded confidence in his job and abilities. Everyone treated him with the deference due a country doctor.

"War is a tough life," Moore said as he wrestled with his rubber lady. It leaked air. He topped it off with a couple of lungsful of air and stretched his sleeping bag over it. He threw himself on top with a sigh and ignored the hiss of escaping air. Kosoglow giggled.

Every day we heard things about what was happening *out there,* beyond the perimeter of the airbase. Sometimes when I had nothing else to do, I strolled through the sand dunes behind Headquarters Company and the messhall where I could look out past the ammo dump and the airstrip into where no man's land began beyond the river that formed the base's southern boundary. Since arriving in Chu Lai, I was getting good at swimming, burning out shitters, training, and moving stuff. How would I do in combat when the time came? Although it was never discussed, I suspected the other replacements asked themselves the same questions in private moments. It wasn't that I wanted to be a hero, something my half-brother Homer warned against, but I desperately needed to conduct myself with courage and honor. I felt almost thankful, however, every time I gazed out into no man's land that nobody so far seemed to have any ideas for using snipers. I shuddered at the very thought of going out there for days at a time, just two of us alone, and hunting down VC to shoot them one by one. Being a sniper in Vietnam didn't seem nearly as romantic as it had in Okinawa.

"I think this platoon is ready to go back on line," Sergeant Howard said one afternoon.

My heart pounded and that furry little something stirred inside my guts. McKinney licked his lips and stabbed a quick look at me.

Two nights later some of us were watching *Ben Hur* in the battalion area. A bunch of old bomb crates had been set up as seats in front of a screen underneath the stars. A voice through the sound system interrupted Charlton Heston's chariot races.

"First Platoon, Charlie Company, hit the road. You got a frag order for a mission."

My mouth went so dry my tongue stuck to my teeth. God protect me. We were going *out there.*

7

Sergeant Howard called a platoon meeting before each patrol. This one was held in the dark under lights provided by a gasoline generator. Shadows crept around the tent's walls and ceiling. Usually he began the meeting with something like, "All right, shitbirds, listen up—" *Shitbirds, ladies, jarheads* . . . terms affectionately complimentary the way he used them. Then he got down to the meat. We would go into such-and-such an area, observe for such-and-such, be in the boonies three days, four, whatever, then come back in, get some real chow and go swimming. We would hump on our backs so much chow, this much water, a basic load of grenades, and ammo.

"Any questions?"

I had none. What did I know? I was a green boot. I went where I was told, did what I was told.

"We insert at first light," he concluded.

Squad Leader Knowles designated me to carry extra belts for Benson's M60 machine gun. Benson, the smallest guy in the platoon, a little redhead, carried the biggest gun. Norman said it was like in Arizona when you knew the runt cowboys always drove up in the biggest pickups.

Into my "782 gear," or "deuce gear," which was what

Marines called our frameless backpacks, I stuffed extra ammo, some cans of C rations, a poncho, a clean pair of socks, rifle cleaning kit, the M60 ammo, and a few personals. Knowles said it was best to travel light. Travel light, freeze at night. Add to that my M-1, my Ka-bar sheath knife, more ammo, canteens, some fragmentation and Willie Pete (white phosphorus) grenades and it made a decent load. Knowles then tossed me a black rubber Mae West, a life saver flotation jacket. I stared at it.

"What am I going to do with this?"

"Put water in it."

"I thought you said to travel light."

"You want to drink, don't you?"

"Yeah."

"Then put water in it."

It made a large rubber canteen that nearly doubled my back weight. I had to add a packboard to my deuce gear in order to carry it all.

"We're going southwest. That ain't so b-b-bad," Ralph Victor stuttered. The old salts seemed to know what he was talking about. He explained for the benefit of those of us who didn't. "The Hiep Duc Valley is northwest. We had to be jerked out twice the last t-t-time we were in there. We kept running into gooks. Lots of 'em. Ask Knowles. He was there."

"Fucking-A," Knowles confirmed. "All the gooks in Vietnam are in that valley."

It stuck in my mind that *southwest* wasn't so bad, whereas *northwest* into the Hiep Duc Valley meant sure trouble.

I hardly slept the rest of the night. I knew Moore got up twice to go use the head. McKinney went outside to smoke a cigarette. I barely touched my breakfast at dawn. Knowles warmed his hands around a tin canteen cup of black coffee as we lugged our gear over to the battalion HQ area to catch the helicopter lift out. It could be surprisingly chilly in the mornings. We stamped around in the tendrils of fog waiting to load. There were few conversations. Some coughing and sneezing, some farting and grunting, but not much talking.

Vietnam was a war unlike any other ever fought by the United States. Lacking conventional battle lines, waged mostly by small actions against an elusive enemy, it had an almost phantasmagoric fluidity characterized by rapid shifting of men and weaponry and insertions and extractions of troops in response to a jack-in-the-box enemy. The prime agent of all that movement was rotary-winged aircraft. Vietnam was becoming known as "the helicopter war."

The helicopter was a fairly new concept, having been invented and developed during Sergeant Howard's own lifetime. A Spanish aristocrat named Juan de la Cierve built an "autogiro" in the 1920s, but the year 1940 saw the introduction of the world's first viable helicopter, the F1-282 Kolbri, or Hummingbird. In 1944, a Sikorsky R-4 was sent behind enemy lines in Burma to rescue and evacuate a downed American pilot and three British casualties. Medical evacuations, or "medevacs," would be carried out on a grand scale during the Korean War with bubble-nosed Bell 47 helicopters flying in support of Mobile Army Surgical Hospitals (MASHes).

Other nations pursued the military potential of rotary-winged craft. The French used about a dozen helicopters, primarily for medevac, in their losing battle to hold onto their colony of Indochina (Vietnam) in the early 1950s. In 1956, Britain loaded twenty-two helicopters with British Royal Marines, lifted them from two aircraft carriers and flew ten miles to Port Said, establishing a toehold for other Marines to land and regain control of the Suez Canal. The French used the turboprop "Horned Butterfly" in its eight-year guerrilla fight (1954–1962) to retain its colony of Algeria.

In the United States in 1956 and 1957, a resourceful staff officer by the name of Colonel Jay Vanderpool conducted improvised experiments with the helicopter as a weapons platform at the Army Aviation School at Fort Rucker, Alabama. He assembled a small fleet of helicopters, fitted them with borrowed machine guns and rockets, and carried out a series of freewheeling field tests. They practiced shooting under various conditions and honed new-found skills in nap-of-the-earth flying—the art of zipping along mere feet above the ground using trees and hills for concealment. Although word of the combat merits of helicopters began to spread in military circles, it was not until the Vietnam War and the development of "airmobile" concepts that helicopters came into wide military use. Airmobility soon became the defining characteristic of the war. By the late 1960s, every branch of the U.S. armed forces, as well as the forces of other nations, had taken to the sky in rotary-winged aircraft.

America's first helicopters—thirty-two big, dual-rotor U.S. Army Shawnees well suited for carrying troops into battle—arrived in Saigon aboard the U.S. escort carrier *Card* on 11 December 1961. In the following months and years, helicopters of various kinds and sizes played a multitude of roles: They were used for reconnaissance, often locating the enemy by intentionally drawing fire; they inserted troops into battle, and extracted them; they delivered ammunition, food, water, and other supplies to the scene of fighting, no matter the terrain; they lifted artillery batteries across the landscapes; they functioned as airborne observation and command posts in battle; they taxied commanders and officials to remote locales; they saved countless lives by swift evacuation of the wounded; they rescued downed aviators. Most visibly of all, they were formidable weapons platforms—gunships—that complemented fixed-wing aircraft in providing close air support to ground troops.

By 1966, more than 2,000 rotary-wing aircraft were in the air over Vietnam on any given day. The Marine Corps used H-34s as troop transports and UH-1 "Hueys" as gunships. H-34s resembled giant, heavy-bodied gnats. Big, dual-rotor CH-47 Chinooks carried the heavy loads.

First Platoon piled onto the bare steel floors of the 34s, six or seven men to a craft, and the trio of choppers lifted off escorted by Hueys flying guns. It was only my second flight on one of the birds; the first had been during training in Okinawa. The doors were open, letting the wind whistle past. I twisted my fingers into a D-ring on the floor to keep from falling out should the helicopter tilt or something. Sergeant Howard sat with his back to me and his feet hanging out the door. Wind whipped his bloused trouser legs. The M-14 held across his trunk-like thighs looked as small as a toy. His face was camouflage-blackened underneath the visor of his patrol cap. He reminded me of a bird of prey as he gnawed on a cigar stub and surveyed the country passing below. Look at him. He was one cool dude.

He had mentioned nothing of the four snipers in his platoon during last night's platoon meeting and mission briefing. I was secretly glad he hadn't. I knew now that I didn't want to go down there with but one other guy. It was scary enough inserting with only a platoon. I would have preferred a battalion, a *division*.

Emulating Howard for coolness, McKinney fished out a pack of C rat *Camels*. After a time he managed to extract a cigarette with trembling hands. He stuck the butt in his mouth and it trembled between his lips. He grabbed it real quick before anyone noticed. Wind snatched it out of his hand. It vanished out the door.

He moved a little closer to Moore, as though seeking a big brother's comfort. He clutched his M-14 with both hands while he stared out the door and down at Vietnam, mesmerized. Moore looked at me. His face appeared to have sunken in around the beak of his nose. It came to my mind that he had uttered not a single word since yesterday about kicking ass and bringing back medals. *Kicking ass* was one thing when you were two thousand miles away from the proposed ass, quite another when you were only ten minutes away.

The other two birds flew close wing on either side, their bellies likewise packed with Recon Marines. All those blackened faces looking back at me as from a mirror made me think of ashes and mourning. I shuddered and tried to swallow. My throat stuck together because I had nothing to swallow except the dry dread of landing in that horrible terrain below.

The chopper banked in a steep turn, its blades thumping. I peered down onto a crazy checkerboard pattern of greens and browns. Hedgerows squared out rice paddies. Villages of no more than a few thatched wooden huts each hunkered in groves of palms and stands of bamboo behind mud dikes. Everywhere else, on the rolling hills as well as in the swamps, grew tangles of jungle. It scabbed over everything, like fungus.

The jungle was a mean place to fight, I recalled being told during Vietnam orientation training. Gooks weren't the only thing down there to kill you or to make life miserable. Tigers, elephants, wild boar . . .

"There are 133 species of snakes in Vietnam," instructors had lectured, "of which 131 are poisonous. Kraits, cobras, and bamboo vipers are the most common. Bamboo vipers are called 'ol' one step,' because that's about how far you get after he bites you . . ."

If that wasn't bad enough, there were scores of pests— red ants whose bites could make you jump up right in the middle of a firefight and drop your drawers; leeches that crawled up your anus or into the opening tract of your penis to suck blood; swarms of insects that bit and sucked and stung and bugged you insane.

If *that* wasn't enough, parasites got into your guts and grew like alien life forms. There were all the tropical diseases that caused diarrhea, cramps, anemia, headaches, foot and crotch rot, malaria, fevers . . . The Vietnamese lived with tapeworms and other tormentors that would kill an American.

Why were wars always fought in the worst possible places?

A Huey gunship suddenly darting across my vision startled me. We were flying at about 1,500 feet to stay out of small arms ground fire. But now the Huey went into a steep-angled glide. The H-34s followed immediately, the floors dropping out from underneath our asses in a weightless moment.

Very quickly we were racing breathlessly along just above the treetops, whipping branches and vortexing funnels of leaves. It made me want to pull my knees even tighter into my chest. My heart pounded in rhythm with the *whump-whump-whump* of the rotors. McKinney's eyes resembled white saucers in his blackened faces.

We were going in. I was scared. Scared spitless, shitless. What if they were *waiting* for us?

The choppers reined up, skidding like horses to the bit, and dropped above a small clearing surrounded by seemingly impenetrable forest. They hovered above grass violently beaten by wind blast from the whirling blades.

"*Go! Go! Go! Go!*"

Sergeant Howard leaped out the door first, disappearing, then reappearing head and shoulders above the elephant grass. Waving his rifle. Looking back and up. His words sucked up by the blades, sliced, then dispersed like sown seed. But you didn't have to hear to know what he wanted.

"*Go! Go! Go!*"

I tumbled out into the tall grass behind Moore and

McKinney. Tripping and falling. Panting and already sweating from the excitement and exertion and heat. Marines in the field, all over the field, scattering like cockroaches to set up a hasty perimeter until we got organized and consolidated. Gunships drifted over the drop zone perimeter, keeping watch until the 34s completed their insertions.

It only took seconds. The now-empty birds jinked back into the air. Pilots threw the coal to their engines. They were most vulnerable near the ground. Most of the helicopters destroyed were shot down in that thirty feet of space above the ground between landing and takeoff.

Gunships rapidly disappeared like insect specks against the morning sky. An awful quiet settled over the field after the noise of the choppers. Vietnam, as I was learning, was at best a nervous place. This was the worst time of my life, this first time dropped off out in the middle of *them*, not knowing if we had been discovered or not. Out here by ourselves, just us and the dinks and the snakes. I had never felt so alone in my life. I wanted to shout for the helicopters to come back and get us.

8

I have always thought medics and corpsmen were the heroes of the Vietnam War. Kids my age were taken fresh out of high school, sent to boot camp and ITR, then provided ten weeks or so of medical training. After that, they were given control of medicines that could be fatal if given in excess or at the wrong time and then sent off to war to take care of other post–high school kids who had been shot up or blown to pieces. On paper it wouldn't work. In reality, it happened again and again in Vietnam.

Combat medics and corpsmen like Billy D. Holmes had to be as brave as they were committed. They were the most visible targets on the battle ground, running or crawling through danger to reach buddies who took a slug or tripped a booby trap. While bullets snapped over their heads, they sealed a sucking chest wound, got IV's started in collapsing veins, stopped bleeding, prevented shock, administered morphine, provided encouragement to the critically wounded or dying, and dragged or carried the shattered bodies of the men they loved as brothers to safety. They went to work when things went to shit. They swallowed their own terror and risked their lives to render aid and comfort to those mangled and torn by the horrid mechanisms of combat.

Ironically, the first American serviceman killed in the Vietnam War, on 22 December 1961, was a man sent to *save* lives. Just as ironically, Specialist Fourth James T. Davis, an army combat medic, died not in the process of tending the wounded on the battlefield but instead while wielding a rifle himself, fighting back against a Viet Cong ambush.

All medics and corpsmen in Vietnam were referred to as "Doc." An ordinary guy—then again maybe he wasn't so ordinary—became a medic and in a very short time began to think of himself as a doctor. Not just any doctor. He became the generalized family doctor, the old country sawbones, the idealized physician who made house calls and knew his patients' first names, their personal and medical histories, what C rat in a can they liked best, where they came from, the names of their wives and/or girlfriends. Vietnam docs did more than patch wounds and tend injuries. They carried a bagful of aid for everything from hemorrhoids and blisters to diarrhea and athlete's foot. They band-aided *ouchies* and administered M&M candies as placebos to those too broken up for morphine.

If Sergeant Howard was platoon papa and Binns platoon mama, Doc Billy D was like the loving aunt who shared the house in a special room on the second floor. The lanky, freckle-faced Doc from Tennessee was twenty-three, the oldest man on the platoon, except for Howard. He was an inspiration to the rest of us. We looked up to him. Not only would he save our lives when the shooting started, he also never lost control or appeared to be frightened of anything. I asked him one time if he was ever scared.

"I'm frigging scared every time we go out," he replied, but I never really believed him.

Billy D arrived in Vietnam back in June 1965 with the shore party battalion before the Chu Lai defense area had an airfield or even a comfort station. For the first six or

seven months, the only action he saw were a few quick skirmishes when Viet Cong sappers attempted to filter onto the
base by way of the beach. In February, a month before the
U.S.S. *Whitfield County* came, he heard the Recon people
needed corpsmen and that Recon jarheads were gung ho
go-getters. The Marine Corps had no medical people of its
own. Combat medics were squids, sailors chopped over to
the Marines from the Navy. Hospitalman Third Class
Holmes packed his seabag, his suitcase, shouldered his aid
bag and went down to First Recon Battalion to volunteer.
Sergeant Major Turner assigned him to First Platoon, Charlie Company. Sergeant Howard's outfit.

Corpsmen in the Marines were combatants the same as
every other swinging dick. They made the same sweaty
humps into the bush, endured the same leeches and bugs
and rain and heat, patched us when we got fucked up, then
went back to fighting. In addition to his deuce gear, Billy D
humped a well-stuffed aid bag, carried a .45 Colt semiauto-
matic pistol in a holster, and armed himself with an M-14
or sometimes a Thompson submachine gun some Marine
transferring out had left him.

We took care of Billy D. Troops looked after their docs.
Corpsmen were the first to get a share of any CARE package we received from home. They didn't do shit details. We
made certain Doc Holmes knew our names, just in case. It
was kind of like paying a premium on a life insurance pol-
icy in advance. Troops well knew that a lot of guys lived to
go home only because a corpsman was there.

In return, Billy D took care of us. Saw after our feet and
blisters, crotch rot, and allergies. After insertion onto the
drop zone, after the platoon got straightened out and on
the march with Binns walking point, Doc worked up and
down the file, checking on *his* men to make sure no one
was hurt when we came in. After that, he took up a position
with the command element near the center of the forma-

tion. The soft tinkling of the men's gear sounded almost musical after the roar of the choppers. The platoon moved single-file, a long gray-green caterpillar. Walking cautiously like hunters moving through a cornfield to minimize our changes of hitting a booby trap or triggering an ambush.

9

The world closed in around the platoon until nothing existed outside the shadowy tangle of jungle. Mattings of vines and bushes clutched the heat and magnified it so that we seemed to be moving through an oven filled with steam. The odor of decay and dampness clogged in my nostrils. We had to sling weapons in places and pull vines apart with our bare hands. Men visibly hunched shoulders against the heat and were soon caked with a thin, dusty layer of salt. We chewed on salt tablets and tried to remain alert in the somnolent heat.

My eyes felt as bulged as dinner plates. They jerked from side to side and up and down in an attempt to capture and analyze each new sight and sound and odor. In my newness, everything threatened. I was a stranger in a strange land in which monsters dwelt. Rustling leaves foretold a skulking VC. Birds flushing set my heart racing. I staggered back in alarm when a bright run of mercury slithered into and out of a rare patch of sunlight where I was about to place my foot. A bright green snake. The dreaded bamboo viper? Ol' one-step?

I was learning that fear and discomfort were constant companions in the jungle. A cold, slimy stranger hooked its claws into the lining of my stomach. The two of us would soon get to know each other only too well. I had a bad feeling this stranger whose name I knew as *fear* had moved in to stay.

McKinney a few places ahead appeared even more unnerved. Corporal Knowles kept reminding him to take his finger off the trigger.

The platoon strung itself out twenty to thirty feet between each man as we emerged from a wide open area dotted with palm trees and came upon a faint trail leading up the side of a hill. I didn't know where the hell I was—somewhere in Vietnam, lost for all I knew—or where I was going. All I could do was trust Sergeant Howard.

The hill steepened until the trail went up at an angle of at least sixty degrees. Footing was slippery and precarious. Downed rotted logs or patches of new bamboo often blocked the path, necessitating our climbing over or cutting a new trail around the obstruction. I was soaking wet with sweat and dying a little at a time from burnout. I thought I was in good physical shape, but I was starting to reassess my condition. My thigh muscles felt singed. Breath rasped against the raw walls of my throat with the sound of a wind-broke horse. A vise slowly clamped around my chest. I stumbled simply placing one foot in front of the other.

Shoot in here amongst us, I almost pleaded, not totally in control of my thoughts. *Some of us gotta have some relief.*

One good thing though. I started to loosen up out of sheer exhaustion. A man could stay on an adrenaline pump only so long before he crashed.

The explosion went off just at the moment I thought I was getting used to things. Up forward where Binns walked point the sharp bang was muffled by the foliage. The concussion rattled leaves as it blew down the hill through the scrub brush and trees.

I froze, unsure of what to do. Had we been attacked? For

a moment I let despair overcome any instinct for survival. *I'm so damned exhausted. I can't fight. I can't do anything. I'm dead.*

"Get down!" somebody shouted.

I dropped in my tracks. McKinney was already on the ground. He looked back at me, his eyes filled with horror. Sergeant Howard sat cross-legged next to the trail with Mulvihill the radioman sprawled next to him and the PRC-10 radio between his legs.

I didn't know what the hell was going on. I was so close to the ground I tasted dirt in my mouth. If possible, given just a tad more incentive—say a burst of rifle fire—I might have burrowed into the earth and pulled it around me. My hard, excited breathing blew forest debris out of the way. I was almost hyperventilating. And of all the stupid things to notice—a line of red ants crawling directly across my line of sight, oblivious of the drama being played out around them. I watched, almost hypnotized, as an ant scampered onto my hand and took a savage bite. I looked at it, too scared to move and brush it off.

I breathed a little easier after a moment or so. It wasn't an ambush, of that I was reasonably certain, as there would have been more than the single detonation. It occurred to me that someone had tripped a booby trap. The majority of booby trap casualties, we were told back in California at the fake Vietnamese village, occurred when soldiers became tired and lost concentration while plodding through slush and mud or steam bath heat. As we were. A large percentage of the deadly devices were simple mechanisms applying a grenade, a trip wire and an old C ration can discarded by careless American troops. The grenade had its pin pulled and was then attached to a wire and stuffed into the can. Springing the wire jerked the grenade out of the can, releasing its handle and arming it.

What seemed like an eternity passed, but in reality must

have been only a minute or so, before word came back that Binns had indeed hit a grenade trip wire.

Oh, my God! I thought. *Binns is dead. Is it that easy to get killed?*

"Corpsman!" Sergeant Howard gestured toward the front.

Billy D was already moving. The corpsman crawled past me like a lizard with his eyes fixed straight ahead toward where Binns lay out of sight about fifty yards up the trail. He and Binns were close pals. He was crawling fast, having shucked his deuce gear and now dragging his aid bag with one hand. He disappeared behind some foliage, then reappeared again on his feet jogging up the trail toward Binns. The rest of the platoon waited, ready for action.

I wasn't ready. I felt wasted. It was like I heard a giant clock in my head measuring off long intervals between each echoing tick while I waited for news that Binns was dead.

At long last, word came back from man to man. Doc had spotted Binns lying in the bushes to the side of the trail, just as cool as could be, scanning the terrain with narrowed eyes while he kept his M-14 at the ready. He suffered only minor injuries from a few minute scraps of shrapnel lodged beneath his skin. He did not even require medevac. His pack took the brunt of the blast, a can of C ration peaches possibly saving his life by stopping a slug of steel about the size of a nickel. Relief flowed down the green crippled worm of a column.

Our respect for Binns grew. Green troops too often froze when they heard the pop, click, or other sound of a booby trap activating, followed all too soon by the explosion. Not cool dude Binns. He hit the dirt instantly. That saved his life, or at least it saved him from getting really fucked up.

"You new guys—remember that," Sergeant Howard pointed out.

10

Typically of Binns, he said nothing else about his wounds after Billy D patched him up. He resumed point. Normally, he was the best man for spotting booby traps and other dangers. The rest of us, especially the new guys, were still nervous.

"Look, it's over," Sergeant Howard growled. "He's all right. I can abso-fucking-lutely guarantee you that every sorry bastard who starts worrying out here about getting waxed sure as hell is going to get his fucking ass blown away. So don't worry about it."

How did you stop worrying? How did you get rid of that knotted feeling in the pit of your stomach?

What you remember most in life are the first time things happen. The first time, clammy and sweaty, you made it with a girl in the back seat. The first time you flew in an airplane, your first funeral, your first fistfight. . . . Later, the routine of patrols became so familiar that I remembered the highlights—the clusterfucks, the few laughs, the tense moments, the contacts—and either forgot the rest or let it all run together in my mind like a stagnant and ignored swamp. But that first time on recon deep in enemy territory was the longest, tensest day of my life. Sometimes, unexpectedly, details later ran through my mind like an often-seen movie that never changed. Sweat would pop out all over my face and soak my collar. I had to mentally push it all back inside and hoped it stayed there. What I kept seeing were the napalm and the people running.

Line grunts accused Recon of having a pud job. We went out there and sat on our butts and waited for gooks to show themselves so we could either call in artillery or air on their raggedy asses or radio back SALUTE and spot intel reports that went into the "Big Picture" for planning future operations. In a way, we did have it made. Most of the time our job was to *avoid* direct enemy contact.

Regular grunts went *looking* for trouble. They spent weeks at a time tramping around in the boonies getting picked off one here by stepping in a punji pit, another there in a hasty ambush, while their socks and feet and crotches rotted and their faces burned and turned to masses of sores from insect bites. The Ninth Marines up at Da Nang spent almost eight solid months in the bush. No sleep, little food, and only basic medical care showed on their shrunken, battle-hardened faces. Like skeletons in green rags.

Story had it that two Air Force policemen watched when the outfit returned to regimental headquarters. It was they who gave the Ninth Marines its label.

"Would you look at that?" said the first.

"Yeah. Those guys look like *walkin' death*," said the other.

The Ninth Marines—*The Walking Dead*.

Maybe we did have it pud, compared to the rifle company Marines.

"It's hours and hours of boredom," Ronnie Knowles cautioned, "followed by sudden stark terror."

By noon of the first day, Sergeant Howard selected an OP—observation post—on the military crest of a heavily wooded hill tangled with undergrowth. The site overlooked a flatland of squared rice fields, beyond which, snugged into a woodline about two kilometers away—a mile and a half or so—sat a "wild" Vietnamese village. Marines had a number of CAP UNITS—Combined-Action Platoons—whose mission it was to eliminate VC from villages and win the loyalty of the populations. CAP had not pacified this village, nor most of the others in the area.

While the squad and fireteam leaders took turns with Sergeant Howard glassing the rice paddies and village for suspicious movement, the rest of the platoon formed a tight perimeter and went on fifty percent alert. With two men together in each position, one man could chow down or nap while the other kept vigil for any threat. I partnered with Moore. After a while my stomach settled down.

The foliage was so thick I couldn't see shit more than thirty feet in front of me down the side of the hill. Insects burred. Ants crawled. Always crawling, always biting, a constant factor in the jungle. Moore and I sat on the ground side by side with our backs against a jungle giant and watched a lizard come out and look us over. It was about half the length of my forearm. It blinked one eye and rolled the other, then switched back, like it was trying to figure out who we were and what we were doing here.

"*Phuoc ieu, phuoc ieu!*" it said and darted away. Moore found that funny.

"A *talking* lizard," he chuckled. "Fuck you, fuck you!" he hissed back.

He became serious again, and watchful, an expression that seemed to enlarge his Texas nose.

"I read statistics somewhere," he drawled, whispering, "that on the average two guys out of every hundred sent to Vietnam get killed."

That kind of pessimism was more characteristic of McKinney and Victor than of Moore.

"Not everybody that comes over here goes to a combat

outfit," I pointed out, also whispering. "Those statistics include clerks and jerks and the rear echelon pukes."

"How much higher is it for guys like us, you s'pose? One out of every platoon? Two?"

"How should I know?"

Moore took a deep breath. "Jesus," he said, as though considering which two of us it would be. "Binns was sure lucky."

He took out a picture of his girlfriend, Fama Tankersley, and unfolded her last letter. He could draw her picture faster than an Old West marshal whipped out his six-shooter. The letter looked worn at the creases. It smelled faintly of perfume. He let me sniff it.

"It's the only thing in this whole country so far that don't stink," he said, looking a little homesick. "It keeps me from forgetting what real girls back in Texas smell like. We're getting married when I go home on leave. Do you have a girl back home, Ray?"

"Not in particular. A girl named Shirley and a few others from high school write to me."

"Maybe it's easier if you don't have somebody to miss," he said.

"Maybe."

Night in the tropics arrived as suddenly as turning out the lights. One minute before the sun went down I could distinguish Moore's familiar features and see McKinney and Knowles nearby in their position, Knowles dozing off, and make out individual trees and creepers and ferns. The next minute I had to concentrate to see my own hand. The jungle was eerily quiet at night. It gave me the creeps.

Fire bases were seeded at various points all over a TAOR in order to provide support on a grid when called upon. Big guns routinely fired harassment and interdiction on preregistered target sites during the night. I heard the 105mm howitzers intermittently whumping and thumping

H&I into distant valleys and against far hillsides. I prayed they knew we were out here and had us correctly plotted on their maps.

In between shell bursts, a dog yapped far off in the ville, interrupting the heavy silence. It was my turn to sleep first while Moore kept watch. I stretched out on my poncho and looked up through jungle canopy to the few visible stars. I was exhausted, but still had a hard time sleeping in such unfamiliar and potentially hostile surroundings. Finally, I dozed off to the accompanying sounds of the barking dog and an infrequent far-off shell detonation.

While I was asleep, a short round landed at the bottom of the hill with a terrific crack that literally jarred me off my poncho. I was on my feet instantly. Basic instinct—flight or fight—took over and told my feet to make tracks. I was hauling ass out of that AO, letting no grass grow, no moss on the stone and all that, before I was awake enough to realize what had happened. I covered about ten yards before I froze in my tracks. Hoping my own guys hadn't mistaken me for the enemy or that I hadn't given our position away.

I didn't sleep again the rest of the night.

Armed VC began entering and leaving the village the next morning. Sergeant Howard radioed in a SALUTE and was informed to stay down and wait for an air strike. It was difficult for me to see through small openings in the jungle, especially since I hadn't access to binoculars. We jockeyed around to get a better view and watch the show. I waited with a combined sense of morbid curiosity and guilt.

To our astonishment, Vietnamese started streaming out of the village in an exodus a quarter-mile long. They pushed carts full of chickens and ducks, balanced heavy loads on their backs or heads, carried babies, and drove water buffalo, pigs, and geese. Hurrying and not looking back. Like they had done this before and it didn't do any good to look back. They reminded me of fleeing refugees in old World War II news reels. Rootless, displaced people on the move.

There was some speculation that Marine patrols must have taken fire from the village within the past few days. Vietnamese knew to expect retaliation when that happened. But how did they know it would be today? It was one of the war's many sundry mysteries.

People were still strung out across the rice dikes on the trail when a pair of F-4B Phantoms soared in over the hill from the direction of the South China Sea, so low the trailing resonance of their engines boomed painfully in my ears. They seemed to suck up all the air from the ground. The earth vibrated. Trees stood on tiptoe and rustled their leaves.

Phantoms were long-range, high altitude interceptors adapted for ground attack. Each carried about 16,000 pounds of rockets and bombs beneath its fuselage or underwing points, along with napalm canisters. The pair of them buzzed the gooks on the trail and screamed in above the village, inscribing in the low air their long, characteristic plumes of cruddy exhaust.

Gooks began to run, snatching up their kids and running harder. Those remaining in the village abandoned it on the double-time. The planes were after the village, not the people. The two jets, still on the deck and already a mile away, broke one to the left and the other to the right and disappeared from sight. I heard them thundering, the sound diminishing, then growing louder again as they angrily returned.

Moments later, the shadows of aircraft flitted over us, followed by the same deafening roar shattering the air. The planes pulled up just before they reached the settlement, releasing bright barrels that tumbled toward the village.

The napalm canisters hit, skipping toward the houses, bursting into skittering ribbons of flame, all culminating in a gaseous whoosh as they consumed their first targets.

The birds made two more runs, adding to the conflagration. Hell devoured the village. Dirty smoke rose, blocking out the sun. Heat and concussion seared the surrounding forest, blackening it. In a short time, nothing remained to show that anyone had ever lived there. Backdropped by fire and smoke, the villagers kept running. They still didn't look back, I thought, lest they be turned to pillars of salt.

"Fuck 'em," Powles lisped. "Burn 'em out like ratth."

Everything these people owned, except for what they had in their carts and on their backs, was destroyed in a matter of a few minutes. Undoubtedly, that was a VC village, but surely not everyone in it was a VC.

"They are after this," Kosoglow commented.

Napalming scenes like this one inspired GI's in Vietnam to compose a wry and macabre fighting song that later became popular in certain areas. It was called "Napalm Sticks To Kids":

> *Eighteen kids in a free-fire zone.*
> *Books in arm going home;*
> *Last in line goes home alone.*
> *Napalm sticks to kids.*

> *Viet Cong woman on the run,*
> *Struck by napalm from the sun.*
> *When they're pregnant you get two for one.*
> *Napalm sticks to kids.*

> *Charlie in his boat sitting in the stern,*
> *Thinks his goddamned boat won't burn.*
> *Those fucking gooks will never learn.*
> *Napalm sticks to kids.*
> **Anonymous**

11

It was in 1966, the year I arrived in Vietnam, that U.S. forces consciously began searching out the VC and NVA rather than simply "advising" ARVN forces and pulling defense security. U.S. Marines as well as army units like the First Air Cavalry Division and the 173ᵈ Airborne in other Corps Tactical Zones launched operations such as *Double Eagle, Masher, White Wing, El Paso,* and *Attleboro,* all meant to carry the war into communist strongholds.

The North Vietnamese Army (NVA was also known as PAVN—People's Army of Vietnam) began building up its strength in the northern provinces to counter the Marine bases at Da Nang and Chu Lai, establishing stations from which to launch attacks against populated areas. This buildup increasingly served to draw Marines out into the boonies. Among the hills and valleys less than thirty miles west of Chu Lai, NVA troops and VC Main Force units kept Recon platoons of the First Marine Division hopping frantically about in attempts to locate them so Marine rifle companies and their heavy support could rain death and hellfire on their heads.

The more any common grunt serving in Vietnam came to know the enemy, the more he grew to respect if not exactly admire him. Any way you looked at the guerrillas, they were tough little fuckers. There was no way an American could have fought under the Spartan conditions that confronted the average NVA or VC fighter in South Vietnam.

"Viet Cong" was a pejorative term meaning "communist" and was the accepted name for the armed forces of the National Liberation Front (NLF). The NLF, which claimed to be nationalist, was actually a communist front run by the politburo in Hanoi. However, very few of the VC peasant recruits were communists. Most had never even heard of Karl Marx or his manifesto for the "working class." Although every unit had a political officer, lectures and classes all centered on the history of Vietnam's popular struggles against foreign invaders rather than upon any ideology. It was a simple approach for simple people—and it worked.

The VC core was made up of 10,000 or so former members of the Viet Minh, who had defeated the French in 1954 and remained in the South after the partition of the country. The leaders were all experienced guerrilla commanders. By 1966, local recruitment by this hard-core cadre had swelled the ranks of the VC guerrilla army to some 300,000 men, supplemented by at least three complete NVA regiments, about 5,800 soldiers, along with support units and political cadres.

The Viet Cong operated from two main sections—Regional Force paramilitary units whose members farmed by day and undertook sabotage and other actions at night; Main Force full military units able to act in large, self-contained formations, all armed and trained as well as the NVA.

Main Force units, the true guerrilla army, were overwhelmingly recruited from the rural villages and were usually men in their teens. Women were enlisted when there was a shortage of men. Although there were city dwellers in the ranks, they were an insignificant minority. The average VC was a field hand who, as Robert McNamara once noted, was "no stranger to deprivation and death." Life had always been hard for him. Accustomed to backbreaking work on a handful of rice a day, he went to war expecting no comforts or ease. Death was as much a part of his equipment as his rifle or his helmet, if he had one.

In those villages supportive of the VC, it was seen as a young man's duty to volunteer when the recruiters came around. Elsewhere, many were conscripted, often at gunpoint. No matter, the organization of the military units lent itself to cohesion, self-discipline, and mutual support, no matter the origins of the members. Each new recruit joined a three-man cell, which included at least one veteran. This cell in turn was attached to a three-cell squad. Three squads formed a platoon. Cells, squads and platoons lived together and fought together, forming strong ties as comrades for as long as they survived.

Paid about sixty piasters a month, approximately two dollars, the field hand–turned–VC carried everything he owned with him. It was never much. Other than weapons and ammo, his possessions might include a few pairs of underpants, some socks if he had boots to go with them, a square of light nylon for use as a raincoat or tent, a hammock and mosquito net, an improvised oil lamp, a water flask, a digging tool, and a long tube known as an "elephant's intestine" for carrying his rice.

Contrary to popular myth, because farmers and villagers did not live in the jungle, the jungle was as strange and threatening to the average VC as it was to a Marine from Chicago or New York. For all the Vietnamese were impervious to many local pests and parasites, the VC were vulnerable to malaria and mosquitoes, malaria causing more deaths among them than any other single cause. Poisonous snakes also took a dreadful toll from among the sandal-wearing guerrillas.

Malnutrition levied its own fee. A VC soldier's normal consumption of food consisted of a ball of cold, glutinous rice spiced with a few chili peppers and maybe some *nuc mam* sauce in the morning and again in the afternoon. A little diced fish or meat and perhaps some salt supplemented the rice, if the soldier were lucky. A single chicken often provided a meal divided among thirty or more men.

When possible, they farmed. B-52 bomb craters filled by rains became duck ponds and fish farms. Hunting for elephant, monkey, rat, and even tiger added meat to the diet. Dogs were eaten. So was the rare cat. Some soldiers snacked on moths attracted to lamp flames.

No matter what the men did, however, usually they went hungry.

Because of poor medical facilities, the VC were dogged by fears of serious wounds that promised a long and lingering sickness followed by death. They likewise feared not having a proper funeral, which was of highest importance to ancestor-worshipping villagers. Some VC wore a leather band around their wrists so that if they were killed in battle a hook could be inserted under the band to drag away their bodies for internment.

Periods when the VC in the northern provinces could kick back and R&R (rest and recreation) at their base camps became rarer and rarer as Marines pressed deeper and deeper into what VC considered "their" territory. Such pressure meant the guerrillas were mostly either out on operations or, as one VC put it, hiding out like "hunted animals."

Still, the little fuckers just kept coming.

12

After a mission or two into the boondocks, I began to get *more* comfortable out there. You were never ever really *comfortable*. You were always scared—like you could feel the fires of hell lapping up at your buttocks and even hear ol' Satan snigger every now and then—but at least you knew a bit more about what to expect and weren't liable to go off half-cocked every time something happened. You started to think maybe most monsters were more threatening in your imagination than they were in real life. Most of them, not all of them.

When you got comfortable with something, secure with its operation, you didn't relish the idea of somebody throwing an unknown factor into the machinery to take a chance on fucking it up. Like with Sergeant Howard. Sergeant Howard was our father, our mother, Uncle Sam, and Jesus Christ all rolled into one mean, lean, green two-hundred-pound package. You're in combat, you're standing in the mud with fixed bayonets and no ammo, ten thousand screaming dinks are charging up the hill at you—and Sergeant Howard wasn't going to bug out on you. Sergeant Howard was going to get your ass out of there. That was the reason none of us in the platoon was any too happy when

First Lieutenant Clinton E. Braley, cherry greenhorn new in-country, got assigned to take command of First Platoon. Maybe he *would* bug out on us.

"We got Sergeant Howard," Victor stammered. "We don't n-n-need any fucking lieutenant to screw things up."

Everybody kept a close, nervous eye on Braley the next time we went on a hump. He was tall and so light-complected he might have lived in a cave. Vietnam would take care of that pallor; Vietnam was going to *burn* his ass. He was from Oklahoma too, even the Tulsa area like I was, but it didn't take him long to shatter any misbelief on my part that common geography gave me any brownie points. Unlike the informality of Sergeant Howard's leadership, Lieutenant Braley was your basic Mod O Marine Corps officer—do what I say, don't ask questions.

"Take your empty C ration cans back to the battalion area with you," he ordered.

I didn't want to put that shit in my pack and get juice and stuff all over my socks. I finished eating and scratched out a place in the ground and covered my can with leaves. Braley checked out the area before we saddled up and pulled out.

"Who's C ration can is this?" he exploded. "Hildreth, you were over here. Is this your can?"

Caught red-handed.

"I thought I told you to put this in your pack."

"Yes, sir," I added, knowing that I had fucked up.

"Do what I tell you or I'll have your ass. Did you ever see what a VC can do with a tin can?"

Sure I had. I was starting to feel like an old salt. Had he? Of course, the lieutenant was right, but I still didn't like a greenhorn first lieutenant dressing me down. It was a booby trap made out of a C ration can that got Lance Corporal Binns. VC were ingenious little bastards. From the tin of C ration cans they made knives and repair parts for their weapons, warning devices, punji stakes . . . Drop a can of C's outside a VC village and the little fuckers would live off the chow for a month while they built tanks and mortars out of the cans and a hooch out of the box.

Sergeant Howard had an even more direct way of putting things. He took me aside.

"The lieutenant is right, Hildreth," he growled. "We don't want to advertise to the gooks that we're out here. Don't do it again or I'll bust your head."

I stuffed cans in my pack from then on, socks or no socks. You didn't question Sergeant Howard.

Binns was especially resentful of the new officer. He had become accustomed to acting informally as Sergeant Howard's platoon sergeant. This meant a psychological demotion for him. He regarded Braley with a wary, watchful eye, like one dog stiff-legged confronting another encroaching upon marked territory.

"The fucker better not try having the platoon stand full-dress inspection," he grumbled rhetorically.

As usual, Binns walked point most of the time we were in the bush. He called a silent halt when the jungle suddenly turned brown, brittle, and dead. He sent word back for Sergeant Howard to come up, not Lieutenant Braley. Braley dutifully held down the fort while Sergeant Howard checked things out.

On Braley's first day with the platoon, he had called us one at a time down to his tent in officers' country for a little informal talk. It probably said to do that in his OCS manual: *Get to know your men one on one in an informal setting, make them comfortable, let them know you're fair but that you're the one in charge.* Something like that.

"Why are you carrying an M-1 rifle?" he asked me.

"I'm a sniper, sir. Me, Norman, Moore, and Kosoglow."

"What do you do?"

"Nothing. So far."

"I see. Well . . . good to have you in the platoon, Hildreth."

"Yes, sir."

"If we ever have need for a sniper, I'll, uh—"

"Yes, sir."

He didn't know what to do with us either. Good.

We all imagined what Sergeant Howard must have had to say during their first get-acquainted confab. Military was ingrained in the sergeant from his thick burr cut to the soles of his combat boots, but Sergeant Howard wouldn't have let a *general* come in and fuck with the lives of his Marines. I could almost hear him saying, "Lieutenant, *sir*, with all due respect, you may command First Platoon, but the platoon sergeant *runs* it. That's me. These are my men. They're good Marines. You don't fuck with 'em. When we're out on mission, you listen to me and do what I do. God willing, I'll keep you alive and your ass intact until you learn what you're doing so you don't get my men killed. Understand? Sir?"

To Braley's credit, he seemed to take Sergeant Howard's advice. We all breathed a little easier. He might not be such a bad Joe after all. I watched him up ahead as he knelt with the radioman and Billy D to wait for Sergeant Howard to return. We were stopped on the edge of a large area that had been sprayed with Agent Orange, a defoliate so called because of the color of its container.

Marine leaders didn't discuss tactics and decisions with the grunts. Sergeant Howard came back and talked things over with the platoon leader. They decided to move the platoon straight across the dead zone rather than waste half a day going around.

"Get thirty-meter intervals and keep your eyes open," Sergeant Howard instructed.

The use of defoliation to strip the forest cover from outlying VC strongholds was reaching its height in 1966.

"Ranch Hands," as the U.S. Air Force and CIA operators of the defoliation program called themselves (Their motto: "Only you can prevent forests"), arrived in Vietnam in 1962. At that time several methods of forest clearance had already been tried.

Napalm canisters fell through the canopy and smothered themselves in the damp undergrowth or caught in upper branches and only burned one tree. Bombing was too expensive. Bulldozing with giant Rome Plows was also expensive, time consuming, and did not work well in mountains. Plus, it effectively fertilized the soil and produced undergrowth denser than the original.

Agents White and Purple—again named after the color of the cans—were tried, but neither worked as effectively as Orange. For dispensing the evil-smelling purple agent, spray booms were fitted underneath the wings and tails of C-123 Providers and 1,000-gallon tanks and pump systems installed in the cargo holds. The Ranch Hands did not confine themselves to defoliating the jungle. They also used Agent Blue to destroy crops that might fall into enemy hands and to persuade peasants to move off the land and into cities and refugee camps where they could be "pacified" and watched.

Hundreds of thousands of acres of forest were destroyed. While the tactics deprived the Viet Cong and NVA of some cover in the short run, it rebounded against U.S. ground troops by making them more visible and susceptible to ambush. I felt exposed, like I had dropped my drawers and was walking naked through a shopping mall.

Everything in the dead zone, even the birds, were either dead or gone. It was a *Twilight Zone* episode, eerie and unsettling. Sunlight bore down in dirty orange-brown shafts filled with the rotted carnage of an expired forest. Dead leaves crumbled into powder. The powder got into our clothing and chafed our skin and clotted in our nostrils.

Dried creepers reached out to trip us. The air tasted as dead as the inside of an ancient closed tomb.

I don't think I breathed at all until we reached live forest again. McKinney sucked in a long sigh of relief.

"Jeez! I just *knew* we were going to get shot," he confessed later.

When we were in the bush conducting recon and observation, we might set up and move two or three different times in as many days, depending upon enemy activity. Vietnamese villages all looked more or less the same as the one the Phantoms napalmed. See one gook village and smell it, you're seen and smelled them all. The first one this time out turned out to be a dry hole with nothing other than ordinary activity.

Sergeant Howard saddled up the troops for a move at 0430 in the morning when the tops of the jungle were barely becoming visible. The heavy night air muffled sounds as watches started rolling people out of their ponchos. We were always on at least fifty percent alert.

We set up a new OP in thick jungle on the crest of a hill overlooking diked, checker-boarded rice paddies covering a total of about eighty or ninety acres, the opposite side of which was occupied by a small village of perhaps a dozen hooches scattered among coconut and banana palms. It was about a half mile away. It was April, at the end of the winter rains and before the summer monsoons, and people were out in the fields early to work. Men, women, and children alike wore straw cone hats and black pajamas with the trouser legs rolled up to their knees. They tramped around barefooted in the leftover black mud, their backs bent almost constantly as they planted or weeded or did whatever it was they were doing.

"Half of them are probably VC," Norman whispered suspiciously.

"Ninety-nine percent," Kosoglow corrected. "Oh, by the way, happy birthday, Hildreth."

I had just turned nineteen. I thought of the CARE birthday package I got from Shirley back home, half of which I kept in my locker at Chu Lai for a welcome-back treat when we were extracted. I watched a kid ride a black water buffalo on the trail that circled the fields. He beat it relentlessly and to no avail with a long stick, for the beast continued at its same slow, steady pace. The scene was off some exotic postcard: *Having a good time, wish you were here. People are wonderful, although they've been known to shoot tourists.*

Because Recons were inserted into jungles and remained hidden in jungles, this was as close as I had come so far to a rice field, a Vietnamese village or hooch, or, for that matter, a Vietnamese if you didn't count the ones working on the base at Chu Lai. Spying on the villagers provided a perverse sort of diversion, sort of like window peeping, but it got boring after awhile. Division wanted in the worst possible way for the Recons to find the enemy in order to unleash upon him the dogs of war. But how could you find the enemy when he didn't *act* like the enemy?

There was only one sure way—if they carried weapons.

Just before dark, things started to liven up. A patrol of five VC—they were armed—departed the village and walked along the trail that encircled the rice fields and passed directly below our hill. I watched with as much curiosity as alarm. They were runts. Small, inoffensive-looking men dressed in black with cone hats, looking exactly like the field workers with whom they undoubtedly mingled during the day. Evidently, they put in a day's work before they went to their hooches, dug up buried weapons, and set out to join with others for a night's fun and mischief. Little old men and women standing next to their huts watching their sons leave might only that morning have changed the batteries on land mine booby traps that would be blowing Marines all to crap. What kind of people were these?

The enemy patrol strode along the dikes with their AK's and remnant firearms from the French war balanced on their shoulders or backs, chattering without restraint. Clearly, they felt safe. Marines seldom operated in force this far out, and the ARVN took to their forts as soon as night fell. The five passed unsuspectingly below the hill, not a football field's length from us. One of them laughed loudly.

I sprawled on my belly, holding my breath and my M-1 as the black-garbed figures floated in and out of view through the trees. They quickly disappeared against the low-slung red sun and into the lone evening shadows.

Lieutenant Braley made a radio SALUTE to the battalion S-2, Intel, and Ops, and asked for a go-ahead to take action. Word passed through the platoon. Braley wanted a body count. Recon wasn't about body counts. Recon was about *observing*. Eager beaver officers could get our asses waxed. Still, Binns and Sergeant Howard both seemed pleased. So did Corporal Knowles and Osorio.

"Tomorrow," went the word, "we are going to waste their sorry butts if they come strolling out again chattering like a bunch of women."

We were going to *kill* these guys! Was it really that easy, that casual?

13

Ambush when you were out in the boonies was always on your mind. It was a favorite technique of the VC, which meant you had to guard against it. Truth was, we ambushed them as much as they ambushed us. That was especially true of units like Recon who operated in country the enemy claimed as his own. The VC felt safe and confident and would often do dumb things—like walking in plain sight out across the rice paddies chattering and cackling like hens, or using the same trail day after day.

Ambushes were divided into two categories—hasty and deliberate. Hasty was when you suddenly spotted the enemy coming toward you and grabbed the chance to quickly get in position to bushwhack him. Deliberate was when you selected a location, planned the action, got into position—and waited and waited. Patience was the number one rule of the successful ambush. Number two was KISS—Keep It Simple Stupid.

Number three rule, if you wanted to stay the hunter instead of the hunted, was to haul ass and get out of Dodge after you sprang the ambush and searched the bodies for intel. Put as much distance between you and the scene as quickly as possible.

Sergeant Howard prepared for the ambush the next afternoon by our occupying a Vietnamese cemetery located on the side of the hill next to the dike trail used by the VC patrol the previous day. He figured the gooks, feeling safe and at home and being creatures of habit, would do it again. A wry thought occurred to me that a burying ground was an appropriate place for an ambush. The graveyard consisted of three or four single gravesites guarded over by a large stone Buddha, whose features through a tangle of lianas were worn almost smooth by decades of weather. A low, stone horseshoe-shaped wall surrounded the graves, with the opening toward the rice paddy trail and the hedgerows. Undergrowth grew thick enough to provide easy concealment.

Corporal Knowles's squad hid behind the stone wall, with the little machine gunner, Benson, posting his M60 at the opening of the horseshoe where he could sweep the kill zone with it. Binns's squad tied into the line ambush by burrowing into foliage to our right and nearer the trail. Knowles, whom Sergeant Howard placed in charge of the assault, moved up with Binns to attain the best location to initiate the action.

McKinney and Moore, along with Osorio, took up positions on the wall to my left. Lieutenant Braley, Sergeant Howard, Billy D, and radioman Lance Corporal Daniel Mulvihill established a CP and rally point back in the bushes from which to oversee and supervise the operation.

"I'll open up first when they all get in the kill zone," Knowles said matter-of-factly. "Then everybody start shooting."

We went still and quiet and waited. My heart hammered against my ribs at the thought of first contact and first combat. After a while, however, even it went quiet. Back in Oklahoma, I had gone deer hunting a time or two with my cousins. I walked out in the woods with them, climbed a tree, and sat there on the stand for miserable hours in the cold waiting for a deer to happen by so I could shoot it. Ambush it. At first, I anticipated the moment when I knew that big buck would show up. After awhile, when nothing happened, the edge wore off and I stopped expecting it to come. It was a real heart-pounding jolt when the deer finally appeared. I got buck fever and missed the shot.

We waited. Hours passed while I grew stiff and bored, unable to talk or move or scratch my balls. It was so hot in the jungle thickets that I stewed in my own sweat. Norman later commented how the dead people in the graveyard must have all gone to hell because we seemed to have encamped right over hell's front door.

Mangrove and nipa palms restricted my view of the kill zone. All I saw by peering through a small opening in the undergrowth was about two or three feet of the trail. I almost hoped none of the VC were in my space when the shooting started. Sure I had been trained as a sniper, instructed in and practiced placing crosshairs on an unsuspecting target and blowing him to Kingdom Come. Faced with that prospect now, I was discovering within myself a big difference philosophically between a man-target and a man-live. The ability to shoot another human being when it came down to it was more within a shooter's psychological makeup than it was in his mechanical aptitude with a rifle.

Like Marine Captain and sniper instructor Jim Land said, "When you look through that rifle scope, the first thing you see is the eyes. There is a lot of difference between shooting at a shadow, shooting at an outline, shooting at a mass, and shooting at a pair of eyes. Many men can't do it at that point."

I squinted, peering through the scope of my M-1D. I honestly didn't know at that point if I could let the hammer down or not. At first excited at the prospect, I now felt ashamed because I was hoping the VC wouldn't show up at all. Some sniper!

Just as relief was turning to complacency and the sun getting low toward another tropical night, Knowles issued a hiss that sibilated along the line and brought everyone to alert. My small opening in the undergrowth presented a better panorama of the distant trail and village than it did of the nearer kill zone. Sure enough, five VC, apparently the ones from yesterday, strolled out of the village and followed the same pathway as before. Still feeling secure, unaware of hostile eyes, they were chattering and grabassing with each other and having a good old time of it. Their shit was weak. It was a cardinal rule that you never used the same trail more than once, and certainly not at the same time of the day.

I eased OFF the safety of my M-1 and felt myself hyperventilating from excitement. Buck fever. I closed my eyes and took a deep breath to control my heart rate and breathing. I shifted positions. I opened my eyes again and got ready by leaning over the wall and sighting in on my little piece of the KZ.

I could do this thing. I *could*.

It took the VC ten or fifteen minutes to reach us. They were out of my sight during that time, but I knew they were coming. How could they not feel the tension generated by this patch of woods and not be warned? My hands sweated. Sweat trickled into my eyes. I badly needed to take a leak.

I heard the murmur of voices and laughter. I almost jumped out of my skin when Ronnie Knowles's M-14 opened up on full automatic, prematurely as it turned out. The Vietnamese were still not in the kill zone. Later, Knowles explained that he thought they were about to turn back, and that was why he pulled the trigger.

There was nothing else I could do except point my rifle in the general direction of where I figured the enemy ought to be and start popping rounds. The entire platoon did the same thing at the same moment. It was a mad minute of noise and confusion, of the air crackling with death, of bullets slapping and ripping through the underbrush. Relieving tension. Benson lay on his machine gun, lashing out with streams of red tracers.

Panic-stricken figures in black darted among the trees. I snapped shots at them. One fellow sprinted past the cemetery wall across my front, so near I saw the terror in his eyes. I could have jumped up and tackled him if I hadn't been caught by such surprise. A young kid. That boy possessed motivation. He had already dropped his weapon. Here he was—and there he went at the same time. *Whish!* Streaking right through our lines. I doubt in his blind fear if he even saw us. He wouldn't have spotted an elephant standing right in front of him.

Binns let out a loud guffaw. "Did you see that silly sonofabitch?" he roared.

He was also one lucky sonofabitch. He was gone into thin air before anybody thought to take a shot at him.

Sergeant Howard walked up behind the lines as cool as if he were out for a Sunday stroll with his wife and kids back in Iowa. Lieutenant Braley followed. He tried to look cool, but his hands trembled.

"Cease fire, Marines!" Sergeant Howard shouted. *"Cease fire!"*

Firing spattered down into uncommon, contrasting silence. My hands shook worse than Braley's as I slapped a fresh clip of ammo into my M-1. I thought I must have done all right for my first time, at least as well as any of the other new guys. McKinney stood up, looking pale and shaken.

Out in the fields, the workers scattered, bolting toward their village in the distant treeline. It didn't take long before the only thing left out there on the paddies was a barking dog—and he didn't stay around long.

"Binns, you and Powles go take a look," Sergeant Howard ordered.

Rustling in the bush as the two Marines hurried out to the trail.

"We got one down over here," Binns called out. "He's wounded bad. I don't see any others."

Sergeant Howard left a fireteam behind to pull rear security in case we had to di-di. The rest of the platoon poured out onto the trail to take a close look at our handiwork.

The wounded dink looked as small as an American sixth grader. He lay on his back with one trembling hand stuck up in the air from the elbow, as though reaching for something. Blood spread and soaked into the ground around his scrawny body. His eyes were heavy-lidded and getting dull. He gasped for air, the effort wracking his body and resulting in a sound somewhere between a whistle and a tortured groan. Next to him lay a rifle nearly as long as he was tall, a leftover from the French Indo-China War.

I kept staring, feeling vaguely criminal. Surely shooting a guy was more consequential than breaking into a Laundromat soap dispenser for gas change. People went to jail for things like this. Didn't they?

Adrenaline was still pumping. Guys shouted and talked and some laughed nervously. Powles shot an M-79 grenade round into an abandoned hooch that set next to the trail in the direction two of the bad guys fled. A flash of fire and smoke shook the hut. The roof collapsed. Nobody ran out.

S-2 Intel people would want to question the gook, if he lived. Sergeant Howard radioed for a dust-off. That meant we had to wait out in the open until the helicopter arrived. Across the field in the village, people gathered on the outskirts and glared across at us. I felt as jumpy as a grasshopper in a hot skillet. I kept thinking: *We really ought to get out of here.*

What seemed like an eternity passed before a lone H-34 medevac soared in over the top of the hill real quick and touched down to yellow smoke Sergeant Howard tossed to designate a landing site. The field was still wet and sloppy from the last of the winter season, but the chopper kept light on its wheels with its blades revving. A couple of the guys—Kosoglow and Adams—grabbed the VC by his legs and shoulders and tossed him into the bird's belly, leaving his rifle lying on the ground. The H-34 jumped back into the air and was gone.

Lieutenant Braley was on the horn, talking to the CP back at Chu Lai. He called out to Sergeant Howard that more helicopters were on the way to extract the platoon.

I stood looking down at the pool of darkening blood and the rifle when Knowles nudged me.

"Do you know how to use it?" he asked in a funny voice.

"No."

He gestured toward the village. "Maybe you'd better learn how. Fast."

The village sightseers were gone. In their places appeared men in black pouring out onto the rice fields. The sudden distant popping of rifle fire left little periods and commas of smoke in the air above their heads. Heavy bullets thucked and rattled through the trees. I knew we *really* ought to get out of here.

14

None of us, not even Sergeant Howard, suspected the village of harboring such a force. *Five* guerrillas in a hamlet this size pushed its limits. But twenty or twenty-five soldiers with helmets and bush hats, well-armed and pissed off . . . that meant Main Force, and it meant something was about to go down before Recon Platoon stepped in the middle of it. It happened sometimes that you blundered into something without knowing what you were getting into. Not even Lieutenant Braley, inexperienced as he was, would have had us blast away in an ambush if there was any indication of an enemy outfit this size only shooting distance away

They came at a jogging trot across the open fields, spreading out into a staggered skirmish line as they advanced. Rifles popped, crackling right and left on the line. Some of the attackers yelped like dogs excited on a fresh game trail.

"This is a piss-poor place for a fight," was all Sergeant Howard had to say. "*Haul ass!*"

Translation: Withdraw with haste. Marines *never* retreated; we merely attacked in a different direction. I didn't have to be told twice. Steel and lead buzzed around my head like demented hornets, this first time I had ever been shot at. I attacked in a new direction straight up the hill toward the old OP and the ambush's far rally point.

I stampeded past the blood on the trail, past the cemetery, puffing up the hill through the brush like a bulldozer on high-octane fuel. Creepers grabbed at me with hostile hands, tree branches slapped me in the face, but a concrete wall couldn't have stopped me by this time. I knew now how that silly sonofabitch gook felt when he dashed through our lines at the cemetery wall.

Run! Run! Damnit, run!

Things were getting scarier and scarier out here. We were about to be in some deep shit.

Corporal Knowles was already at the OP when I arrived with my heart pounding. He pointed me into position to begin a perimeter. I took a knee as squad leaders caught other guys storming up the hill and threw them into the perimeter. We were going to make a defense, fight these cocksuckers? *Here?* That wasn't our job. Our job was to get the hell out of here. Jesus, we could get killed doing this kind of grunt rifle company stuff.

"Get back in your position, Hildreth," Knowles growled.

Mulvihill with the PRC-10 radio on his back knelt in the middle of the perimeter. Sergeant Howard had his map out and, unruffled, was making commo with the nearest fire support base.

"Garden Time Five, this is Red Ball Six. Fire mission . . ." He quickly provided grid coordinates and an azimuth, advised of the target, requested HE (high explosive), superquick and delay fuses. "One round, spotter will adjust . . ."

Military wisdom argued that if the enemy could be located and held in place by ground units, calling in artillery and air power would guarantee his destruction at minimum cost. With a maximum effective range of 11,000 meters, the 105mm Light Howitzer M01A1 was deployed by the thousands in Vietnam and provided the ideal fire support weapon when dug and sandbagged in. Howitzers at U.S. Army Special Forces camps in the mountains and boonies, at ARVN posts, and at fire bases covered large surrounding areas of a TAOR to allow ground troops in the bush to know that if they got in trouble they had support able to crash down 105mm rounds within seconds of a call on the radio net. The leader of every mission knew the location of his nearest fire base and its call sign and radio frequency in order to call in fire quickly should it be needed.

A unit in a bind transmitted his location and other pertinent data back to the fire base, where the Fire Direction Control Center (FDC) quickly checked the calculations on a plotting board and relayed the exact required elevation and deflection to the gun crew. Seven men made up a gun crew, with six guns in a battery. Number Six gun was the base gun. Number Six fired the first round to adjust. Once it was on target, the other five guns of the battery aligned themselves with it and lay the firing data on their sights.

The crews loaded forty-two-pound rounds into the breeches and, firing for effect, began pulverizing the distant target in barrages of three or six rounds per gun. The howitzers could fire twenty different types of ammunition, including HE, white phosphorus (WP), smoke, flares, antitank, and anti-personnel (beehive). Fuses could be set quick, or point detonating; timed (two seconds out of the barrel, five seconds, and so forth); delayed, or timed to go off whenever you wanted; and variable, in order to explode at different heights above the ground.

Sergeant Howard's marking round went wide and long. He adjusted and called for three rounds. Everyone was really wired, waiting for arty. McKinney chanted, "Jeez! Jeez! Jeez!" His favorite epithet. Excitement exacerbated Powles's lisp. "They are thooting!" Shooting. I couldn't see the dinks in the rice paddies because of the intervening jungle, but they were coming.

The shells hurtled in six at a time, three different barrages, with whooshing sounds like freight trains roaring down through a narrow canyon, right over our heads. The first rounds exploded on the rice fields with a single *CRRRRUMMP!* Within seconds, the second six slammed into the enemy, followed by the third six. Explosives stomped across the lowlands, banging and cracking in bursts of red and green and gray. Smoke rose into view above the treeline.

"Blow them fuckers *up!*" somebody cheered.

Nothing prepared you for your first exposure to *real* war. Not boot camp or Recon and sniper training, not Wallace Beery movies. While there was something surreal about it, it was also so simple and straightforward. Two forces on opposite sides shooting at each other. I thought there ought to at least be music playing to add drama and suspense to the event. Maybe "Ballad of The Green Berets" or "Halls of Montezuma."

I crouched panting and sweating in the undergrowth, blackguarding Wallace Beery for ever making me want to enlist in the Marine Corps.

Huey gunships whooped in when the 105s lifted. It was spectacular. All those individual duels going on while we watched like spectators at a Cardinals game.

Huey machine guns chattered, answered by the sledge hammer sounds of RPDs from the VC field. A gunship slid across the opening in the trees directly above, trailing little wisps of smoke as its door gunner leaned out over his M60 and laid fire on the enemy, blistering him. Hot brass rained out of the sky onto my back. The bird's M-60's sounded like the magnified ripping of cloth.

Sergeant Howard saw our chance to di-di and we took it, with Knowles on point. While the wicked little choppers with their guns and rockets held the VC at bay, killing or dispersing them, the platoon bugged out the back door to reach a prearranged extraction point. H-34s snatched us to safety. Not a single Recon man had so much as a scratch. We shouted and laughed from pure exhilaration and pounded each other on the back.

The lesson was clear and gratifying. We had nothing to worry about out in the boonies. If we got our asses in a crack, all we had to do was get on the radio with Uncle Sam. He didn't mind burning up a million dollars worth of pyrotechnics to get us out. I was now combat tested. I had followed orders, stood fast, and survived my first firefight.

We all felt pretty cool. We were combat vets.

15

The ambush and the breathtaking escape afterward, with no casualties on our side, worked wonders for morale. At our ages, at least until something happened to change our minds, we really believed we were going to live forever. Even Binns's wounds only won him a few Band-Aids and the platoon's first Vietnam Purple Heart. Nothing bad was going to happen to us. We were too lucky. We were too smart. We were so valuable to the war effort that all we had to do was call in if we had a problem and, like Western Union, the money would be there to bail us out.

Once you overcame your fear, Vietnam was a great adventure, something like climbing Mount Everest or canoeing the Amazon. We were kids, boisterous, bragging young men emerging into full prime in a land that prized and rewarded natural aggression.

The unwinding back at base camp meant a lot of grabassing and wisecracking while we minimized actual or imagined dangers so we didn't have to deal with them right then. The immediate swimming in the ocean, in which even Lieutenant Braley enthusiastically participated, served as a symbolic cleansing of our souls as well as an actual cleansing of our boonie-soiled bodies. The platoon tents rocked far into the night. Sergeant Howard had to come over twice to quiet us down. The rear echelon paper pushers complained because they couldn't get any sleep. Poor babies. Sergeant Howard shook his head and kind of grinned.

Fuck the rear echelon. Let *them* go out there and get shot at and see how they felt.

Adams, Norman, McKinney, and a couple of other guys got in a loud card game using one of the cots as a table. Moore showed Binns his picture of Fama Tankersley. Kosoglow wore a mischievous gleam in his eyes and his Pennsylvania laugh with lots of nasal in it hovered over the tents, like he was thinking of a new prank to pull on somebody. A portable radio tuned to an Armed Forces station played in the background: "Over and Over" by the Dave Clark Five. I played chess with Osorio. One of the fireteam leaders, Lance Corporal Alcadio Mascarenas from New Mexico, pulled up a cot on which to sit and watch.

Mascarenas was probably the quietest member of the platoon. Short, medium build with dark brown skin, fluent in both Spanish and English, he was nonetheless so softspoken that he almost blended into the background.

Lance Corporal Ralph Victor darted by, chasing Benson the machine gunner with a wet towel. He paused. "B-B-Boy, Hildreth. Are you so g-g-good it takes two of them to play you?"

"They've each got only half a brain," I joked.

Neither the card game nor chess could be pursued too zealously on a night when everybody remained on a loud high, rattling on and on. Trying to relive what it felt like out there. Make it funny to rob it of its darker significance.

"Goddamn!" said Kosoglow. "There was fire here and fire there and everybody was shooting. This one goofy fucker comes running right at me with a wild look like the devil was fucking him in the ass, and he just keeps right on going. Nobody even took a shot at him."

"I hope that's me if we ever get ambushed—nobody takes a shot at me," Norman said.

"I'm running through that brush like a motherfucker when the bad guys start coming," said Billy D, laughing. "I look up and a streak goes by. It's Hildreth and he's *moving on home, baby.*"

"Don't look back. Right, Hildreth?" Adams chided. "Something might be gaining on you."

"My daddy didn't raise no fool," I said.

"Then who raised you?" Moore asked, grinning.

I ignored him. "Your move, Osorio."

Benson sang out one of our little ditties: "Rock 'em, sock 'em. Go, God, go!"

Over in the card game somebody got to talking about An Ton, the Vietnamese village outside the gates, wondering if there was any pussy there and if we could sneak out to find it. Something about escaping death made you horny.

"You'll get black syphilis and it'll rot off your dick and eat your brain," Mulvihill warned.

"Adams's dick *is* his brain," Billy D laughed.

I boxed in Osorio with my queen. "If you lose, Osorio, you gonna get us some Spanish fly?"

"Is that the only way you can get poo-sy, Hildreth? Get her doped up?"

"It's for McKinney."

Norman laughed and assumed his best Arizona Zane Grey stance, tipping back an imaginary Stetson with his thumb and mimicking McKinney's Louisiana swampland accent. "Pardon me, mamsalle bebe. Do you have any pussy for two dollars?"

"Jeez!" Over in the card game, McKinney ducked his head and actually blushed.

During Marine orientation at Camp Schwab in Okinawa, the base chaplain, a Navy commander, informed us horny young Marines that there were two hotels—Hotel Ginza and Hotel Tokyo—outside the gates in Henoko where the chances of catching clap or something even worse were decreased because mamasan brought her girls on base once a month for VD checkups. Naturally, since the chaplain recommended it, Norman, Moore, Kosoglow, and I had to look things over and research the goods. Even lowly Marine Pfc's could afford the fees: two dollars for a short time, five for an all-nighter, plus a buck for the hotel room.

"You still a virgin?" Benson the redhead teased McKinney.

"Jeez!"

Moore and I had introduced our little Marine brother to the carnal pleasures offered off base at Okinawa. At least we assumed we introduced him. I even paid the two dollars. A skinny Japanese girl with big teeth grabbed his hand and dragged him into a crib. Moore and I waited outside, sniggering.

McKinney came tearing out in short order, appalled and indignant. The entire platoon now roared with laughter when I finished telling the story. Once alone with him, the big-toothed girl lit a cigarette and placed it in an ashtray. A short-timer, she informed the shy Cajun, ended when the cigarette burned down to the filter.

"I refuse to perform on demand," McKinney alibied, still blushing but grinning good-naturedly.

Binns, the serious one, said, looking at Knowles, "It was a screwed-up ambush. We shouldn't have fired so soon."

Powles won a hand with a pair of kings. "Why did you do that, Ronnie? Why didn't you wait until we all could see them? One little VC shot up out of five ain't very good shooting."

"All right. All right, I fucked up," Knowles acknowledged with a scowl. "I thought I was going to lose them all. I didn't know they were coming up through the hedgeline. I thought they were getting ready to go the other direction. I wonder if the slant-eyed little bastard died. The platoon gets a body count if he did."

It started to rain outside, a thick drizzle pelting on the tents' canvas roofs. We had got back just in time. Recon really had it knocked compared to the rifle companies. We went into the field for a few days at a time, then came back in to showers, hot chow, and sleeping dry off the ground without having to worry about Charlie pulling reveille on us in the middle of the night.

The poor suckers on the line moved first here and dug in, then moved there, slogging through rice paddies and bamboo and villes with hostile natives, Arkansas-skinny pigs, bare-assed chickens, and kids equally bare-assed, and dug in again among more rice paddies and bamboo. After that, they got up and moved again to a place that looked exactly like the last place, but wasn't, and dug in again. All the time the sun baked their brains during the day and the rains followed in the evening and made them stiff and wet and irritable and filled up their sleeping holes.

Booby traps blew off their legs and gouged out their eyes. Firefights and ambushes stole away their buddies wrapped in bloody ponchos. Foot rot and crotch rot and fungi and parasites gnawed them down to moldered skin and bones. Leeches sucked what blood remained.

Every man's war was different in Vietnam.

Adams stretched back on his cot, clasped his fingers behind his head and sighed contentedly. Rain drummed on the tent and splashed at the open flaps.

"Wonder what the *real* jarheads are doing on a night like this," he mused. "The poor bastards."

Victor and McKinney were the platoon pessimists and cynics. For them, Murphy as in Murphy's law—Anything that could go wrong, *would*—was a real guy and bunked out next to them.

"One of these days," Victor stuttered, "we're gonna get in a real sh-sh-shitstorm and nobody can get us out. What happens then?"

Kosoglow laughed.

"We'll be all right," I interceded quickly, "as long as we don't go northwest."

16

Division was still looking for the enemy and wanted him in numbers instead of piddly-assed squads of VC Regional Forces and an occasional Main Force platoon. Division wanted VC Main Force and NVA companies or battalions in order to wax some major ass. We kept hearing they were in the TAOR. But *where?*

That was about all we common grunts knew about the "Big Picture." In the crotch, they really never told you shit. I assumed someone at Division or MACV knew everything that was going on, back in some war-gaming room with maps on the walls with colored pins stuck in them. Sometimes I had my doubts that the paper pushers and rear echelon motherfuckers really cared about what happened to us. To them, we were nothing but colored pencil marks or pins on maps. Green meant we were lucky and safe back at Chu Lai; red signified we were in some kind of danger; black signaled we were in it deep and taking casualties. If we got creamed, I assumed, some asshole simply wiped off our mark, removed our pin, threw it away, and put somebody else in our place.

Lieutenant Braley and Sergeant Howard decided the platoon could double its coverage and expand our chances of finding the enemy if they split us into two elements. Captain Geraghty, the Company CO, apparently concurred, the idea being that each of the two squads would insert at different points and patrol back toward each other to eventually reunite at a common rendezvous. Sergeant Howard took Binns's Second Squad, leaving Braley with Knowles's First Squad. I felt reasonably comfortable with the lieutenant by this time, although he was no seasoned warrior like Sergeant Howard and Binns still felt uncomfortable with him. There was even some scuttlebutt that Sergeant Howard and the lieutenant weren't getting along.

Deep penetration Recons were supposed to travel light, but Sergeant Howard insisted the platoon go heavily armed even if it meant leaving food and comfort items behind. "Carry enough ammo to hold out if we have to until we get support," he demanded. Humping anything on your back in the jungle eventually became agony. We bitched about the weight, but Sergeant Howard ultimately proved to be right.

It started to rain early in the afternoon shortly after H-34s inserted First Squad with Lieutenant Braley. I took point first; I carried a lighter-weight M-14 like everyone else by this time. It had become clear that snipers in Recon were never going to be utilized as such. I had to admit I wasn't particularly disappointed. I went over to supply and traded in my old M-1D, thus reducing weight and doubling my firepower at the same time. Kosoglow, Norman, and Moore readily followed my example.

Sergeant Howard approved. "Good decision," he said.

Clouds continued to roll in, the sky became darkly overcast, and the rain was a cold, drenching highland rain that chilled us to the bone after our bodies had grown accustomed to tropical heat. Eerie twilight settled over the forest, muting sound. I found little comfort in the realization that the jungle was neutral and that the VC got wet and cold and leeches too. Ponchos went slickety-slick in the down-pour and clothing underneath became sodden, filthy, and stiff and chafed against our skin. Because we didn't take off our clothes or remove our boots for days at a time while we were out on mission, minor problems quickly became major ones—jungle sores, small cuts, boot blisters, mosquito bites wouldn't heal. It was a little taste of what the rifle company grunts endured day after day. Osorio, Hawkins, and some of the other short-timers due for transfer back to the World began taking peroxide baths so their faces would clear up. McKinney's face looked like he was going through pimples and puberty all over again. Mine didn't look much better.

Braley pointed and told me to lead to the top of a hill shrouded in rain fog. It was tough going. We moved through a thick, live, wet curtain. Everything green was circular and grew from the top down rather than the bottom up. Vines intertwined with one another and hung from forest giants whose roots crawled along the ground to trip you. Bamboo-like plants six and eight feet tall shot up straight as palms and as tough as steel. Footing was precarious and as slippery as snot. Slopes became mudslides almost impossible to climb, while downed trees made passage even more difficult. Stagnant pools and rotting vegetation hatched evil clouds of mosquitoes. Everything stank. *We* stank.

Distance to the top of the hill proved deceptive in the rain. We crossed a swamp and halted on the other side to burn off leeches with cigarette butts held underneath ponchos or to scrape them off with Ka-bars. Point man had to be rotated frequently under such strenuous conditions. Mascarenas took my place and the lieutenant selected an easier route to the top of the hill. It was getting dark by the time we reached our destination. Braley contacted Sergeant Howard's squad on the PRC-10 and informed him we would remain overnight where we were.

Trying to stay warm, I hunched underneath my poncho while the rain made puddles off it and the inky blackness of night seeped around us. Sleep would be tortured and intermittent at best, no matter that we were all virtually collapsed from exhaustion. My stomach gnawed from hunger. I used a P-38 to open a C ration can and attempted to eat.

Life in the bush afforded few pleasures. One of these was eating, if you could do it right. C rats not done right had to be something wished upon us by a sadistic enemy. Most of the guys split open the little boxed meals and took with them only what they liked. Some of us—gourmets, if you will—took the entire box and relished in the preparation of it when we had the opportunity.

Each boxed meal contained a canned main course of either ham and limas, turkey loaf, ham and eggs, pork or beef slices with potatoes and gravy, spaghetti, and one or two other choices. *Everything* was canned except the accessory pack that contained plastic eating utensils, a P-38, salt and pepper, toilet paper napkins and toothpick, instant coffee and cocoa mix, a chocolate bar, and a little pack of three cigarettes. Since I didn't smoke, I traded my cigarettes for canned fruitcake, white cake, fruit cocktail, peaches, or pears. Peaches were best.

Everybody hoarded a little bottle of Tabasco hot sauce, the idea being that you could eat your combat boots if you had to, as long as you sprinkled them with hot sauce. Mascarenas was a good combat cook, as were Binns and Billy D. You could mix and match, heat everything in your canteen cup over a heat tab or a little pinch of burning C-4 explosive, dash in salt and pepper and Tabasco—and actually enjoy it, followed by a desert of white cake under peaches. It wasn't steak and lobster or fried chicken, but it wasn't bad, not bad at all. Considering.

You couldn't really appreciate C rations, however, until you tried to eat cold pork slices with potatoes and gravy as rain mixed with the thick grease in the OD-green can. At least the water drowned some of the insects that crawled into the can.

Huddled underneath my poncho, sheltering my food as well as possible, unable to heat it in the rain, I dug at the mess with a heavy plastic spoon while my stomach churned at the thought of eating it. Truly, war was hell.

17

Even though we knew our enemy were runts, little bitty motherfuckers, in our imaginations they were monsters, almost superhuman. They could do anything. Sneak up while we slept and snip buttons off our uniforms—or cut our throats. Break any barriers. Mass any number of men. Never run out of supplies. Live off a pocketful of rice mixed with muddy water from the tracks of a water buffalo. They never got sick. They were invulnerable.

As First Squad slowly worked its way toward a rendezvous with Sergeant Howard and Second Squad, Lieutenant Braley kept us busy on scouting parties looking for the VC. That was another thing the VC were good at—hiding. They were like wisps of fog. Like ghosts. Binns said they probably thought *we* were ghosts.

The rain stopped after the first night, leaving the jungle soaking and sloppy. The sun came out and heated everything up to steam. Tendrils of mist writhed among trees and clotted in pockets. Lieutenant Braley pointed to a map and sent Osorio, Moore, Adams, and me out to watch a jungle trail. The lieutenant had lost his pale stateside complexion and replaced it with one raw and red and bugbitten. Welcome to Vietnam, the world's armpit and crotch.

"Division is asking for a prisoner," he said. "If you get a chance, snatch one of the little shitballs."

Roger that. And while we were at it, catch a leprechaun and make him tell us where he hid his gold.

We watched the trail most of the morning and saw nothing except mosquitoes. We hid in a small clearing behind a wall of thicket about twenty paces from the trail. After two or three hours of tedium, Osorio indicated the PRC-10 radio and told me to make commo with Lieutenant Braley.

"Tell him this is a dry hole," he whispered.

Unlike newer radios such as the PRC-25, on which you merely set the frequency and started talking, the PRC-10 first had to be calibrated. To calibrate it, you pushed in one knob to release the frequency selector and fiddled with the selector to fine-tune it on channel. Sort of like finding a station on a regular AM/FM radio. I had never calibrated one of the damned things except in training. I couldn't get it right. Frustrated, I lay my weapon aside and crawled about ten feet over to ask Osorio a question. You never spoke out loud while you were in bandit country. Moore and Adams lay in bushes nearby watching the trail.

I knew I had fucked up the instant I saw Osorio's face. It darkened even more than normal so that he suddenly looked constipated.

"What—?" I began.

His eyes snapped at me and he stiffened. I followed the movement of his eyes until—There they were. Ghosts. Enemy soldiers swinging down the trail toward us. These guys were hard core Main Force too. The type we were looking for. No black PJs and straw cones for these fellows. They wore camouflage uniforms and bush hats. One sported a helmet. They approached so rapidly I dared not chance giving us away by any movement.

The first thing I thought of was my rifle. There it lay, ten feet away, as though mocking me at the moment I needed it most. It may as well have been on Mars. If shooting started, I would be one dead piece of meat long before I reached it and started shooting back. You had to go to stupidity school to get this stupid. I could almost hear Binns snarling. *You dumb ass of a boot.*

Drill instructors back in boot camp had taught us a little chant:

> *This is your rifle*
> *This is your gun.*
> *This is for fighting,*
> *This is for fun.*

"Ladies, you got a rifle—" holding up the weapon—"and you got a gun"—grabbing his crotch. "At least, I assume most of you do. From now on, you will treat your rifle the same as your gun. If you can reach and touch your pecker anytime you want, make sure you can touch your rifle anytime you want. Your rifle can save your dick. Your dick can't save shit. The rifle is your friend. Clear?"

"Sir. Yes, sir!"

My dick was hanging way out.

We froze in the thick brush, hardly breathing while the VC passed. They were a fairly large element, far too many for us to take on under any circumstances. How could they keep from seeing us, we were so close to the trail? Fortunately, they weren't paying a lot of attention; they weren't hunting. You didn't see what you didn't expect to see; these guys obviously never expected to see us so deep in their territory. They traveled single file with six to eight feet between and, again fortunately for us, no flankers. It was old home week on the farm. They yakked up a storm, jabbering like crows on a fence. Just like the five we ambushed on the rice paddy trail.

I counted them as they passed. Thirteen all in a row, carrying AK's and SKS's, and one of them an RPD light machine gun. Ho Chi Minh sandals made out of tire treads on their feet. Smelling like fermented fish. They kept going, vanishing so quickly around a bend in the trail that it was like we had never really seen them. Unreal, like ghosts.

When I could breathe again, I scrambled for my rifle. Osorio didn't have to say a word. I knew I'd fucked up. From now on, I vowed, I wouldn't let that rifle out of my hands even to take a crap in the woods.

Osorio rallied the team and we beat feet back to Lieutenant Braley's CP. Braley made a SALUTE to battalion S-2—we had found some of the little bastards. S-2 came back up on the net to tell us to rendezvous with Sergeant Howard. I was jittery the rest of the day over what happened and what *could* have happened.

By early dusk, the squad moved around the edge of a rice paddy next to the jungle. We had been humping hard all afternoon and our tongues were slapping our ankles. Cooking fires and oil lamps in the small village across the way reminded me of pictures of Indian camps in 1870s Oklahoma or Nebraska. Dogs yapping, people talking. Sound carried long distances at night.

I walked point again. Braley looked at the village, then motioned me back into the woods to break brush again. He called a halt once we were in the shadows. He and Osorio got underneath a poncho in order to use a red-lensed flashlight to study the map. I had a hunch the lieutenant had gotten us lost.

Word came back up for me to lead out on an azimuth of ninety-five degrees. Moore came up to run compass for me. Point carried a special responsibility and a special danger and mustn't be distracted. Point watched everything out front, the entire 180 degrees, from eye level and below. Slack took the left overhead and the ninety degrees to the left. The third man took the left overhead and the ninety to the left. The fourth and subsequent men scanned the areas to their sides and overhead. Tailend Charlie covered the rear and brushed out tracks if he needed to.

It was tedious and nerve-wracking work. In enemy country, you walked at a slow march, putting your feet down carefully and stopping every five or ten meters to look and listen and sniff the air. You developed a feeling, a rhythm, when you moved like that. That was the way it had to be or else you got caught. You got in a hurry, you got careless, you got fucked up. Sooner or later you got fucked up.

It was point's ass first if he led the element into a shitstorm. He could trigger an ambush or, like Binns had, blunder into a booby trap—a punji pit, a canned grenade, a Malayan whip, a Bouncing Betty, a buried mine, or toe popper. The Vietnamese were ingenious little fuckers when it came to booby traps, and booby traps were their bread and butter. They could mess you up in a dozen ways without your ever even seeing them.

I didn't know where the hell I was going or to what destination. I simply followed instructions. Full darkness settled, and I couldn't see shit. I couldn't even see my own feet. Monsters lurked in the night. I led the patrol around the village, then began climbing through thick stuff, breaking trail. Sweeping out ahead with my rifle barrel to feel for wires, praying I didn't hit one. God, I hated booby traps. They were evil.

Click.

Like a rifle safety snapping *OFF*. Or a booby trap activating.

I aged ten years in a tenth of a second. I dropped. It was amazing how long it took, even from a crouch, to get completely flat. The rest of the squad went to cover behind me like dominos. I lay tense on the ground with my nerves jangling like bursts of electricity going through them. I thought about spraying everything out there in front where the sound came from.

Lieutenant Braley crawled up beside me. He had been on and off the radio all evening with Sergeant Howard. He touched my arm.

"Easy, Hildreth."

Directly ahead, a red-lensed flashlight blinked on and off. I heard Braley break squelch on the radio. The red flashlight winked again.

"That's Howard," the lieutenant said, sounding relieved. "Move on up to the perimeter."

I lost it. I simply lost it. "You dumb sonofabitch," I hissed into the lieutenant's face. "Why didn't you tell me we were almost there? I could have shot 'em."

"I thought you knew."

"Fuck I knew. You didn't tell me shit."

"All right, Hildreth. Can it. I'll take the hit. It won't happen again. Now, move on out."

"Yes, sir. *Sir.*"

My rage wasn't entirely reasonable. Nerves can get raw in the bush. I still seethed as the platoon reconsolidated.

"You guys almost gave me a heart attack," I said.

"Heart attackth are common in the buth," Powles said with his mild lisp.

18

I was always hungry in the bush. I couldn't carry enough food in my deuce gear to replace all the calories I burned. I lost as much as ten or fifteen pounds on each excursion and had to eat everything in sight once we returned to base camp to replace the weight. By the end of any particular patrol, we often resorted to living on water and, for those of us who smoked, cigarettes.

I was hungry now. The platoon had been sitting on an ambush site all afternoon in the somnolent heat. Division and Lieutenant Braley still wanted a prisoner for the spooks to question. It was getting toward evening, cooling off some, and the "fuck you" lizards were coming out. *Phuoc leu! Phuoc ieu!*

Fuck you back, I thought.

Concealed in the bushes, I glanced up and down the trail and decided it was safe. I eased a peanut butter tin out of my pack, but then couldn't find a P-38 with which to open it. I used my Ka-bar instead and ended up scooping out peanut butter with my finger. I spat out the bugs.

I was just finishing it off when a cone head on an old balloon-tired bicycle came riding along as happy as an

Arkansas hog in slop. He was even humming a little tune, oblivious to everything around him.

"Get that silly sonofabitch!" Sergeant Howard shouted.

That brought the gook back to reality. The bicycle wobbled on the trail as a half-dozen black-faced jarheads in green leaped out of the bushes and piled on the guy. Even in war, there were some funny times. It was an Abbott and Costello moment, a Keystone Kops spectacle. In short order, the prisoner had his hands quick-cuffed behind him and sat on the trail. Marines were laughing and going on and looking the guy over. This was as close as most of us had ever come to one of them. The gook managed a sheepish grin.

Lieutenant Braley and Sergeant Howard made commo with S-2. Somehow they all decided the kid wasn't a VC or that he wasn't worth sending out a helicopter for. We still had to keep him overnight. Just in case he *was* the enemy and would send back bad guys to look for us. Sergeant Howard kept a guard on him overnight and turned him loose the next morning as we moved out of the AO. The kid pushed his bicycle off through the trees without looking back.

"Maybe we should have cut his throat anyhow," Corporal Knowles said.

For breakfast I had water and a John Wayne chocolate bar. We came across a couple of single huts out by themselves and I found myself sniffing the air for cooking smells. My stomach growled. I was so hungry I might have eaten rice with *nuoc mam,* that shitty-smelling rotted fermented fish entrails-and-eyes-and-lips sauce. Now *that* was hungry.

I spotted some pineapples growing in a small patch and liberated one for the betterment of the Free World. I peeled and ate it during a rest break. It tasted especially sweet but more acidic than the ones back in the World. I offered Norman and McKinney some, but they declined.

"Do you know what the gooks use for fertilizer?" Norman asked, then answered his own question. "Night soil. Human shit."

I looked at the pineapple pieces and shrugged. I had juice all over my face and hands.

"I thought you cowboy-types ate rattlesnakes and coyotes," I commented.

"We don't eat *gook shit*."

We had barely reached the landing zone for our extraction when the first excruciating pains wracked my guts. They almost bent me double, but they quickly passed.

One lone tree about six inches in diameter and fifteen feet tall grew in the middle of the clearing where the helicopters, one at a time, had to sit down to load us.

"Hildreth, you and Powles chop down that tree," Sergeant Howard ordered.

"Okay." I looked at it. "What with?"

"Use your Ka-bars."

We hacked at it. It was a palm-type with a soft trunk. I grabbed my stomach and doubled over.

"I gotta go."

"When you gotta go, you gotta go."

I almost made it.

Powles whiffed the air when I got back, making a face. "God," he complained, "you smell like thit."

"I feel like shit."

Gunships always escorted the H-34s for a pickup. They hovered above the edges of the clearing, keeping watch, while the slicks glided over the jungle canopy on approach. Radios crackled.

"*Snake Two-One, Red Team Leader. Mark your Lima Zula with smoke, now. Over.*"

Sergeant Howard tossed an M18 smoke grenade spewing yellow smoke.

"*I have yellow smoke. Confirm that, Red Team Leader?*"

"Roger that, Snake."

The choppers roller-coastered in and hovered one-by-one over the landing zone until the last man, Sergeant Howard, clambered aboard. Then they poured on the power, climbing fast and jinking right and left to avoid possible ground fire. I lay sick on the cold metal floor, up on one elbow to relieve the mounting pressure, smelling the essence of the bird—a combination of hot oil, gasoline, grease, mildew, sweat and cigarettes. The crew chief wore a scarred helmet with a legend inscribed on it: *If I die in a combat zone, bury me face down so Vietnam can kiss my ass.*

Nobody wanted to sit next to me. I had the cramps bad. The helicopter wasn't flying fast enough. *Hurry, hurry, hurry . . .*

I almost made it.

19

The Chu Lai SubDefense Zone appeared to be transforming itself almost overnight. Seabees—Navy Construction Battalion engineers—were busy from sunup to sundown measuring and hammering and bulldozing. They built officer and NCO and EM clubs so we didn't have to wait in line for two hours at the chow hall to get our daily allotment of two hot beers. The clubs even had electricity for a few hours at night, provided by gasoline-powered generators.

In the beginning, the chow hall was a GP tent (large) with freight pallets fitted together for flooring. Seabees built a hardback messhall. The first few days back in, we ate everything in sight. After that, we didn't feel much like eating. It was so hot and miserable. Sergeant Howard issued an order that every swinging dick had to go to chow whether he ate or not. He didn't want anyone flaking out on mission due to lack of nutrition.

We returned from the field to find that the Seabees had even constructed wooden floors for our platoon sleeping tents. No more walking barefooted on the sand.

"Oh-h-h, a *hardwood* floor," Victor cooed with sarcasm. "I think I'll p-p-put in for the penthouse suite when it's finished."

Sergeant Major Turner wanted the battalion area looking especially good. Chu Lai was our home, he said. At least it was our home temporarily and should look like a home. Maybe it looked like home to him, his being a lifer, but I had other images of what home meant: girls who smelled good; movie theaters with air conditioning; a hot dog stand on the corner; a drive-in where everybody hung out.

Sergeant Major grabbed every man he could to put him out on work details—installing metal bomb crates as seating for the outdoor theater; digging wells from which water could be pumped into a retaining pressure tower; replacing the cold outdoor field showers with privately enclosed gravity showers heated by the sun. . . .

If any brass were scheduled to come down and see the battalion commander, Sergeant Major had somebody on a Mighty Mite, the USMC version of an all-purpose vehicle, leveling and smoothing the sand by dragging a section of old airstrip runway metal around. While it gave the grounds a graded, symmetrical appearance, it never lasted long because of the wind and vehicular traffic. I suspected Sergeant Major might have had us out painting rocks, if there had been any rocks.

Recon platoons on stand down proved to have no immunity from Sergeant Major's obsession. Usual garrison routine called for only a half-day's training: rubber boat handling in the surf, recon techniques, patrolling, radio, fire mission procedures, weapons. . . . First though, every morning, Sergeant Major came calling to the companies to get his quota of men for battalion shit details.

It's a fact of military life that colonels get the medals and privates and corporals clean the latrines. I literally volunteered for the shit detail—burning the accumulated deposits from the outdoor comfort stations. It was shitty work, like Osorio said, but it was quick work. I dragged the half-barrels out from the multiholed toilets, mixed fuel oil with the contents, and lit them up into boiling black smoke. Burning excrement was one of the many unpleasant odors that marked bases in Vietnam, the others being insecticides, urine, asphalt, jet fuel, cordite, and general man smells.

While the excrement burned, I sat upwind and either read or wrote letters to my girlfriends. *Having a shitty time, wish you were here.* Few officers chose to defy the stench to violate my privacy. After that, I had the rest of the day off to hang out while everybody else remained on detail.

"Orderly of the shithouse," Moore started calling me.

"It's good work if you can get it," I shot back. "Where are you headed? Oh, you're on KP? All night? Gosh, that's tough. Where am I going? I think I'll go for a swim and work on my tan."

Otherwise, we lived a rather bucolic and tolerable existence in garrison, with lots of free time to wait and anticipate the next mission. We loafed around the tent scuttlebutting and grabassing, playing cards or chess and talking about girls. Swimming was almost a daily ritual, as was a movie at night. Mail call provided the single major social event of the day. Guys competed for the privilege of walking to battalion to pick up the mail. It was almost as good as getting mail yourself. It broke the boredom and drudgery of war as physical labor and provided an opportunity to circulate and see how the war was going elsewhere.

I received plenty of mail. Ex-girlfriends and girlfriends from high school. I liked to show off by showing off their pictures. "They all love me," I bragged, waving my pages of sweet-smelling letters. I was their "soldier boy" away from home. They were contributing to the war effort and the morale of the troops. One time two of them were injured in a bad auto accident and none of the others wrote me about it until weeks afterward. Shirley said they didn't want me to have to worry about anything back home, as I must have enough to worry about fighting the war.

Moore, who had his Fama Tankersley, whom he declared enough for any one man, suggested I have some of my girl pen pals write to the guys who didn't have girlfriends and who received few letters. I asked Shirley about it.

I don't know them, she fired back. *What'll I say?*

Tell them they're wonderful, I proposed. *Write to them about home. That's what they want to hear about. Put perfume on the letters.*

"Perfume is okay, but have them rub the letters in their crotches," Kosoglow said. "That's what we *really* want to smell."

For some reason unknown to the common grunt and known only to the enemy, and perhaps to the Marine brass, Chu Lai remained relatively secure. No one seemed particularly concerned that the U.S. Marines were encamped in the middle of hostile territory. People in swim trunks ran up and down the beach barefooted and unarmed during daylight hours. There were no attacks, no probing fire or nighttime mortar harassment.

The base didn't even have wire for the VC to probe. The defensive outside perimeter consisted of a series of sandbagged bunkers one hundred meters apart, starting about one mile south of Recon Battalion at an inlet where the Cau Dai River emptied into the ocean. There were other bunkers around the ammo dump and the airfield and an occasional wooden watch tower, but very little concertina wire and no guard dogs sullied the neighborhood.

SubSector Five Defense was laid back. Like Sergeant Major said, the First Marine Division was at home. Like good neighbors, the enemy didn't disturb us at home.

Quite in contrast to Chu Lai, the Da Nang airfield, a mere ten or fifteen minutes' chopper ride north, had fought for its very existence since the beginning. Only one month after Seabees completed construction of the airstrip, on 1 July 1965, a sapper team crept onto the airfield and destroyed three aircraft and damaged three more. Small arms fire wounded three Marines as they chased the sappers off the base.

That was the way it had gone ever since. VC and NVA troops frequently probed the wire. Rifle and mortar fire erupted regularly from the surrounding rice paddies. Only this month, while Chu Lai basked in peace, the situation at Da Nang had so deteriorated that American civilians, nonessential military personnel, and foreign nationals were being evacuated. Marine elements were pulled back out of the field to guard the installation.

Chu Lai had been attacked only one time, that being seven months ago on the night of 27–28 October 1965. About twenty sappers snaked onto the base to destroy two jets and damage six. At the same time, some 90 Main Force guerrillas attacked under a barrage of mortar fire. Three Marines were killed and 91 wounded. Everything had been quiet since then.

Perhaps Chu Lai's relaxed atmosphere contributed to the at-ease flavor of its units. Division hounded Recon and the rifle companies to find the enemy, fix him, and fuck him up. Still, few major clashes occurred. Just little ankle biters, annoying as hell but unable to settle anything. It seemed foe and friendly alike moved around on the chess board trying to avoid one another. In two months of "fighting," First Platoon had suffered a single casualty—and that a minor one. You could enjoy a war when your buddies weren't getting hurt and you could watch Steve McQueen or Robert Mitchum on the silver screen every night and listen to the Rolling Stones on Armed Forces radio.

We felt pretty good about ourselves. I was beginning to think that war wasn't that bad after all. The lack of major contacts prompted a joke that passed around base. New meat were real suckers for it when it was told with appropriate gravity and dramatic inference. Victor's deadpan delivery and innocent little clicking stutter were particularly effective.

"There was this one mission where we were p-p-pinned down on this hill all night," he began, dropping his chin and shaking his head as though in emotional denial. "Heavy fire b-b-blasted us from three sides. I really thought the platoon was about to be marked off black. But we fought like tigers. All night we f-f-fought. When dawn finally came, we fixed bayonets and, out of desperation, counterattacked the enemy in vicious hand-to-hand combat."

His voice broke as though he lacked the fortitude to continue. That was the break the enthralled new guy required in order to ask his breathless question: "What happened then?"

There were two ways to finish the story. Victor took a deep breath. It could be either, "They killed us all!" or "We killed them all—all t-t-three of them."

Private First Class Charles Bosley, nineteen, who had reported in only that morning, stared at Victor with a mixture of awe and incredulity. He was a soft-spoken Hoosier with hair the color of ripe wheat.

"He's pulling your leg, Bosley," I said.

He looked surprised. "You mean . . . it really didn't happen?"

"You believed that? You've got to be shitting me, right?"

"Did you really think three gooks could pin down a *Recon* platoon?" Adams demanded, swaggering over. "Bosley, you cherry asshole. I could whip three gooks all by myself. Right, Powles?"

"Roger that, good buddy."

We were cocky, all right. Almost half the platoon was made up of inexperienced new guys barely out of boot camp, who didn't know enough *not* to be brash. I was one of the old hands, a veteran, and I hadn't been in-country hardly two months yet. And all I ever shot up were some bushes in a botched ambush.

One by one, the old hands like Corporal Ronnie Knowles, Hawkins, and Osorio transferred back home to the land of the Big PX, their tours of duty complete. Lieutenant Braley was neither an old hand nor a short-timer. But one day Sergeant Howard came over to the platoon tents and said the lieutenant had received orders to report to Okinawa. No other explanation. We wondered if the transfer had something to do with the scuttlebutt about Howard and Braley not getting along.

Sergeant Howard once more became acting platoon leader *and* platoon sergeant. Binns moved back up, unofficially, to second man in charge.

It seemed the platoon was mutating even as the base transformed itself. New guys took the short timers' places almost as soon as they left.

Private First Class Thomas Glawe was another new guy who came in about the same time Bosley did. He was a tall, slender eighteen-year-old who, being from Chicago, felt compelled to adopt a tough gangsterlike talk and walk.

"Man, them gooks ain't tangled with me yet," he blustered. "Man, I am gonna *pop* some of them."

Did we all come in full of ourselves like that? His first time out he'd be as scared as the rest of us.

Late that afternoon, some doofus in Alpha Company accidentally fired off a 40mm round while he was cleaning a loaded M-79 grenade launcher. The grenade ripped a hole through the tent roof and exploded on the west side of the chow hall. That generated some excitement; we thought we were being attacked. Everyone snatched rifles and ran outside. Binns glanced at the wide-eyed Glawe and sniffed.

"How are you going to kill gooks?" he asked. "Dumb ass. You left your rifle in the tent."

20

By April 1966, the First Marine Division's "Old Breed" was fully deployed in its TAOR and approaching 17,000 men in-country, including two regiments of infantry, the Fifth and Seventh Marines, four battalions of artillery, and supporting units. The First along with the Third Marine Division at Da Nang composed the III Marine Amphibious Force. The most savage battles fought by the Marines in I Corps occurred before I arrived in Vietnam. Although things had been relatively quiet in the months since the end of March, the amount of patrolling and reconnaissance laid upon the Recon companies told us the brass wanted major enemy contact in the worst possible way, along the line of those operations conducted in early March. Commanders down to the platoon level spoke of "another *Starlite*" or "another *Utah*" in which the VC and NVA would once more be found and defeated.

It wasn't that the enemy hadn't designs on Chu Lai. The October attack against the base was the only one simply because Marine activity kept Charlie off-balance and prevented his massing for another attempt. By luck, aggressive patrolling, and good intel, the Marines managed to keep the fighting confined inland away from the seacoast and the airbase.

As at Da Nang, the enemy had intended to wipe out Chu Lai before the U.S. established a firm toehold. On 15 August 1965, when Chu Lai was barely an enclave and the airfield still under construction, a member of the First VC Regiment surrendered to the ARVN. Interrogation of the prisoner revealed that his regiment of 1,500 soldiers had established a base fifteen kilometers south of Chu Lai and about two kilometers inland. It was from there that the VC prepared for a full-scale attack.

Major General Lewis W. Walt, commander of both the III MAF and the Third Marine Division, did not wait for the Vietnamese to strike. He launched Operation *Starlite* on 18 August. First Recon Platoon, Charlie Company—my outfit—was involved in the early patrolling before General Walt committed two battalions to the attack.

Three Marine companies made an amphibious landing to the south and east of the Van Tuong village complex where the VC were staging, blocking the southern escape routes. A fourth company moved overland from Chu Lai to block escape four kilometers northwest of the landing beaches.

Immediately after the anvil set up, three companies of Marines dropped the hammer by helo-assaulting into three separate landing zones south and southwest of Van Tuong. Everything was in place and ready before dawn.

Despite a great deal of confusion, the Marines won the battle after two days of bitter fighting. Heavy artillery, close air support, and the six-inch guns of the light cruiser U.S.S. *Galveston* made the difference. What was left of the First VC Regiment withdrew, leaving nearly half its number, 614 men, slain on the battlefield. The Marines lost 45 KIA (killed in action).

General Walt continued battering the VC regiment in September by launching Operation *Piranha* to pursue the retreating enemy. Although 178 VC were killed in the operation, compared to five Marines and ARVN KIA, the operation could hardly be deemed a success. In fact, the First VC Regiment had already fled the area—but would return again as soon as allied troops withdrew. The Batangan Peninsula south and west of Van Tuong remained an enemy stronghold.

For three months following the operations, the Viet Cong refused to meet the Marines in battle while the First Regiment resupplied, rearmed, and replaced itself. That didn't mean the VC were idle. On the night of 27–28 October, VC hit both the helicopter facility at Marble Mountain near Da Nang and, for the first and only time so far, the Chu Lai airfield.

In November, a revitalized First VC Regiment moved northwest of Chu Lai and overran the small ARVN garrison holding Hiep Duc in Quang Tin Province. Hiep Duc was the district capital at the western end of the fertile Hiep Duc Valley, also known as the Que Son Valley, one of the most strategic areas between Da Nang and Chu Lai. This region, bordered on both the north and south by rugged mountain ranges, remained bitterly contested. Fighting in the valley had led to Ralph Victor's admonition upon my arrival in First Platoon that southwest of Chu Lai wasn't so bad but that *northwest* into the Hiep Duc Valley meant trouble.

In December, the Seventieth VC Battalion all but wiped out the Fifth ARVN Regiment near Hiep Duc and drove the surviving ARVN troops into the hills. During Marine efforts to relieve the ARVN and reestablish dominance, an operation known as *Harvest Moon,* Foxtrot Company, Second Battalion, First Marine Regiment found itself cut off and raked by vicious blasts of enemy fire. Echo Company of the 2/7 went to the rescue. It in turn was attacked and isolated. During a ten-hour ordeal, the two companies suffered more than 100 casualties, including twenty dead.

Shortly thereafter, Hotel Company 2/9 found itself in a similar predicament when attacked from the rear and both flanks. The Marines lost eleven KIA and 71 WIA, compared to 104 KIA left on the battlefield by the Eightieth VC Battalion.

Operation *Harvest Moon* ended on 20 December when all Marine maneuver battalions returned to their enclaves at Da Nang and Chu Lai. That left the enemy once more free to build up his forces in the Hiep Duc Valley. The allies chalked down on their dich boards for the operation 407 enemy KIA and 33 captured. ARVN forces lost 90 killed, 141 wounded, and 91 missing. Marine casualties were 45 killed and 218 wounded.

No major Marine operations had been conducted in the Hiep Duc Valley since then, although 1966 began a year of bloody fighting in the highlands between Chu Lai and Ban Me Thuot. During Operation *Masher/White Wing*, small elements of Marines joined with the U.S. Army's First Cavalry Division, ARVN units, and Korean White Horse Division troops to attack strongholds in Binh Dinh province in II Corps; 2,389 enemy soldiers were reported killed.

Operation *Utah* saw Marines tangling for the first time with NVA regulars in fierce combat along Highway 527, killing more than 600 North Vietnamese soldiers while losing 98 Marines. Lieutenant Colonel Leon N. Utter, battalion commander of the 2/7, assessed the NVA this way: "They're not Supermen. But they can fight."

Both *Starlite* and *Utah* were considered stunning victories for the Marines. Although Marines launched ten more battalion-sized operations in the Chu Lai TAOR between April and June, only one of these, *Hot Springs*, resulted in anything other than minimal contact. The Seventh Marine Regiment killed 150 men from the ranks of our old enemy, the First VC Regiment.

The First VC Regiment appeared to be moving northward. Its elements had been spotted in the Hiep Duc Valley as early as February 1966, but Operation *Double Eagle* failed to locate and close with it. The Eighteenth and Ninteenth NVA Regiments, along with the Second VC Main Force Regiment and a dozen Regional VC companies were also believed to be operating in, around, and out of the valley—an estimated 6,500 men.

Since I was merely a common grunt and nobody told me shit, it was only in aftermath that I learned the First Marine Division planned to expand its TAOR control northward and westward beginning in June until it joined with the Da Nang TAOR at Tam Ky. Of course, there were rumors. There were always rumors. Guys kept saying that we were going back into the Hiep Duc Valley, that another operation was about to be launched into this enemy-rich environment northwest of Chu Lai.

The Recon Battalion would be the first to know. I decided not to worry about the rumors until the Recons started receiving missions to the northwest.

21

Restless, voiceless men stamping about in the fog-tendrilled dawn while the helicopters warmed up and the pilots and crews conducted preflights. Yawning, coughing, shuffling, adjusting the straps of our web gear, checking equipment, counting grenades, having a last gulp of hot, black coffee. Sergeant Howard had called us out of the movie last night for the mission briefing. It seemed we always missed the last half of *The Green Berets* or *On The Beach*. We knew the routine. Saddle up at dawn, form up outside, amble off down to the helipad for chopper pickup, go roam around in the boonies or sit on a hilltop for a few days. SOS. Same old shit.

"Which way are we going?" I asked. I always asked that.

Binns looked at me. "Does it make a difference, Hildreth?"

"It does to me. I want to keep up with our colors on the map."

"You're weird, do you know that, Hildreth?"

"Southwest," Sergeant Howard said. "Around the Song Tra Bong River."

"That's good." And it was. My stomach settled down.

The platoon made up a new traveling song:

> *Strollin' down the Song Tra Bong,*
> *Lookin' for the Viet Cong.*
> *Comin' back to Chu Lai,*
> *Ridin' in a Six-by . . .*

"We put the 'Six-by' in because it was the only thing that rhymed," Benson explained.

Bosley looked scared to death, and Glawe's gangster talk disappeared before we reached the helo pads. He looked like I felt my first time out. But, hey, I was an old vet, right? Moore and I even went into a little comic routine to break the preinsertion jitters while we waited for the birds. To show how little this shit affected us by then. Skinny Moore stuck a pretend microphone underneath his ample nose and began pattering like a sports announcer.

"Well, well, good morning, sports fans of Vietnam. Here we are back at USMC University. It's a beautiful morning to renew the grudge match between our heroes, the Mean Green Team of wonderful downtown Chu Lai—*Yay! Yay!*— and the Little Yellow Men of the jungle—*Boo! Boo!* Both sides appear ready for the kickoff. So far, the Mean Green has had a winning season, but I think we can safely predict some real fireworks today. For our man in the stands interview, we go to a typical sports enthusiast. Private First Class Raymond Hildreth, what do you think about today's game?"

He thrust the microphone at me.

"Well, B.E., if you want my opinion, I always say it ain't the size of the guy in the fight but the size of the fight in the guy. The Little Yellow Men of the Jungle are gutsy little fellas with an excellent ground offense. They don't seem to know when they're beat. They just keep right on coming trying to wear you down. It's going to be a close one today, B.E., but I'm still putting my money on the Green and their air offense. . . ."

"There you have it, folks. Bookies are offering three to
one odds in favor of the Mean Green. . . ."

Bosley and Glawe still looked scared. We piled into the
helicopters. The giant rotors yanked us into the air and the
choppers departed like bumblebees in a panic. We crossed
the line between the First World and the Third World, leaving behind clean water, relatively, warm showers, relatively,
hot chow and coffee, relatively, and entered a world where
people still died of toothache and believed in demon *pratas.*

The helicopters set us down in a clearing low on the side
of a hill. We labored our way through thick virgin jungle to
the military crest. Sergeant Howard, along with Binns, who
had regained his unofficial position as platoon sergeant
now that Lieutenant Braley had left, selected an OP position where we could survey a wide checkered valley of rice
fields without our being seen in return.

As usual, we felt safe after we scouted the area to make
sure it was secure, then burrowed into a perimeter. Undergrowth grew so dense we could hardly find each other.
Sergeant Howard put the platoon on normal in the bush
fifty percent alert; half of us could kick back and catch a little R&R. We were going to be here for a couple of days.
Might as well make ourselves at home. Adams broke out a
can of C rats. McKinney decided to take a nap. Four or five
others had paperbacks. Fuck books were passed around in
the field until the covers wore off.

A lot of trails crisscrossed the valley, all of them apparently well used. Here and there sat a peasant's hooch. Poor
fuckers. Guy worked his whole life, strong back and weak
mind, and what he ended up with was a tin- or thatched-
roof shanty, six or seven chickens, two pigs, two pairs of
black pajamas, a patch of rice, bare feet—and people shooting at him and burning or bombing his shanty if he failed
to choose the right side in a war he knew little about. You
could almost feel sorry for them if you let yourself.

There were certain AO's designated as "free fire zones" where you could legitimately shoot or drop bombs on anything that moved. That made war simpler. This wasn't one of them, however. Anybody you spotted here, you had to make a judgment call: *Is he or isn't he? Is she or isn't she?* About the only way you could tell for sure was if you observed a weapon. I had heard of outfits who considered a spade or a planting stick to be a weapon, making the bearer eligible for the dich board. Kill 'em all, let God sort 'em out. Sergeant Howard didn't work that way. He let fireteam and squad leaders practice map reading and calling artillery fire missions on the newly issued PRC-25 radios, but he stressed that you didn't kill anybody unless you were reasonably certain the guy was VC. It was up to you to make the final call. You lived with your conscience if you were wrong.

The first two days on-site dragged. Binns took Norman, Kosoglow, and Powles on a hump a couple of hills over to pick up a resupply of chow and water from a helicopter drop. Their uniforms were soaked with sweat and crusted with body salts when they got back. They hadn't caught even a glimpse of the enemy.

Activity picked up that afternoon and the following morning. Somebody opened the barn door. During a SALUTE report, Sergeant Howard requested permission to bring smoke down on targets. That opened the shooting gallery. There were targets all over the valley. Usually singles, sometimes doubles. All it took was a little call on the radio.

"Salton Two-Three, this is Rover One-Six, fire mission, over."

"*Rover, Salton. Fire mission, over . . .*"

"Take out Victor Charlie in open . . . Will adjust . . ."

It took only a few seconds before a thundering rumble disturbed the air as the projectile shrieked overhead. A yellowish plume of smoke erupted around a bright splashdown in the valley, followed by the bang of the explosion. It was a thrill. It gave you a hell of a rush, having all that awesome power at your beck and call. Spending a few hundred thousand dollars of U.S. taxpayer money to waste a few hapless dinks trying to walk across a field. Killing them dispassionately and with such raw, youthful enthusiasm.

"Why'd you shoot that man?"

" 'Cause it's fun."

"Move out of the way. Let me get a shot at the next one."

It was too late for the guy by the time he realized he was targeted. Through the binocs you could see Charlie Gook bopping along with his rifle over his shoulder, not a care in the world, feeling like nobody was around for miles. The first thing you noticed was how he froze in terror when he heard the shell coming. It was always the same. He froze, then looked up at the sky. Like that old cartoon of a mouse gaping up at the talons of a descending hawk. Then he started to run even though he didn't know which way to run.

Shells generally fell in volleys of three or six. Sometimes the guy made it, darting through the erupting geysers in a broken field run that would have made Hollywood Joe Namath proud. Other times, he vanished in a flash of flame and a puff of smoke. More commonly, he tumbled like a shot rabbit when shrapnel caught him.

"Now that's my kind of gook," Binns said, glassing the field. "Dead."

McKinney climbed a tree to get a better view. After a while, he climbed back down and said he didn't want to watch anymore.

In order to keep Charlie from getting suspicious that ground observers were in the area, battalion dispatched a "Bird Dog" FAC (Forward Air Controller) aircraft to act as a decoy. The VC would think the FAC was responsible for putting fire on targets. Right off, the pilot spotted a Viet

Cong hot-footing it for the woods, zigzagging across the paddies and really putting them down.

The little single-engine prop dropped right on the deck and gave chase. All he had were WP marking rockets. The first one missed, flaring up in a pod of smoke and flame to the runner's left.

The second rocket caught him dead center in the back. The poor bastard tumbled and whooshed up in a blaze, like the Buddhist monks who used to immolate themselves in Saigon to protest the Diem government.

"That was some good shooting!" Mascarenas cheered.

The little plane climbed out and sailed off down the valley, looking for other targets.

Charlie Company ordered First Platoon pulled back in after four days of fun and games interspersed with long hours of sweat and lethargy. Helicopters lifted in a company of grunts to sweep the valley while we humped down the hill to the extraction point and caught the same choppers back to Chu Lai.

This was getting to be old hat.

Sergeant Howard stopped me the next day as I headed for the showers. Uh oh.

"Congratulations, *Lance Corporal* Hildreth," he said.

"Huh?"

He grinned. "You've been promoted."

You only got promoted if your platoon leader recommended you. I grinned back. He must have thought I was doing okay. Norman, Moore, Kosoglow, and Powles also made it. Hey, that extra twelve bucks or so a month meant another hundred bucks in our accounts by the time our tours were up. Dad and my half-brother Homer would be proud of me, considering the manner in which I had ended up joining the Marines and leaving home.

Part II

*For he to-day that sheds his blood with me
Shall be my brother.*

WILLIAM SHAKESPEARE,
KING HENRY THE FIFTH

22

The nature of VC designs on the Chu Lai TAOR became increasingly clear to U.S. war planners. The enemy intended to concentrate on wearing down and exhausting the ARVN, both psychologically and militarily, while they attacked and destroyed isolated government outposts, picking them off one by one until they could apply the same strategy to larger communities such as district capitals. As for the Americans, the guerrillas and NVA would avoid large-scale battles with them while hammering away with constant attacks on smaller American units in order to create a climate of caution and defensiveness.

To counter this strategy, General Lewis W. Walt, III MAF commander, called for the First Marine Division to extend its influence into the Do Xa region southwest of Chu Lai near the western border of I Corps. Intel sources placed an enemy headquarters in the area. Brigadier General William A. Stiles, First MarDiv's assistant commander, began planning a new operation. Before he could complete his work, however, III MAF intelligence officers uncovered information that changed the scope of the operations.

Ever since Operation *Harvest Moon* ended the previous December, Marines had attempted little work in that range of steep mountains and twisting valleys in the Hiep Duc (Que Son) region northwest of Chu Lai. Hidden deep in this bandits' lair, VC and NVA had had nearly six months uninterrupted time to train and plan for assaults against the heavily populated seacoast hamlets. According to the recent intelligence, a mixed force of Viet Cong and North Vietnamese Army regulars, including the Second NVA Division and Chu Lai's old enemy, the First VC Regiment, was gathering by the thousands. Instead of marshalling in large and vulnerable assembly points, the units were currently widely dispersed and moving eastward in squads and platoons. They would mass only when it came time to attack.

Recognizing the threat to this vital area. General Walt postponed the Do Xa operations and changed its focus from the southwest to the northwest. He placed eight full battalions on alert—four Marine and four ARVN. They would not beat the bushes for the enemy bands. Instead, they would wait, prepared to air assault, until reconnaissance units located the enemy.

On 13 June, General Walt ordered an extensive reconnaissance effort to be made between Tam Ky and Hiep Duc. Operation *Kansas* began that afternoon when he detailed Lieutenant Colonel Arthur Sullivan's First Reconnaissance Battalion to scout the mountains. Over the next twenty-four hours, seven recon platoons and teams would be planted on sites around the high rim of the Hiep Duc Valley. They were to report on enemy activity and, when possible, call in artillery and air strikes on the formations. Once NVA positions were verified, the battalions on-call would helicopter in to engage and smash the enemy.

An air of excitement infested the Marine base at Chu Lai. There was a feeling that this was the long-awaited beginning of another Operation *Starlite* or *Utah*. Colonel Sullivan expressed confidence that his men could perform the mission.

"The Vietnam War," he said, "has given the small unit leader—the corporal, the sergeant, the lieutenant—a chance to be independent. The senior officer just can't be out there looking over their shoulders. You have to have confidence in your junior officers and NCOs."

23

Much of the First Marine Division had had the weekend off to watch movies, catch up on reading, go to tent services provided by either the Protestant or Catholic chaplain, or simply to sleep in on Sunday morning until it got so hot in the tents that the heat drove you out. There were some combat security patrols, a few units out on fire bases with the artillery batteries, a couple of companies of various battalions beating the bush half-heartedly—but for the most part the Sunday of 12 June 1966 was laid back. If you were a common grunt, the first thing you thought when things were that easy was, *Uh oh, they're about to fuck us.* As in, sung to the tune of the Mickey Mouse theme song:

> *F-U-C . . . K-E-D A-G-A-I-N*
> *Fucked again.*
> *Why?*
> *Because we love you . . .*

There were rumors, of course, many of them suggesting something big was coming down. And that it was coming down in the Hiep Duc region *northwest* of Chu Lai. Of course, there were always rumors. One said we were getting ready to make a mass beach invasion against Hanoi, another that Hanoi was getting ready to make a mass invasion against *us*. Most of the time rumors didn't mean shit. My nervous stomach warned me, however, that this time there might be something to it. When I stepped out of the platoon tent on Monday morning, 13 June, and saw Sergeant Howard striding at a good pace in the direction of battalion operations, my stomach did flip-flops. It was the look on his face. Stern, calm, but otherwise emotionless. That kind of look meant a mission.

I watched him until he disappeared. I kept standing there, shirtless and in flip-flops and a pair of cut-off utilities. Laid back. Thinking about going swimming since Sergeant Howard had already informed Binns to cancel the normal training routine.

Things were too good to last. It wasn't even exceptionally hot this morning. A breeze from the ocean brushed against my cheek. Sun devils sparkled on the smooth sheen of blue-green ocean only a minute's walk away. People back in the States paid big money for seaside vacations. I turned and went back inside. McKinney looked up from lying on his cot reading a book.

"Weren't you going swimming?" he asked.

"I changed my mind. Get ready for a mission."

Victor turned over and opened one eye. "How d-d-do you know that, Hildreth?"

I shrugged and went over and sat down on my cot to wait.

Staff Sergeant Jimmie Earl Howard continued his brisk walk to the hard-sided GP tent that housed the battalion S-1 and S-2 shops. Officers and NCOs alike exhibited a great deal of respect for the tall acting platoon leader of First Platoon. It was common knowledge that, although Howard had been busted in rank at least once, maybe twice, he had also turned down battlefield commissions an equal number of times. He must have been something of a heller during his younger Marine days.

"Howard's a very personable fellow," Charlie Company's commander, Captain Tim Geraghty, had said of him. "The men like him. They like to work for him. He wants to stay in the field with them."

The battalion exec, Major Scotty Harris, was equally complimentary. "Jimmie's a very intelligent man, a cautious man. He thinks his place is with the enlisted."

No one was laid back in S-1 or S-2 when Howard paused outside the tent, then went in to find himself in the middle of what he always termed a clusterfuck. The battalion ops officer, Major Jack Cooper, was busy presiding over a gaggle of company commanders and other need-to-know personnel. Operation *Kansas* was just kicking off. Cooper and his staff were "jumping through our assholes," as he put it, preparing for airlifts into the Hiep Duc Valley. Maps were spread on field tables amidst copies of radio messages, operations orders and the other paperwork necessary to launch large-scale movements. Major Cooper glanced up as Sergeant Howard entered.

"Come on in, Jimmie."

Cooper liked to be on a first-name basis with his battalion's platoon commanders. Howard stood loosely at attention among the tentful of brass.

"Sir, my boys going back out?" he asked.

"Yeah, Jimmie. Come on over here and take a look. We may have them this time, if we can get them into a position to make them fight. The old man's going to be in on this personally."

Recon platoon commanders were being called in one at a time to receive mission briefings informally and on a one-on-one basis. The "old man," Colonel Sullivan, wanted the importance of the operation stressed individually to his leaders. Cooper pointed to a map.

"This is the Hiep Duc/Que Son Valley," he began. "Enemy has been spotted as early as *this morning*. Here, about twenty-seven miles northwest of Chu Lai. Unknown numbers and unit designations at this time. G-2 thinks we may have as many as two divisions of NVA and VC hiding in the valley. For the past few days, they've been drifting east toward the coast where they're expected to reconsolidate and become a nuisance. Division wants Recon teams inserted in the highlands around the rim of the valley to observe and report large concentrations while calling in fire on smaller elements. You'll have artillery on-call and air standing by. You'll be provided call signs and frequencies."

Sergeant Howard cleared his throat and, mostly to himself, murmured, "Northwest?"

Major Cooper raised a questioning brow.

"It's just a superstition among the men," Howard said dismissively.

"Well, the further north you go, the more likely you are to run into something."

Sergeant Howard shrugged it off. This mission was little more than a replay. He and his platoon had been inserted numerous other times to check out enemy movements. Most of the action they saw came from a botched ambush, blundering into a booby trap, or eating green pineapples. Why should this one be any different?

"Your platoon, Jimmie, designated as Team Two, will be inserted today at 1830 hours—here on Nui Vu Hill, Hill 488, about nine miles southeast of Nui Loc Son, where we'll have another Recon OP. There's an ARVN outpost and Army Special Forces camp here at Tien Phuoc, about seven klicks to the south of Nui Vu. It will provide artillery support. You are to observe terrain north and west of your position, which is into the valley. There's been lots of activity there. Get your men ready, Sergeant. Any questions?"

My nervous stomach was right: There *was* a mission.

Sergeant Howard assembled the platoon for a warning order. It was routine, we'd been over it before: Out five or six days sitting on the top of a hill. Pack the usual boonie stuff—radios, extra batteries and ammo, signal flares for extraction, chow, and water . . . Routine.

"How did you know?" McKinney asked me.

"I'm a lance corporal now."

"If you know so much, where are we going?"

My mouth felt dry. "Northwest," I finally managed. It was a feeling, an unpleasant feeling.

"I don't want to go northwest," McKinney said.

Sergeant Howard requested a fly over order to recon the operating area by helicopter while the platoon got ready. An H-34 took him and other battalion unit commanders out above the AO. It was the beginning of summer in Vietnam. The weather was clear and sunny. Not a cloud in the sky, not a hint of the rains that often swept in from the South China Sea across the coastal lowlands in the afternoons. It was always drier and more windy in the mountains.

The chopper soared high enough to avoid ground fire, but low enough to provide a good look at the terrain. The brown-and-green countryside looked as though some careless giant had crumpled it in his fist like a sheet of paper. The Hiep Duc Valley cut out a deep trough in a gentle half-moon running generally toward the northwest from the Chu Lai area and then gradually curving back to the southwest. Brutal country, especially in the surrounding escarpment.

There was a fire base of 105mm howitzers on heights at the near end of the valley and another at the Tien Phuoc ARVN/Special Forces camp south of it. Howard was especially interested in the batteries at the ARVN camp. The big guns were capable of bringing under heavy explosive fire virtually any point within a range of roughly seven miles. Nui Vu Hill lay well within artillery range.

Nui Loc Son Hill lay nine miles northwest of Nui Vu. A

Recon, Team One, had already been inserted there, but there was no sign of it from the air. The team had burrowed into the undergrowth like groundhogs afraid of seeing their shadows.

Hill 488 rose to an elevation of just over 1,500 feet and dominated the surrounding terrain. The chopper circled it once while the Marine sergeant leaned out the open door against his safety harness to study it. The hill was a barren, grass-covered knob whose stark countenance made it appear ominous and forbidding. It was devoid of almost all foliage. Even the grass, knee-high and thick as wheat down from the crest, grew patchy and short on top, like a man with cancer losing his hair.

Howard estimated the hilltop was less than twenty-five yards across at its widest. It was slightly concave to the northeast before it shallowed into decline toward the south and southeast into a saddle connecting it with the easterly-running ridgeline. Otherwise, it formed a sort of triple finger design that resembled a three-bladed airplane propeller assembled lopsided. One hogback blade extended north from the crest into the valley. It looked steep off its east side and descended in a more gradual gradient to the west.

The shortest blade at the southeast corner overlooked a steep gradient into the saddle east of it while shallowing into descent toward the south and southeast. The longer of the blades on the southwest overlooked a moderate gradient that dropped deep into the valley to the west and northwest. The only cover on the entire hilltop was a boulder at the upper base of the northern blade. It was about the size of a Volkswagen Beetle with its top chopped off.

Rolling, grassy hills lay to the south and east. Jungle and other foliage grew in some abundance in the lower creases and crevices. Farmer huts and a number of small villages dotted the floor of the valley, all of which were linked by well-worn trails and small cart roads. Hedgerows and patches of woodland broke the rice land into various-sized squares, like a patchwork quilt.

What interested Sergeant Howard most were likely avenues of enemy approaches and routes by which his platoon might bug out if it came to that. Any enemy, he decided, would likely close in using the more gentle slopes on the hill's northwestern face. That left escape routes to the east and south. He marked on his map several locations helicopters might use to drop in and extract his men.

He cast a final look at the hill. It seemed to glower back at him around the boulder that served as its bulbous nose. He didn't like the looks of it. His boys would be exposed to the world.

He settled back in the chopper and rubbed the tension out of his eyes. A long time ago, there had been another hill like this one. It was called Bunker Hill.

24

A big, rather private man of few words, Staff Sergeant Jimmie Howard rarely spoke of that September night in Korea over fifteen years ago. Some people went through their entire lives without having to make any kind of a stand, certainly not one that required wagering their lives on the outcome. Howard was twenty-three years old and a Marine Corps corporal the night he won a Silver Star, the nation's third-highest award for valor, along with a third Purple Heart for combat wounds suffered during that "last stand." He was assured then that that night was a "once in a lifetime" experience that few men in the world had to live through more than once.

Howard had enlisted in the USMC on 12 July 1950 after having played football for the University of Iowa for a year. Two weeks before he signed up in a fervor of patriotism and adventure seeking, on 25 June, more than 80,000 North Korean soldiers poured across the partition line separating the two post–World War II Koreas. Their intent was to conquer South Korea in a blitz and reunite the two countries. The ex–football player from Iowa remained in training during the perilous months when the communists stormed almost the full length of the peninsula and then were driven back, thanks in part to General Douglas MacArthur's landing Marines at Inchon.

The war was well into its second year by the time Howard arrived in Korea and was assigned duty as a forward observer with a 4.2-inch mortar company in the First Marine Division, the same outfit with which he would later serve in Vietnam. Armistice negotiations begun in July 1951 dragged on. Fierce fighting continued, although the battlefront remained stalemated in the raw mountains north of the post–World War II boundary, developing into what became known as "the battles of the outposts." The same ground was fought over day after day, the tide sweeping back and forth. An outpost held by the North Koreans today might have been in the hands of the Marines yesterday and would be back in their hands tomorrow.

United Nations raids, along with communist counterattacks, stretched into the summer of 1952, each side hoping to win an advantage for the peace talks. U.S. warplanes operating with Australia and Britain launched a massive airstrike against the North on 25 August, the heaviest of the war so far. Hundreds of bombers and fighters hammered the North Korean capital of Pyongyang, targeting communist supply installations, repair shops, troop concentrations, military headquarters, and other vital sites.

The Chinese Reds retaliated with a series of harassing attacks against the U.S. Marine hill outposts along the front lines. On a single day in September, 45,000 mortar and artillery rounds pounded UN defensive positions. Bunker Hill was one of these outposts not too far from the village of Panmunjon where the peace talks were being conducted. All during the day of September 5, shells walloped Bunker Hill. Howard and the other leathernecks of his outfit hunkered down in their trench line defensive bulwarks on the northern crest and endured.

Hardly a blade of grass survived. The hill was cratered

and trenched and pulverized until it resembled a cold and dark moonscape. The shelling ceased toward nightfall, replaced by a chill moaning wind iced with the threat of coming winter. Silence descended with the darkness. Under its cover, hundreds of enemy soldiers began marshaling in well-camouflaged foxholes at the base of the hill.

Marines waited in their positions, listening to the sounds of enemy preparations in the night winds. Finally, the peal of a bugle racing its notes signaled the charge. Enemy officers used bugles, whistles, and clacking sticks to control and direct their units. Human waves of men—silhouettes, shadows, ghostly figures—poured from cover and stormed up the steep slopes. Muzzle flashes spattered and glittered in a sparkling wall. Tracers in contrasting reds and blue-greens stabbed and floated back and forth, punctuated by the white-hot bursts of grenade explosions. The noise was deafening. It was total chaos, insanity.

Young and scared, Howard fought savagely for his life. He stacked clips of ammo close at hand in his trench and heated up the barrel of his M-1 squeezing rounds into darting shadows and at blossoming muzzle flashes. One figure rose out of the ground directly in front and ran at him, screaming and firing. Howard emptied a full clip into the man—eight rounds—before he tumbled dead into the trench at his feet. He kicked the body out of the way.

A second enemy soldier charged before Howard could reload. The burst of an exploding grenade etched his wild figure against its strobing light. Screaming back, Howard leaped to his feet to meet the threat. The Chicom wielded a weapon as long as he was tall, affixed to the muzzle of which was a bayonet that added another third to the overall length of the rifle. The attacker lunged, jabbing with the bayonet.

Howard parried and stepped into the charge. He felt his rifle knife sink deep into enemy flesh, grating on bone. Hot blood sprayed his face. He fell back against the rear wall of the trench and used the leverage of his rifle and his foe's own momentum to propel the shrieking body over his head and onto the ground behind him. He jerked his bayonet free and turned in time to face his next assailants.

Two more rushed him with bayonets prickling from long rifles. Still not having time to reload, he vaulted from the trench to meet the charge head-on. He crushed the first enemy's skull with a well-timed butt stroke. After dodging a bayonet thrust from the second, he lunged and speared him through the chest, killing him instantly.

That bought him some time. He dropped back into the trench, quickly reloaded, and resumed firing. Savage hand-to-hand fighting like that went back and forth over the crest of the hill for the next two hours. Screaming and shouting and bugles and bamboo sticks furiously clacking. The fierce rattle of rifle fire, exploding grenades, the blasting booms of artillery shells. Finally, the defeated Chinese and Koreans withdrew, leaving Marines still in control of Bunker Hill.

After daylight, the company commander inspected the length of trench his men were committed to hold. He found young Jimmie Howard grimy and blood-crusted, bleeding from wounds, with enemy bodies stacked up all around him. The Marines to his left and right were all dead. Howard single-handedly defended thirty feet of trench against a determined enemy who would have made a breakthrough but for his heroic resistance.

Korea was a long time ago. Vietnam was a different kind of war, in which hills were not normally defended and attacked. Yet, that morning looking down from the helicopter onto Hill 488, Sergeant Howard suffered a brief, passing sensation that he had done all this before.

25

At some point or another in our lives, we were all new guys—at a new job, at school, in a military unit. Usually, there was time to settle in, get acquainted, learn the ropes. In Vietnam, however, there wasn't always this kind of time. A new guy could come in on Monday, go out on patrol on Tuesday, get in a firefight, and be in a body bag by Tuesday night before he even knew what was going on.

A platoon was family in the closest sense of the word. Tighter than blood relatives. We fought and quarreled among ourselves, but were ready to stand off the entire outside world when one of us was threatened. It took new meat time to bond into the family. Again, there wasn't always time.

New meat were at once a liability. They talked too loud, made too much noise moving around in the bush, didn't know what to take out on recon or how to wear it properly, responded slowly to basic combat commands, fired too much ammunition, and tended to flake out on the easiest ten-klick march. They also got homesick. Most of all, they were an unknown factor.

I had been there before. It occurred to me when Sergeant Howard returned from his aerial reconnaissance of our AOR (area of responsibility) and called a mission briefing that First Platoon was almost *all* new meat. My eyes skipped over the younger serious faces of the Marines squatting or sitting on cots or on the slatted wooden floor around Sergeant Howard. The sides of the tent were rolled up to let in an ocean breeze. Of the sixteen jarheads in the platoon, plus Billy D, the Navy corpsman, three men who had just reported in the week before were about to "bust cherries" on a first mission. Two others—Glawe and Bosley—had been out on only one other.

The rest of us couldn't *really* call ourselves combat veterans, with the exception of Sergeant Howard. How could you call a botched ambush and a Purple Heart from a booby trap *combat.* We might have the training and be badass Recon Marines—*Hoo-ya!*—but most of us were still untested greenhorns.

While there was nothing to indicate, as far as I knew, that this mission would be any different than the others in which I had participated since March, I nonetheless felt apprehensive, jittering in the pit of my stomach. So much new meat going *northwest* was enough to cause me some concern. I tried to placate my stomach by assuring it that, percentagewise, only two guys out of every one hundred sent to Vietnam were ever killed or wounded.

"But you never know when it's *your* percentage," observed McKinney, ever the platoon pessimist.

"Or when you might g-g-get somebody else's percentage," added Victor, the other cynic.

Later, I found myself considering how fate worked in our everyday lives.

Fate (fa"t) n. **1.** *A force viewed as unalterably determining in advance the way things happen;*

destiny. **2.** *That which inevitably happens as though determined by this force; inescapable lot or outcome.* **3.** *Final result or outcome.* **4.** *An evil destiny; doom; especially death or destruction.*

Fate, I pondered, seemed to have worked in unpredictable ways outside the control of ordinary mankind in making its selections for the mission, as though it alone somehow decreed who would go and who would stay behind. Selection started with the new guys.

Lance Corporal Robert Martinez, radioman, came over on Friday from Bravo Company, where he had been a member of a floating reactionary force. He was a young, dark-skinned Mexican-American of medium height and build, but was far from any stereotype of a Chicano. He was born in Kansas and grew up in Oklahoma, where he never learned to speak good Spanish. Mascarenas declared Martinez the first Mexican he personally had ever known who spoke such poor Spanish in a dustbowl *Grapes of Wrath* accent.

A lot of "ifs" could have kept Martinez off the mission. *If* he had enlisted two days later than he did back in Oklahoma; *if* he had been sick enough to delay shipping out for overseas; most significantly, *if* he had waited another few days before transferring out of Bravo Company. None of these things happened, however, and so here he was with fate making sure he went along.

Fate must have had an especially good time bringing Private First Class Ignatius Carlisi all the way from New York to this particular place at this particular time. To begin with, he was drafted into the Marine Corps. Nobody was ever *drafted* into the Marines. If you were drafted, you invariably went into the army.

A New York Italian from a well-to-do family, he was olive-skinned and short with soft-looking arms out of proportion to the rest of his body. He looked totally out of place. It was obvious to me that he had grown up sheltered and protected. He should have been a clerk in some army rear echelon outfit. But here he was—drafted and somehow in Recon on this particular Monday. On his way into the bush for the first time.

Corporal Jerald Thompson, light-skinned, slender, and a fraction of an inch under six feet tall, took Ronnie Knowles's place as First Squad Leader. He also had his *ifs*. *If* Knowles hadn't already departed, leaving his slot open, and *if* he hadn't recently made corporal he likely would not have been with First Platoon and would have gone to another outfit.

Originally from Indiana, with a wife waiting in North Carolina, Thompson had been in the crotch long enough to make rank but hadn't been corporal long enough to become entirely comfortable with his stripes. During Thompson's first or second night on the sand dunes, Mascarenas and some of his amigos started raising hell and having a good time in the next tent, keeping everyone awake. Binns was at a movie, and, of course, Sergeant Howard billeted separately. Thompson finally got pissed off. He jumped off his rubber lady, stomped over to the next tent, and threw the flaps aside.

"All right, you guys," he barked. "We can't get any sleep over there, so shut the fuck up."

Instant silence. He came back to bed.

"Wow!" he murmured. "They listened to me."

Fate worked with equal determination in making selections from among the platoon regulars. Doc Billy D, for example. Billy D had only a couple of weeks left in-country before he was due to be transferred Stateside at the end of his duty tour.

"You're a short-timer, Doc," Sergeant Howard said.

"I'm not short, Sergeant, I'm *next*."

"You've done your share. You don't have to go out on this one."

Combat corpsmen had this chaplain-like thing whereas they believed it was up to them personally to take care of their flocks. Doc glanced at Binns, his best friend.

"What am I gonna do while you're out in the bush—sit on one thumb and play switchies? I'll go. It's a last chance to work on my beautiful Vietnam hillside suntan."

On the other hand, B.E. Moore, my oldest bud in the platoon, and Private First Class Benson, the little redheaded machine gunner, were both selected *out* of the mission.

Moore was on mess duty over the weekend and on the roster for KP the entire week. All the platoons, without exception, had to contribute manpower for running the chow hall. That meant the duty watch dragged Moore out of the sack at 0200 for the breakfast rush and he spent most of the rest of the day scrubbing pots and pans and getting dishpan hands. But for that he would have gone out with the platoon.

We were preparing for mission, on our way to the company area bunker to draw munitions, when he stumbled in to catch a few hours sleep before the evening meal call.

"Wish I were going out with your guys," he said. "The only medal I'll ever win in the chow hall is the Good Housekeeping Seal of Approval. God, I hate mess duty."

"Better you than me," I said.

"Well, you guys be careful out there. I'm catching some Z's."

Fate must have taken a liking to Benson and found him too funny and boisterous to send out that particular time. Powles joked how Benson was like Norman's analogy of guys who drove pickup trucks. The bigger the pickup, the smaller the guy who climbed out of it. That was why the smallest guy in the platoon packed the biggest gun. In the field, Benson absolutely refused to let anyone spell him on carrying the M60 machine gun.

"It's like his dick," Powles said with a laugh. "He's always got to have his hands on it."

Benson would have been humping the M60 to Hill 488 on Monday except for Fate stepping in on Sunday. A bunch of the guys got to grabassing and horsing around, as young men will when faced with time on their hands. Powles was a good-natured likeable Californian and therefore almost always in the middle of any mischief. Some of us wrestled him into submission while he was wearing nothing but his skivvies and tied him to a tent pole, where he was sprayed with shaving cream. During the scuffle, Benson caught his toe in a crack of the new wooden Seabee floor and ripped off a toenail. Scrub him from the mission roster. The platoon would go to the field without a machine gun or gunner.

The last man Fate selected or discarded, almost at random, it seemed, was Navy Hospitalman First Class Richard Fitzpatrick, a heavy-framed, balding corpsman of about thirty-five, a friend of Sergeant Howard's. Fitz was attached to the headquarters platoon and didn't have to go out, not that day or any other. Somebody said he had to go on patrol in order to draw combat pay. I doubted that. You drew the pay if you served in a combat zone. Chu Lai certainly qualified as a combat zone.

Fitz huffed up with his deuce gear and aid bag as the platoon saddled up for the stroll over to the battalion helicopter pads and requested to tag along as a spare medic. He had never been out on mission before—and he chose this one, or was chosen for it. Fate worked in strange ways.

So there we went, filing through the late afternoon heat to the waiting choppers. Sixteen jarheads and two Navy squid corpsmen. Over half of us were either new guys who hardly knew how to load onto a helicopter or near green-horns untested in any serious action.

Jovial Kosoglow attempted to lighten the mood by wryly chanting an old "Jody call":

> *Ain't no use in lookin' back,*
> *Jody's got your Cadillac.*
> *Ain't no use in goin' home,*
> *Jody's got your girl and gone . . .*

26

A total of eight recon patrols were being planted onto the highlands surrounding the Hiep Duc Valley. Most of them were squad-sized or slightly larger—eight to ten Marines. Sergeant Howard's First Platoon was the largest to be inserted. Deep into territory the enemy considered vital. Beyond Nui Vu Hill lay nothing friendly all the way to Laos.

One of the teams, Team Seven, took up a position on heavily wooded Hill 555 southwest of Hill 488. Within hours, the OP reported enemy activity, most of it in groups smaller than platoons. The VC seemed to be moving east, just as intelligence reports indicated, training as they drifted toward some as-yet-unknown marshalling area where they apparently intended to consolidate into battalions or regiments large enough to do battle. The Recon team noted the sighting of a larger-than-normal man wearing camouflage among one of the groups. The size of the man and the cammie uniform signified a Red Chinese "advisor," probably someone from Manchuria or thereabouts where people were almost as large as Americans. The presence of a Chinese with the enemy usually meant NVA regulars or large VC Main Force elements. It seemed intel about the Second NVA Division and the First VC Regiment being in the valley might be right on target.

Somewhat later in the afternoon, Colonel Sullivan at the battalion CP, whose radio call sign was Iron Hand, received a terse message from Hill 555.

"I think we've been made, sir," the Recon lieutenant whispered into his mike. "We need to request an emergency extraction."

It appeared a VC patrol working a scout dog had picked up an intruder scent. The dog with its owner in tow flitted in and out of woodland at the foot of the hill. The Recon platoon leader waited until he saw the patrol with the eager dog in front hurrying up the slope with purpose before he requested extraction. Recon was never intended to stand and do battle.

Besides, it was still too early in the game to engage the enemy. For now, the Recons would make their SALUTE reports, the data from which was tallied and transcribed to maps in an effort to pinpoint enemy consolidations against which First Marine Division infantry and support might maneuver with greater success. It was cat-and-mouse played large scale.

Colonel Sullivan dispatched a trio of UH-34s escorted by Huey gunships to pick up the endangered Recon team. The lifts dropped into a predesignated LZ on the opposite side of the hill from the enemy advance. Marines scrambled hastily aboard. Soon, they arrived safely at Chu Lai.

27

Boot was a Marine slang term applied both to trainees and in mild mockery to an unseasoned or green Marine. As the men of First Platoon, Charlie Company, headed toward the helicopters, Nancy Sinatra sang "These Boots (Are Made For Walking)" on somebody's transistor radio. We found it wryly amusing under the circumstances.

Ready, boots? Start walking . . .

The weather was clear and bright and the sun still up but sinking rapidly beyond the western mountains. Three H-34s from MAG-36, Marine Air Group-36, sat on the helipad between battalion HQ and the ammo dump, shuddering as they ran up their engines. We clambered through the open side doors, six of us to a bird, and sprawled on the steel floors. There were no seats. Laden with gear and extra bandoleers of ammo, I felt like a turtle tumped on its back.

"How're we supposed to get up?" Norman cracked.

The choppers were designed to lift a full marine rifle squad, including weapons and gear. However, the heat and humidity of Vietnam sometimes turned them into gooney birds that had to hop a couple of times on takeoff before they gained sufficient momentum to get into the air. I held on to McKinney for balance with one hand and on to my M-14 with the other.

The tent cities of Chu Lai receded below. Benson stood outside the flaps of the platoon tent, watching us leave. He lifted a hand in farewell. For some inexplicable reason I found the gesture profoundly cheerless. The red sun tinted him and the Marine base and us in the choppers with the failing light of day's end.

Always before we headed south from First Battalion area, out across the river on the southern perimeter, then turned inland. This time the chopper followed the coastline north for about three miles before cutting across the northern base toward the interior. Division headquarters passed below, with the airstrip to our left.

Then we were flying out across the coastal flatlands toward the mountains. A pattern of dikes and hedgerows and rice fields punctuated by clusters of Vietnamese hooches. Some people still labored in the fields, but they no longer paid much attention to activity from the base. These people were tame, "pacified." At least those were who weren't VC spies.

I shifted uncomfortably on the floor and craned my neck to look out. I felt a little twitter in my belly. I kept hoping there would be a change of mission at the last moment and the helicopters would turn southwest. That wasn't going to happen. The choppers continued flying *northwest.*

These were the members of First Platoon en route to Hill 488:

Staff Sergeant Jimmie Earl Howard,
    acting platoon leader
    Date of Birth—27 July 1929
    Date of Enlistment—12 July 1950
    Wife—Theresa Howard, San Diego, California
    Parents—Edith Schnedler (mother), Sperry, Iowa

Lance Corporal Ricardo C. "Rick" Binns,
    Second Squad Leader
    Date of Birth—25 December 1945
    Place of Birth—Bronx, New York
    Date of Enlistment—29 March 1963
    Parents—Alberta and Cyril Binns, Bronx, New York

Hospitalman Third Class Billy D. Holmes, medic
    Date of Birth—29 December 1942
    Place of Birth—Waverly, Tennessee
    Date of Enlistment—28 May 1962
    Wife—Clarice Holmes, Madison, Tennessee
    Parents—Don and Frances Holmes, Madison, Tennessee

Private First Class Charles W. Bosley
    Date of Birth—15 January 1947
    Place of Birth—New Berlin, New York
    Date of Enlistment—14 August 1964
    Wife—Suzanne Bosley, Geneva, New York
    Parents—Vida H. Ellis (mother), Greencastle, Indiana

Hospitalman First Class Richard J. Fitzpatrick, medic
    Date of Birth—4 March 1931
    Place of Birth—Waltham, Massachusetts
    Date of Enlistment—4 March 1948
    Wife—Mary Fitzpatrick, San Diego, California
    Parents—Laura Kane (mother), Vacaville, California

Lance Corporal Raymond S. Hildreth
    Date of Birth—6 April 1947
    Place of Birth—Tulsa, Oklahoma
    Date of Enlistment—25 March 1965
    Parents—Julius A. Hildreth (father),
       Tulsa, Oklahoma

Lance Corporal John T. Adams
    Date of Birth—23 January 1944
    Place of Birth—San Antonio, Texas
    Date of Enlistment—15 August 1963
    Parents—Dorothy Bartlett (mother),
       Mt. Clemens, Michigan; Bill R. Adams (father),
       Columbus, Ohio

Private First Class Ignatius Carlisi
    Date of Birth—6 October 1945
    Place of Birth—New York, New York
    Date of Enlistment—18 November 1965
    Parents—Frank and Sarah Carlisi, New York

Private First Class Thomas D. Glawe
    Date of Birth—4 March 1948
    Place of Birth—Rockford, Illinois
    Date of Enlistment—9 March 1965
    Parents—Mr. & Mrs. Eugene J. Glawe,
       Rockford, Illinois

Lance Corporal William C. Norman
    Date of Birth—18 January 1947
    Place of Birth—Harvey, Illinois
    Date of Enlistment—10 May 1965
    Parents—Norman and Mildred Norman,
       Sedona, Arizona

Lance Corporal Thomas G. Powles
   Date of Birth—2 March 1946
   Place of Birth—Hamburg, Iowa
   Date of Enlistment—2 June 1965
   Wife—Kathy Lisabeth Powles, Vacaville, California
   Parents—Cyril and Margie Powles, Vacaville, California

Lance Corporal Ralph G. Victor
   Date of Birth—4 May 1947
   Place of Birth—Ogden, Utah
   Date of Enlistment—2 June 1965
   Parents—Erland and Afton Victor, Ogden, Utah

Private First Class James O. McKinney
   Date of Birth—30 October 1947
   Place of Birth—Monroe, Louisiana
   Date of Enlistment—1965
   Parents—Mr. and Mrs. Odas K. McKinney,
      Monroe, Louisiana

Lance Corporal Alcadio N. Mascarenas
   Date of Birth—6 June 1944
   Place of Birth—Sapello, New Mexico
   Date of Enlistment—15 February 1965
   Parents—Mr. and Mrs. José Mascarenas,
      Sapello, New Mexico

Corporal Jerald R. Thompson, First Squad Leader
   Date of Birth—5 November 1941
   Place of Birth—Columbus, Ohio
   Date of Enlistment—30 November 1959
   Wife—Katherine Ruth Thompson,
      Raleigh, North Carolina
   Parents—Elsie Ginbey (mother), Pataskala, Ohio

Lance Corporal Robert Martinez, radioman
    Date of Birth—1945
    Place of Birth—Garden City, Kansas
    Date of Enlistment—7 January 1964
    Wife—Linda Sue Martinez, Santa Ana, California
    Parents—Fred and Esther Martinez,
      Garden City, Kansas

Lance Corporal Daniel Mulvihill, radioman
    Date of Birth—28 December 1946
    Place of Birth—Chicago, Illinois
    Date of Enlistment—18 May 1964
    Parents—Pearl (mother) and Walter Richter
      (stepfather), Chicago, Illinois

Lance Corporal Joseph Kosoglow
    Date of Birth—4 March 1946
    Place of Birth—Greensburgh, Pennsylvania
    Date of Enlistment—25 February 1964
    Wife—Judy Kosoglow, New Bern, North Carolina
    Parents—Anne and Henry Kosoglow,
      Irwin, Pennsylvania

28

A pair of Huey gunships escorted the flight. One flew high, the other low. The choppers maintained a safe altitude of about 1,500 feet to keep out of small arms range. Rice flatlands changed to the rolling hills and sharp ridges of interior mountain ranges. Shadows settled like ink in the hollows and valleys, while the dying sun painted the tops and ridgelines in pale pink. Between the ink and the pink the land glowed with soft purple. Without the war, Vietnam might have been an enchanting country. If you weren't out in the boondocks all the time getting shot at.

McKinney was daydreaming. His dark, sad eyes said he was in another world far removed from here. Back in his Louisiana bayous. His hand rested on my knee, seeking reassurance. I nudged him and smiled. He glanced at me, then turned away to stare out into the collecting dusk, his features as expressionless as those on the other faces also turned toward the coming night. You tried to keep your mind formless and your thoughts neutral. You didn't want to think about home and the soft curves of a special girl. You didn't want to think at all. And you couldn't talk because of the roar of the engines.

A normal tour of duty in the Nam was thirteen months. All you had to do was make it through that period and you went back home. For the first few months, you were scared to death and thought you would never do it. The last few months, you got real careful, almost paranoid, unless you were somebody like Billy D on a mission from God. You didn't want to do something foolish two weeks before you rotated and lose a leg or your eyes, or your life. A short-timer could be worse than a new guy.

In between the first months and the last months were the months when you simply made it through one day at a time. Do this mission, one less to go. Made it again. You developed an almost fatalistic attitude. *It don't mean nothing* was a common grunt phrase. You didn't let it "mean nothing," because if you did something was bound to happen to disappoint you.

That was where I was, approaching the middle months. I kept telling myself that this was just another mission. Southwest or northwest, what difference did it make? Go out there and get it over with. I couldn't let *northwest* psych me out. It was only a direction. I wasn't normally superstitious.

Cut it out, Hildreth. I made my mind go blank.

The choppers followed the valley, banking and twisting with it. Cooking fires and oil lamps twinkled below in pinpricks of light. There were villages and huts all over.

Normally, we dropped in at some distance from where we intended to establish an OP and then snooped and pooped our way to the objective in order to throw off any enemy who might have seen the helicopters touch down. This time, however, the flight swarmed out of the valley in a last, fast ride past the hilltop with the big rock on it. They flared on the grassy southern slope, below the hill and out of sight of the valley. To any observer down in the villages, it would look as though the birds simply turned to go back by another route. At least I assumed that was the intent.

Marines piled out into fields of brown-green grass. The choppers leaped back into the air, pitched their noses to gain speed, and departed as quickly as they arrived. Leaving behind silence and that old alone-in-the-big-world feeling.

1930 Hours

We were left on the back side of a long, dark ridgeline that formed the brim of Hiep Duc Valley beyond. Nui Vu rose out of the ridge to dominate the terrain. Stars started switching on behind its bold knob. We were about a quarter-mile from the top. The mountain was so obvious, so visible, so *present* that hiking up there, it seemed to me, was like that old joke about how could you hide an elephant in a cherry tree. Answer: You painted his toenails red so he could pretend to be a cherry. We would be that obvious.

Bad guys might already be up there waiting on us to blunder into their trap. I could hear John Wayne or Wallace Beery saying it: "Quiet. Yeah, too quiet."

Binns took point. I leaned forward against the incline and the weight of the pack on my back, thankful my M-14 wasn't the old heavier M-1D. I followed the silhouette of the man six or eight feet ahead as we humped to the top. It wasn't bad weather-wise this time of evening in the high country. A slight breeze swept in from the sea. Grass swaying and whispering against my knees reminded me of wheat fields back in Oklahoma and Kansas.

Hardly any grass grew on top. There was the single big rock on the northern aspect, the highest part of the hill. It was larger than a sofa but smaller than the average car. It looked as though some giant hand had dropped it there.

A number of fighting holes dug into the rocky soil gave disturbing notice that the enemy knew this terrain feature well and at some time in the recent past prepared it himself for a defense. We might have enjoyed more privacy, I thought, digging in on the Hollywood Freeway.

The platoon had a number of housekeeping chores to perform before we settled in for the night. Most pressing were the radios. Better no personal weapon than no radio. A radio in the field was an outfit's lifeline. Communications meant you could direct in the wrath of artillery and summon death and destruction from the skies. Communications meant you could call for extraction and get your ass out of there if you had to.

Sergeant Howard set up his command post behind the boulder where he took a commanding view of both the valley below and his defenses on top. Martinez and Mulvihill the radiomen moved in, along with the two corpsmen. Soon, they were running their commo checks. Radio reception in valleys and lowlands sometimes proved tricky. This high up, however, voices from Chu Lai came in startlingly loud and clear.

"Iron Hand (battalion call sign), this is Carnival Time (platoon's call sign), over."

"Go ahead, Carnival Time, over."

"Communications check. How do you hear me?"

"Loud and clear. Over. How me?"

"Same-same. Oscar Papa (OP) secure. Over."

"Roger your Oscar Papa, Carnival Time. Over."

"Turn down the volume," Sergeant Howard urged. "You don't want to disturb the gooks."

Off the northeast corner of what became immediately known as the Big Rock, some previous occupant prepared for any eventuality by hollowing out a shallow depression with a sump hole in the middle. It was designed to catch thrown grenades and roll them into the sump hole. They exploded without doing much damage because the sump directed the blast upward.

Sergeant Howard and Binns established a defensive perimeter, designated fields of fire and zones of responsibility, and assigned fireteams to cover them. Mascarenas was now my fireteam leader. Adams, McKinney, and I were his fireteam. We drew the southwest blade of the propeller-shaped hill. Each of the three blades encompassed a narrow strip of relatively level ground before it fell abruptly away onto the side of the hill.

"Mascarenas," Sergeant Howard said, pointing, "your team covers from that little bush there to your left to that small dead tree over to the right. If something comes up, you know what to do."

I hoped nothing came up.

Binns took Powles, Norman, and Kosoglow with him out on the northern blade-finger to set up an LP, listening post. This blade was the shortest and steepest. It sloped down from the Big Rock and the CP toward the valley.

The rest of the men assumed positions to cover every likely avenue of enemy approach. Victor was now a fireteam leader. The new PFC's—Bosley, Glawe, and Carlisi—were his responsibility. It took them a while to chill out. They kept seeing boogers.

"Cool it," Squad Leader Thompson finally hissed. "There's nothing out there."

I wasn't so sure of that.

2000 Hours

On fifty percent alert, one man could eat or sleep or take a leak while his partner maintained vigil. Mascarenas and I occupied one of the fighting holes. It was about three feet deep with a small cavelike shelter scooped out at one end. Gooks were small men. Off to our right about twenty meters, Adams and McKinney shared another hole facing south. The crown of Nui Vu rose black behind us up into the Big Rock. Everything was dark and silent. I listened to the wind sighing and rasping. It sounded like the hill was breathing through a pair of disease-ravaged lungs. Alive, but just barely.

Mascarenas exuded a quiet self-confidence that made you hope he was on your side if you were ever back-to-back in a barroom brawl. He wasn't much of a conversationalist, however. I found myself a good soft corner of the hole while I opened a can of C rat peaches and surveyed our new domain. It was definitely not a high-rent neighborhood, view or not.

The valley the hill overlooked at this point was about a mile wide. It curved to my left out of sight behind the continuing ridge. I had a good picture of the valley to my right front, to the northeast, framed between the ridge on my left and the forward curve of the hill on the right as the valley went out of sight east toward the seashore and Chu Lai. Below were pinpricks of light in a black curtain—hooches and villages. The largest concentration of lights existed to the north and east, out of my line of sight. On the other side of the valley rose more mountains, the northern rim to our southern rim. Over there, I assumed, other Marine Recon teams were bedding down for the night. They were too far away to provide much comfort.

Enough light lingered at this elevation for me to determine that grass grew thick and knee-high for about one hundred yards off the top downward. Beyond that sprouted small shrubs, scattered, few more than thigh- or waist-high. Heavier vegetation found root in the valleys and crevices where water collected. Anything larger than a small dog would have difficulty moving up on us without being seen, or so I thought; even it would surely leave a movement trail in the grass. Depending upon the amount of light the moon supplied.

I looked up at the sky. God, we were in a closet. The next few days would be in the dark of the moon. After a while I had a hard time seeing Mascarenas in the hole with me, even though I could reach out and touch him.

I ate my peaches.

"The end of another lovely day in paradise," I whispered.
"Uh huh," Mascarenas said.

2200 Hours

Mascarenas took first watch. I drifted asleep in the hole watching the blinking running lights of a jet heading in the direction of Da Nang. I awoke when Mascarenas nudged my boot and indicated in a whisper that I was to look down into the valley. Groggy, I didn't know where I was at first.

"Dinks," Mascarenas murmured.

That got rid of the cobwebs. My stomach did a flip-flop. I sat up.

Across the floor of the valley moved a line of blazing torches in a generally easterly direction. VC used torches for night movement. They were so far away that they resembled lit matches. I stared, mesmerized, as they drifted by like disembodied spook lights, unattached to anything except to their own illumination in the black river of night.

Mascarenas scurried up to the Big Rock to notify the CP. Every Marine on this side of the hill had already alerted to the movement. Sergeant Howard counted fourteen lights for his SALUTE report. The torches were spread out pretty good. He estimated there were perhaps ten fighters marching in the darkness between each torch—perhaps 140 soldiers. A company-sized element. He shot a compass azimuth to where the procession originated in order to determine its genesis when daylight came.

I watched the lights until they disappeared from my view around the north side of the hill. Mascarenas dropped back into the hole with me.

"Beaucoup dinks," he said.

29

Like farmers back in Oklahoma, like farmers everywhere, the Vietnamese peasants got up early. Up with the chickens, as my old pappy always said. People were already stirring down in the valley when Mascarenas tapped my boot with his. It worked out that he had had both the first watch and the last while I took the in-betweens.

"Wake up, Hildreth. I'm going up to the CP to see what's happening."

"Bring breakfast when you come back. I'll have eggs over easy, a rasher of crisp bacon, buttered toast, and coffee. . . ."

Mascarenas snorted. "Huh!"

That was the extent of most conversations between us. I wasn't usually talkative either. He climbed out of the shallow hole and walked uphill toward the Big Rock, making little effort to keep low. Observers lower down couldn't have seen the top of the hill, and we occupied the highest ground around.

My mouth tasted like an entire battalion of VC marched through it overnight, spraying it with *nuc mam*. I smacked a couple of times, made a face, swigged from my canteen, and then propped myself against the low wall of the hole facing in the direction of the valley with the as-yet-unseen sun off to my right site. It got cool nights and I had wrapped myself in a poncho.

It was a quiet, lovely, still morning, like June mornings back in Oklahoma. Not a cloud in sight. I sat there lazy and a little cramped from sleeping in the hole and watched Vietnam come awake. It always made me feel like a spy, like Agent 007 or something, to secretly observe the Vietnamese.

The sun eased into the sky and blinked an eye from east to west, splashing a swath of rich gold light across a section of the valley floor. I remained in the shadow of the hill, as did the little string of villages below me, the demarcation between light and shadow distinct. It was about a mile down to where the first hooches were. They were regularly spaced in the settlement and separated by beaten paths. I watched as activity around the tiny thatched-roofed huts picked up.

Everything appeared normal—children running about, old people going for walks, other men and women and kids heading for the fields with farm implements, not weapons, on their shoulders. *Early to bed, early to rise,* I thought, *made the VC . . .* Made the VC *what?* Pissed off? How could anybody be pissed off on a morning like this? It seemed there was no war at all. Instead, there was light and good feeling and surely hippies were dancing somewhere singing "Kumbayah" with flowers in their hair.

I stretched leisurely, yawned, and thought about breakfast.

A narrow dirt road entered the valley from out of sight to my left, snaked through the village, and continued on around until it disappeared again toward the sunrise, passing not too far from the base of the mountain. It reminded me of the ghost lights last night. It reminded me there was still a war on. That took off most of my good mood.

I fumbled in my pack for a gourmet C rat and came up with chopped ham and eggs. A real man's breakfast. Hooya! I would have drowned the contents with hot sauce had I not forgotten to bring some. Showed what a boot I still was. No vet ever *forgot* the Tabasco. I heated the C in its can over one of the burning blue tabs in the bottom of the hole. The flame burned tiny and emitted little scent to give me away. Breakfast wasn't up to my usual standards of camp cookery, but under the circumstances it would have to do. I enjoyed it long and leisurely washed down with stale water from my plastic canteen, replacing the horrid taste of night mouth with a new but equally horrid aftertaste.

There was no sense of urgency. We were going to be here a few days.

0800 Hours

Sergeant Howard got down to the business of war. From the compass azimuths he recorded last night, he quickly calculated that the torches originated from two primary sources—huts in the village or caves and tunnels dug into the ridge behind the village opposite us. VC often hid like rats underground.

Through binoculars, he noticed that a particular building in the heart of the village attracted more than its share of visitors. Most of the people coming and going were young men of military age. He had no doubt this was a VC stronghold, but couldn't confirm it until he saw more convincing signs. Such as weapons.

Confirmation wasn't long in coming. A little adrenaline surge pulsed through my body when a patrol of sixteen enemy soldiers appeared marching from the west along the road. They seemed to have no concern about being seen, as they had had virtually free rein in the Hiep Duc Valley since at least last December. They considered themselves its owner. They were a mixed bag when it came to uniforms and equipment. Some were hatless in black pajamas. Others wore straw cones or NVA caps. Several stood out in the gray-green uniforms of NVA regulars. Still others, taller, were clad in camouflage common to Chinese troops. All carried combat packs and weapons ranging from RPD machine guns and RPGs (rocket propelled grenades) to Chicom AK-47s and Swedish-made SKS rifles. Every soldier had attached so much shrubbery to his body that he might be mistaken for a bush when he stood still.

Even though we on the hill hadn't access to the "Big Picture" or maps with colored pins or colored markers, it seemed obvious these guys were heading east toward Chu Lai to join with other elements for a pending attack.

The village was a way-stop where they could be fed by the VC-friendly population. They were greeted and soon dispersed among the hooches. What appeared to be the leaders made their way to the lively building in the village center. Sergeant Howard reported it as a possible headquarters or command post.

The VC didn't know it, but eyes were watching them from afar. The enemy's free rein was about to end.

"Shall we go get them, sir?" Sergeant Howard asked Colonel Sullivan through the Chu Lai CP. He had in mind the artillery battery at the ARVN/U.S. Special Forces camp.

Colonel Sullivan rejected the suggestion. *"It's too risky, Carnival Time. You'll give your position away. Stand by. I'll get Bird Dog."*

0830 Hours

Under the curious rules of engagement used in Southeast Asia, bombs could not be dropped in South Vietnam without a Forward Air Controller (FAC) to control the strike. It was FAC's responsibility in his slow, low-flying, single-engine O-1 Cessna Bird Dog to locate the target, identify it to attack aircraft, and ensure they dropped their

PLATOON 345 U.S. MARINE CORPS
SAN DIEGO 1963

(Previous page) Hildreth's Company 345 graduates from marine boot camp. Hildreth is in the second row from the top, fourth man from the right. *(U.S. Marine Corps)*

(Above) Members of the First Platoon prepare for mission prior to Hill 488. From left to right: Ray Hildreth; John Adams; LCpl. Osorio; James McKinney. *(Below)* First Platoon, Recon Battalion, during its early days before Hill 488. Marines on Hill 488 include: Sgt. Jimmie Howard (top, third from left); Ricardo Binns (top row, fourth from left); Ray Hildreth (bottom row, first from left); Ralph Victor (bottom row, third from left). Others identifiable: LCpl. Ronnie Knowles (top row, fifth from left); LCpl. Hawkins (top row, fourth from right).

H-34 helicopters leaving recon battalion helipad at Chu Lai.

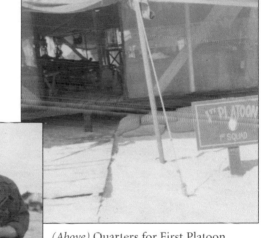

(Above) Quarters for First Platoon at Chu Lai.

(Left) Pfc. Thomas Glawe with M-79 grenade launcher, prior to Hill 488.

(Above) At Chu Lai prior to Hill 488: Cpl. Ronnie Knowles (left, facing left); David Kosoglow (center, brother of Joe Kosoglow); and Joe Kosoglow (right).

(Below) Marine Charlie Company start up Hill 488 to rescue First Platoon after all-night fight. *(U.S. Marine Corps)*

(Above) FAC Lt. Philip Freed calls for air support while pinned down on Hill 488 during rescue. Sgt. Jimmie Howard is to the left. *(U.S. Marine Corps)*

(Left) LCpl. Ray Hildreth is being presented with Silver Star for Heroism on Hill 488, by General Wallace Green, Commandant of the Marine Corps. *(U.S. Marine Corps)*

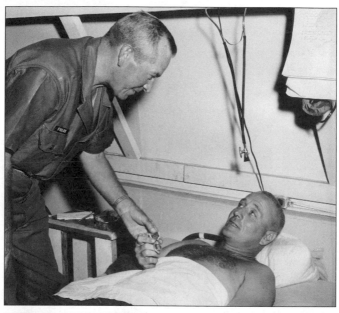

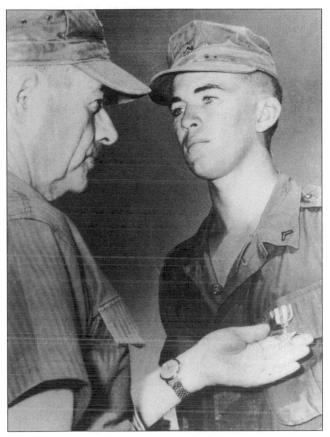

(Above) General Wallace Green, Commandant of the Marine Corps, awards Silver Star to LCpl. William C. Norman following battle of Hill 488. *(U.S. Marine Corps)*

(Opposite page, top) Sgt. Jimmie Howard is awarded a Purple Heart in hospital by Major General Lewis Fields, First Recon Division commander, following battle on Hill 488. *(U.S. Marine Corps)*

(Opposite, bottom) President Lyndon B. Johnson greets Ray Hildreth following Gunnery Sergeant Jimmie E. Howard's Medal of Honor presentation. *(LBJ Library Photo by Frank Wolfe)*

Vietnam War Memorial "The Wall," upon which six names were contributed from Hill 488. *(Photo courtesy Ray Hildreth)*

ordnance in the right place. While Bird Dogs were used in all four Corps Tactical Zones, the rough and mountainous terrain of northernmost I Corps usually proved fatal for any FAC shot down or experiencing engine failure. Bird Dog pilots commonly took reckless chances in order to pinpoint targets and guide in fast-movers.

From my position on the hilltop, I watched the silver little plane appear floating high over the valley. The enemy weren't as likely to get suspicious of being observed on the ground when FAC was in the air. Bird Dog came up on our tactical net.

"Carnival Time, this is Bird Dog."

"Is that you coming in, Bird Dog?" Sergeant Howard asked.

The Cessna rocked its wings. *"What have you got, Carnival Time?"*

"Maybe we have work for you, Bird Dog. I have you in sight. Break off toward the south. See the village west north-west of Hill 488 . . . ?"

The sergeant directed him over the VC command post. The pilot used binoculars to locate and identify the target while he remained at altitude, making lazy circles as though randomly searching. When he was certain he had the site pinned down, he contacted TacAir Control Airborne for any attack aircraft in the area.

Marine jet pilots at Chu Lai flew mainly A-4 Skyhawks, while those at Da Nang chauffeured F-4B Phantoms. Phantom fighter jocks were the first combat jet fliers officially in-country, having arrived at Da Nang in April 1965 at the start of the big buildup. The F-4 was designed as a carrier-borne, long-range, high altitude interceptor for the Navy and Marines. However, it went land-strip in Vietnam and flew all sorts of missions, its main job being to help grunts on the ground with close air support. Capable of a top speed of 1,485 mph, it could carry up to 16,000 pounds of rockets and bombs.

Musket Three responded to the request for help. *"What have you got, Bird Dog?"*

Sergeant Howard and those others of the platoon's command element eavesdropped on the air channel.

"Musket, we have a fixed target. Advise how much play time and what type ordnance?"

"Roger, Bird Dog. We have one-five mikes left and we're carrying twelve Mark 82's . . . slick."

Fifteen minutes was more than ample time at the speed the Phantom traveled. "Mark 82's" referred to 500-pound bombs and "slick" meant they had no retarding devices and thus could be delivered at high speeds and high dive angles.

Bird Dog gave the Phantom its target briefing, describing the target and its location, concluding with, *"I'm going to mark the target with a Willie Pete to make sure."*

Willie Pete, phonetic for white phosphorous, left a large cloud of white smoke when the rocket struck the ground.

"I have you in sight, Musket. Do you have me spotted?"

"Give me a wing wag, Bird Dog. Roger, I got you."

"Okay, Musket. I'm going in now to mark the target. Keep me in sight."

Marking the target was about as close as a FAC came to playing fighter pilot. It called for precision flying. The little silver Cessna rolled into a near-vertical dive and placed his gunsight on the target. The rocket should hit precisely where intended once the correct parameters of dive angle, airspeed, and altitude were met. FACs practiced the maneuver long and hard in order to do it right.

Bird Dog released his rocket and immediately pulled into a steep climb and rolled into a slight bank to watch the rocket hit. A perfect splash! A puff of rapidly spreading expanding smoke billowed next to the target building.

It was the best show in town and I had a box seat on the fifty-yard line. I sat on top of the world watching it. It was like waiting for a train wreck to happen.

"I got your smoke, Bird Dog," Musket said.

"Okay, Musket. Put your egg into the building next to the smoke. You're clear to make your pass."

"Roger, Bird Dog. I'm rolling in hot from the east."

The Phantom streaked in low and fast, inscribing its famous long plume of cruddy exhaust in air just above the ground. It was almost silent at its speed until it was already past the target and its jet roar caught up. Two bombs fell as the pilot pulled up sharply to the right.

Incredible. Both impacted within a few feet of the target. The building erupted in a massive cloud of smoke and dirt and fire. Elsewhere in the village, terrified people appearing the size of ants from my vantage point scurried for cover.

We're back!

Tongues of flame leapt out of the smoke. The train wreck had happened. Fascinated and curious, I couldn't take my eyes off it. Within a few minutes, a secondary explosion destroyed what was left, which was little. The house obviously stored munitions. A dirty chimney of black smoke climbed high into the sky.

Before going off-station, Bird Dog made a second pass to assess the damage. He reported seeing a couple of burnt corpses lying on the ground, but there was no other movement in the village. The inhabitants and the surviving VC visitors had gone to ground in the little homemade bomb shelters they dug underneath their hooches.

The show was over. I settled back in the hole once occupied, perhaps, by some of those little men down there. The sun rose high and heated the air to broil. I watched the column of black smoke tethered to the village.

30

Marines on top of Nui Vu relaxed and sat around talking and visiting, although in low tones. Familiarity can lead to a dangerous sense of false security. It was almost like the hill lured us into kicking back, deceptive though the seduction might be. We realized, of course, that bad guys surrounded us. At the same time, we felt confident in the ability of artillery and air power to protect us and in the prompt response of helicopters to jerk us out if things got too hot. After all, hadn't Uncle Sam always snagged our bacon out of the fire?

The top of the hill was as bare as a nude woman's breast. The Big Rock was her nipple. However, we were so high above the valley and the world that we couldn't easily be seen from below if we stayed in the "safe zone" below the top of the hill and above the break of the slopes. Sergeant Howard required OP/LPs to be manned and alert. As long as that security was observed and nobody got to grabassing, he didn't seem particularly concerned. There were always three or four Marines off-duty lolling around the CP with him and the command element, reading fuck books, chattering, eavesdropping on the battalion net. It was good duty if you could get it.

As the heat and humidity rose, a couple of the guys shucked their shirts and went around in skin. Billy D took his shirt and boots off and rolled up his trouser legs. Chilling out, catching some rays, waiting for the next couple of days to pass. This was his last mission. He was going home.

The other corpsman, Fitzpatrick, took it upon himself to oversee sanitation. That was always a problem whenever a unit bivouacked. Trash, human wastes. Fitz dug a small straddle trench on the back side of the summit and left an e-tool nearby to cover up our deposits after we did our duties. Nui Vu, Powles said, should be renamed Old Shit Top.

I spread a poncho across my hole to provide shade and propped up one end to catch a breeze. I stewed in my own juices underneath it, but at least I was out of the burning sun. Lethargic and half-dozing in the heat, I made myself as comfortable as I could and gazed down the long descending slope of the grassy hill where not a breath of air stirred.

Occasionally, a sound reached us from the village—the sharp hacking of an ax or machete, the growl of a motor scooter without a muffler, dogs barking. It was so hot the dogs never barked more than once before collapsing in the shade. The thin waif of smoke from the bombed-out VC building rose into the air as straight as a pencil mark. I was always amazed at how quickly the Vietnamese recovered from a tragedy and went on about their lives, how well they adapted to war as a constant state. I didn't think Americans could do it.

First Platoon's AOR remained relatively peaceful after the Phantom, but it became obvious as the day wore on that enemy troops were scattered all over the valley and that they were drifting toward the populated areas along the seacoast between Da Nang and Chu Lai. A Bird Dog, sometimes two, prowled overhead as decoys for Recon teams calling in artillery fire on targets of opportunity. HE shells *Whumped* and *Crumped* at different points along the valley floor. Isolated pillars of smoke made more pencil marks against the bright sky. Would those goddam gooks never learn? The Marines had returned.

Mascarenas came back from the CP and from checking on McKinney and Adams and got in the shade with me underneath the poncho. I couldn't see anyone else from my position. At times I felt almost alone on the hill. Just it and myself baking in the sun.

"Anything going on?" I asked him.

"SOS." Same old shit. "It's hot."

I agreed it was.

"Sooner or later," he said, looking worried, "they're gonna figure out what's happening to them. They might be stupid, but they ain't *this* stupid."

"How long are we going to be here?"

Mascarenas shrugged, having spoken his allotment of words.

We sat side by side and watched heat devils rising in transparent squiggles from the earth. Curious how you could be bored under such circumstances. I would have liked to have bunkered up with McKinney or Norman for their company. I talked to McKinney only briefly this morning and hadn't seen Norman since we climbed the hill.

1400 Hours

We were already running short of water. Usually, a chopper brought in resupplies. That wasn't wise under the circumstances. A helicopter sniffing around and setting down anywhere in the vicinity would be a dead giveaway. Billy D proposed to go look for water. Sergeant Howard thought it a good idea.

The corpsman and Powles strung a bunch of empty canteens on belts, slung the belts over their shoulders, and hiked deep into the ridge saddle to the west where verdant vegetation—"Like wild hair around a woman'th puththy," Powles said—suggested the possibility of a spring or small stream. They soon returned soaked in sweat, empty-handed, after having spotted a VC patrol lower down on the saddle. It was also bound for the east. The enemy seemed to be migrating like birds or lemmings.

"We might have to start rationing water," Doc Fitzpatrick said.

1600 Hours

There was no indication that Charlie suspected he was being watched from the ground, although some of the VC undoubtedly began casting suspicious eyes toward the surrounding mountains. Apparently, most of the enemy figured the FACs were extraordinarily good at spotting movement, or incredibly lucky. Others might have considered the bombing fate, pure coincidence, aberration. There might even be traitors in the villages. Pity these poor bastards who received undue VC attention, justly or not. They were going to get strung up by their heels and disemboweled as a warning to other government sympathizers. The VC played rough, without rules.

The valley had to be swarming with gooks for there to be so many sightings. They moved in groups of three to five men and kept to the wooded streambeds and patches of jungle, ducking for cover whenever a FAC flew over. Periodically, all afternoon, big shells from the fire bases banged against the valley floor, often with deadly accuracy. There were so many Marine Recons in the mountains keeping observation on the valley that seldom more than an hour passed without shells falling somewhere. The enemy had to be getting jumpy.

Colonel Sullivan became concerned that the VC would start piecing things together and discover one of the Recons. Of all the units in the field, First Platoon on the bare knob of Hill 488 seemed most vulnerable. Much of the enemy activity originated from that vicinity.

"*Carnival Time,*" Iron Hand radioed, "*fire mission requests will be honored only when a Bird Dog is in the vicinity.*"

2100 Hours

A second night on Nui Vu. A mild breeze from the ocean, beginning to stiffen, cooled off the night, a relief after the heat of the day. I dined with only the hill for company while Mascarenas attended a squad and fireteam leaders meeting with Sergeant Howard at the Big Rock. The only time I ever knew what was going on outside my own sensory range was when Mascarenas came down on our finger blade and told me we were going on fifty percent alert, shifting observation to the right or left, or whatever.

I had spaghetti for the evening meal. No garlic toast and no wine. I sipped hot stale water, into which I mixed a packet of C rat Kool-Aid. I pretended it had ice cubes in it. The breeze gave the mountain a voice. I couldn't tell if it was purring or snarling. Whichever, it made me uneasy.

I collapsed my poncho shelter and prepared to wrap myself in it once the night turned chilly. I devoted most of my attention to the immediate perimeter, within the first one hundred yards or so down the mountainside, instead of to the valley itself. That near area posed the most immediate threat to me personally. If you stared at a bush long enough, you swore it stood up and walked.

Mascarenas dropped into the hole with me.

"See those lights down there?"

I blinked. I actually missed them, so preoccupied had I been with walking bushes.

"Keep an eye on them," he said.

It was a rerun of last night. The torchlight parade flickered through the trees like flashlights passing behind a picket fence. Passing like groups of ghosts. I counted twenty two in one bunch, all in a row with spaces between. More of them than last night. All moving north and east toward the seacoast. Migrating lemmings. This valley must be as thick with dinks as maggots on a dead water buf.

After an hour or so, there were no more lights. I didn't see anything else for the rest of the night.

31

Wednesday started out the same as Tuesday. Same suffocating heat. Same C rat without Tabasco. Same hill; the longer we stayed on it, the more it seemed to develop its own personality, not a benevolent one. Luke the gook down in the valley went about his narrow farmer and VC existence. Up on the hill, Sergeant Howard let his squad and team leaders practice calling in fire to blast the little fuckers with arty and with lightning from the sky. Shit happens.

Although it seemed to me that sooner or later the dinks would realize that it was more than coincidence that their formations kept getting blitzed, nothing indicated that today would be any different than yesterday. We still felt secure and hidden on our own little high piece of real estate, impervious to discovery and retaliation. We were almost like gods lurking up there and looking down on petty little mankind and impersonally picking out those upon whom the giant foot from heaven would descend.

It was a well-recognized fact that men in war seldom fight for God, country, and Mom's apple pie and other noble ideals. Men fight for their buddies, for each other. It was no more complicated than that. Although Marines were considered expendable and as replaceable as parts of a machine, they still had to be able to count on one another as though they would in fact endure. That kind of tightness required bonding—and nothing contributed more to bonding than hardships, deprivations, isolation, and living together under primitive conditions. If nothing else, conditions on top of Hill 488 helped form those tight asshole bonds to cement together an outfit composed of so many fucking new guys and combat cherries.

Under normal circumstances, bonding took weeks or months. Events unfolding on top of Nui Vu were anything but normal circumstances. Just during these first two days, Tuesday and Wednesday, I witnessed a remarkable transformation taking place, even though our feet still hadn't been held to the fire. First Platoon became joined. Secluded like that, surrounded by real danger, the platoon developed an *us* versus *them* mentality. Family. All for one and one for all. I saw it evolving in the little exchanges and interpersonal transactions.

Mascarenas relieved me on watch. I took the opportunity to circulate and see how everyone else was doing. Adams and McKinney sat side by side in the grass yakking away like best buddies. Seeing me, McKinney looked up and grinned in that hesitant manner of his. "John's going to teach me martial arts," he announced happily.

I continued to the Big Rock to see for myself what was going on. Mulvihill and Martinez sat leaning against the boulder munching on John Wayne chocolate. Mulvihill composed a new stanza for the Song Tra Bong marching song:

> *Sitting on top of the hill,*
> *Watching Charlie walking down the trail.*
> *He don't know he's bound for hell.*
> *Them gooks will never tell. . .*

Dinks, gooks, slopes. Racist slurs aimed at the VC served a useful purpose in dehumanizing the enemy and making it easier to kill him before he killed you.

Even the kid Glawe, whose smooth cheeks looked as though they had never felt a razor, reclaimed his Chicago gangster swagger and rap.

"Do you still think you're going to kill all the gooks in the world, Glawe?" Norman chided.

"Man, they ain't fucking with us, are they? That's because they know I'm up here."

1200 Hours

Doc Fitz rationed the water supply. We still had the Mae West bladder full and every man had almost one canteen remaining, but lack of water could become a real problem with another full day out in the open underneath the blistering sun. He and Sergeant Howard ordered the curtailment of all unnecessary physical activity in order to conserve body fluids.

1400 Hours

There didn't seem to be as many dinks moving about today as on the previous day. Maybe they were getting smart.

"They're on to us," Bosley worried, looking scared again.

1600 Hours

First Platoon's second full day on the hill was ending and our third night about to start. We had brought down some hurt on the VC from both artillery barrages and air strikes, contributing in a significant way to hampering his marshalling efforts. The possibility that the VC may have gotten wise to us caused some concern at the battalion CP. Colonel Sullivan and his exec, Major Scotty Harris, became a little antsy over the risk of leaving the platoon stationary much longer.

"Carnival Time, maybe we ought to think of getting you out of there," Colonel Sullivan radioed. *"Sooner or later they're going to figure it out."*

"We have a defensible position and we feel pretty comfortable up here," Sergeant Howard reassured him.

The OP *was* situated in an ideal location. We were giving the enemy a headache and, so far, had encountered no difficulty. Sergeant Howard thought we had a secure bug-out route along the ridge to the east. After further discussion, Howard and the Colonel agreed that one more night on the hill seemed well worthwhile. The platoon would remain, with the stipulation that our radiomen check in every quarter-hour with a SITREP (situation report). We would be extracted if action picked up before nightfall.

"Okay, tiger," Colonel Sullivan concluded. *"Keep your boys low and alert and we'll take you out in the morning."*

1700 Hours

As it turned out, the enemy had become well aware of the platoon's presence. In hindsight, Colonel Sullivan theorized that the VC and North Vietnamese Army, harassed, disrupted, and punished by leatherneck Recon units in territory Hanoi arrogantly claimed to control absolutely, determined to annihilate one such unit and thereby demoralize all others.

Late on the afternoon of 15 June, preparations having been made, VC began moving hundreds of fresh, well-equipped, and highly trained troops toward the base of Nui Vu Hill.

1900 Hours

The VC might have caught us entirely by surprise, wiping us out before we knew they were upon us, had it not been for members of the U.S. Special Forces A-Detachment, "Green Berets," on patrol from their ARVN/CIDG (Civilian Irregular

Defense Group) camp located at Tien Phioc. Also at the camp were the ARVN 105mm batteries that had provided fire on demand into the Hiep Duc Valley over the past two days.

The French withdrawal from Southeast Asia in 1954 and the growing influence of communism helped bring about the introduction of U.S. Special Forces soldiers to that part of the world. Operational detachments from the Seventy-Seventh Group (that shortly became the Seventh Group) were sent to Vietnam in 1956. President John Kennedy's interest in Special Forces and his belief in their capabilities led to the activation of four more active duty SF groups by 1963. The first Congressional Medal of Honor awarded for heroism in Vietnam was earned by Special Forces Captain Roger Donlon in 1964 for leading a successful defense of the Nam Dong Special Forces camp.

The Fifth Special Forces Group (Airborne) was handed the Vietnam mission and became formally established in South Vietnam on 1 October 1964. In 1966, 1,598 SF personnel were advising 28,200 CIDG, 2,300 Nungs, and 28,800 "Ruff Puff" troops—RF/PF, Regional Forces and Popular Forces. Special Forces soldiers found themselves in a number of different roles and missions under the "unconventional warfare" concept. Eclipsing all others, however, in both size and scope was that of the so-called CIDG program, in which Special Forces found themselves involved in every conceivable aspect of counterinsurgency: military, economic, psychological and political. It involved thousands of Green Berets in approximately 100 camps spread from the DMZ in I Corps to the Gulf of Siam in IV Corps. These camps prevented large areas of South Vietnam from being swept under VC military domination. Without the crucial presence of SF, the U.S. Marines that arrived in May 1965 would have found much more of South Vietnam under effective enemy control.

Special Forces advisors were crammed into dirt-walled,

under-gunned campsites carved out of steaming, disease-ridden swamp and jungle. These crude compounds were usually isolated, lacked mutual support, and deliberately placed in areas controlled by the VC or astride major VC infiltration routes. They offered lucrative targets to the VC. That was especially true of those camps in I Corps.

Camp Tra Bong, west of Chu Lai, lost 47 men, including four Green Berets, on 30 January 1966 when the CIDG unit there responded to reports of an attack on the nearby Long Phu outpost. One hour before noon, the patrol radioed, "We're going into attack. Request all support you can give us." That was the last heard from it. A reaction group sent from Da Nang found thirty-nine bodies of the lost patrol in two shattered jungle charnels. Seven were never recovered.

The heaviest losses for Special Forces in 1966 occurred shortly thereafter in March when VC overran another contested region of I Corps. The A Shau Valley, sometimes called "The Valley of the Shadow of Death," perched on the rim of Vietnam's northwestern border in one of the most forbidding primeval stretches of tropical terrain in Southeast Asia. VC overran the A Shau SF/CIDG camp during three days of savage fighting beginning on the night of 8 March. The entire 141st CIDG defected en masse to the assailants. The camp was abandoned and never reopened.

In 1966, most SF A-detachments were on "clear, hold and build" assignments, charged with constructing and garrisoning fortified camps to hold the VC at bay in contested territory. Special Forces and their CIDG commandos provided highway security and convoy escort, defended airfields, cleared projected base areas, and swept critical VC avenues of infiltration.

On the afternoon of 15 June 1966, Green Beret Sergeant First Class Donald Reed and Specialist Fifth Class Hardy Drande led a platoon of CIDG on patrol into the vicinity of Hill 488. By sundown, the patrol moved into the Hiep Duc

Valley less than two miles from the hill that dominated that part of the terrain. Friendly units operating in the same AO commonly eavesdropped on each other's radio channels. The Green Beret call sign was "Skip Balls," but Sergeant Howard misinterpreted it as "Stiff Balls." Stiff Balls immediately caught Howard's attention when he came on the air to report enemy movement.

"Elements of PAVN (Peoples Army of North Vietnam, also known as NVA) and Main Force VC heading east," Reed advised his base camp.

"Roger that," responded base. *"What size element? Do you have coordinates?"*

First reports indicated a platoon. Sergeant Howard plotted the coordinates on his map and nodded his head. Nothing unusual so far. Enemy elements had been moving east for the past two days. Stiff Balls called down an artillery barrage, but the platoon disappeared into heavy forest.

Stiff Balls spotted even more enemy over the next hour. His estimation of the enemy's size grew from the original platoon to a company, then to a battalion. Hundreds of hard-core NVA and VC were on the march, later identified as a battalion from the Third NVA Regiment.

"There's at least a battalion," the Green Beret reported, *"and they look like they mean business."*

Night fell. Darkness meant the cessation of air-to-ground helicopter operations until daybreak, especially in such rough terrain. First Platoon was stuck on the hill for the rest of the night, come what may. Sergeant Howard continued to anxiously monitor Stiff Balls's transmissions. He overheard Reed and Drande proposing the CIDG, reinforced by additional units from the camp, hit the enemy from the rear and disrupt him. However, these ARVN and CIDG forces, like most others, were reluctant to move from their fortifications after nightfall when the VC went on the prowl. No matter how much Reed argued with the Vietnamese camp commander, he steadfastly refused to send out more units. Reed's language turned blistering: *"What the fuck is with these chickenshit asswipes?"* he raged. *"Why the hell do they think they're out here—to sit on their asses and hide?"*

Sergeant Howard chuckled. "They sure didn't learn that language in communications school."

The situation deteriorated while Sergeant Howard and his command element listened. Stiff Balls obviously had CIDG in the platoon whose balls weren't so stiff. Reed and Drande were having a tough time keeping their men from panicking and disappearing into the woods.

The picture became even worse when the point element tripped a booby trap and killed two and wounded two. We on Hill 488 could only guess at what was going on down there. Stiff Balls on the air sounded both angry and distressed. *"The chicken-livered fuckers have bugged out on us. The cowardly bastards have ghosted."*

The Green Berets had problems. There was nothing we on the hill could do to help them. Thus warned, Sergeant Howard began preparing his own defenses—just in case the enemy headed our way.

"Iron Hand," he radioed matter-of-factly to Colonel Sullivan, "just make sure we have plenty of air support if we need it."

32

While in the distance, barely audible and sounding like distant thunder, artillery shells banged against the suspected locations of the enemy and his likely routes of movement, Sergeant Howard summoned squad and fireteam leaders to the Big Rock and briefed them on the situation. He didn't bother with a "win one for the Gipper" speech. Instead, professional, blunt, and Marine, he simply told them that we had movement in the neighborhood and that we should prepare. Colonel Sullivan, he said, had earlier offered the option of extracting us. That was before nightfall and before Stiff Balls encountered VC. Sergeant Howard made the call to stay on the hill another night. Now the platoon had no other option.

"Put the men on fifty percent alert until we have something more definite," he instructed.

The defense would be a three-sixty perimeter. Initially, it consisted of two-man listening post positions arranged around the sides of the hill twenty yards or so from the top. He also shifted the men around. Marines dug into one position over time sometimes got too comfortable with it. Moving them often restored the edge.

"Don't try to fight them out there if anything happens," Sergeant Howard emphasized. "I want everybody back here on top. Fast."

He designated the Big Rock as rally point, around which the Marines would form our final defensive line. If time and opportunity permitted withdrawal rather than defense, Mascarenas's fireteam would take point and head east on the ridge, down into the saddle and back up on the other side. Otherwise, the platoon would be extracted after sunup tomorrow.

"Any questions?"

"Yes," Victor said. "Like General Custer said, 'Where d-d-did all them goddamned Indians come from?' "

Again, there would be no moon. The air appeared faintly hazed from two days of explosions and fires in the valley. Leaders crept off in the darkness to brief their men and reposition us around the hill. Sergeant Howard, the two radiomen and the two corpsmen remained at the Big Rock to monitor radio traffic. Billy D lay back on his poncho to catch a few winks.

2030 Hours

I was watching a whole string of the ghost lights floating past on the trail below when Mascarenas came back from the meeting.

"Gather your shit, Hildreth," he ordered. "We're moving places."

The strain in his voice told me something was about to shake loose. "What's going on?" I asked.

"Taxes, death, and *them*." He nervously indicated the lights. "Sergeant Howard wants us to be ready."

He collected McKinney and Adams. The four of us in the fireteam switched from the southwest propeller blade to the southeast one overlooking the saddle in the ridgeline. Victor's fireteam from Thompson's squad took our places.

McKinney and I hunkered together in the grass above the saddle. Mascarenas took Adams and disappeared in the darkness to our right. I heard the swish of their legs in the tall grass. Then there was more silence as they went to ground together. Even the hill seemed expectant, waiting for something to happen.

I still didn't know what was going on, other than that an Army Special Forces team had spotted a large number of VC not far away. As I always said, if you were in the common crotch, a grunt U.S. Marine, you went where you were told, did what you were told, and tried in the process to keep your butt from getting shot off. The brass back at Division or MACV moved your colored pin from place to place on the map and you simply followed it. You rarely saw the "Big Picture." What you saw of the war was what there was of it in your immediate vicinity.

Right now, what we saw of it wasn't much. It was so dark I could barely make out the top of the hill behind me against the slightly lighter sky. Below lay only inky blackness. If I scratched my nuts, I had to ask McKinney if the were mine or his I was scratching. Vietnam defined the word *dark*.

"Daylight belongs to us," Lance Corporal Osorio explained when I first arrived in-country. "The dark belongs to *them*."

As far as McKinney and I were concerned, we could have been on another planet twenty-five *million* miles away from Chu Lai instead of a mere twenty-five. There didn't seem to be a sound anywhere in the world except the soughing of a freshening breeze through the grass. It sounded like soft weeping. Darkness hid danger while at the same time promising a false security that it also hid you *from* danger. For all we could tell, we might have been the only two people left on earth.

"Ray?" McKinney whispered, nudging me.

"Yeah?"

"I'm really going to be glad to see the sun again."

"Me too."

"I wonder what Moore's doing."

"Sleeping. Getting ready to go back on KP."

"Lucky asshole," he said. "Him and Benson both."

We sat in the still of the night.

"Ray?"

"Yeah. I'm awake."

"Reckon there's still a world out there?"

Always a bit of the pessimist.

"The world is what you can see, James."

"It's a small world, Ray. Jeez! I can't even see my feet."

He edged closer. Our knees touched. Touching another human being provided a great deal of comfort when you were two nineteen-year-olds in the dark a long way from home and surrounded by people who wanted to kill you. We talked for a while, whispering about home and family and girls and cars. After a while, McKinney pulled a poncho over his head so the glow wouldn't be seen while he smoked a cigarette. He yawned and nestled down under his poncho, saying he was going to catch a few Z's.

"Wake me in a couple of hours and I'll let you grab some rack time," he promised.

He was soon breathing deep and regular, sitting up. I repositioned my M-14 across my knees. The renewed rumble of distant artillery reminded me of thunder and the storm season. It was tornado spring back in Oklahoma. When a storm was brewing in the evening, you stood outside and watched lightning flickering on the horizon. You knew a storm was coming, but you never knew for sure whether it was coming your way or not. Nor did you know how bad it would be.

2100 Hours

Lance Corporal Bob Martinez hunkered over his PRC-25 behind the Big Rock on top of the hill. Sergeant Howard and his friend, corpsman Richard Fitzpatrick, leaned with their backs against the rock and listened to the low, barely audible mutter of the radio. Billy D napped on his poncho. Second radioman Dan Mulvihill had been placed on perimeter watch a short distance below the Big Rock.

Starting from the twelve o'clock position on the north, Lance Corporal Ricardo Binns, Bill Norman, Thomas Powles, and Joe Kosoglow occupied the OP/LP out on the narrow finger overlooking the most likely avenue of enemy approach. At one o'clock sat Mulvihill in the grass. James McKinney and I occupied three o'clock. At six o'clock were John Adams and Lance Corporal Alcadio Mascarenas.

On the other side of the hill, Ignatius Carlisi and Lance Corporal Ralph Victor took up the eight o'clock. The outspoken Chicago kid, Thomas Glawe, and Charles Bosley were at ten o'clock. First Squad leader Jerald Thompson stayed near the top of the hill to supervise his squad.

The Recon patrol was armed with eighteen M-14 rifles equipped for full automatic fire; eighteen combat knives, mostly Ka-bars; one M-79 40mm grenade launcher; two .45-caliber pistols carried by the two corpsmen; at least four fragmentation grenades per man; two or three flares total for signaling; and approximately 3,000 rounds of 7.62 ammunition. A basic load of ammo per Recon Marine called for him to carry five twenty-round magazines of M-14, 7.62 caliber, plus a sixty-round bandolier. Some of us carried more than that. Of course, Benson and his M60 machine gun stayed behind, which might have been a good thing. At least for him or anyone else who attempted to fire a machine gun in close-range fighting. A machine gun drew enemy fire like a magnet attracted steel shavings.

We were low on water and food, but what the hell? We were out of here tomorrow anyhow.

The platoon waited for daylight.

33

Someone crept up behind me through the grass, stooped over and low to the ground to cut down on his outline against the stars. Corporal Jerald Thompson, First Squad Leader, dropped on one knee next to us. Although this was his first mission into the bush, everyone seemed comfortable with him. He was confident and authoritative while at the same time good-natured and approachable.

"You guys awake?"

"Yeah," I said.

McKinney stirred and leaned against me in his sleep, like a little brother. It had been a long day.

"Sergeant Howard has put us on one hundred percent alert," Thompson said. "Hildreth, move over to your right about twenty paces."

"What's up?" Something cold and slimy stirred inside my gut.

"There's been lots of movement," Thompson whispered. "If we have to bug out, Hildreth, you're point man. Lead us down that draw in front and then around to the right. Got it?"

He indicated the middle of the ridge to the east, toward the coast and "home."

"Yeah. Okay."

I shook McKinney, wrapped in his poncho as though insulated against the world. I hated to disturb his dreams.

"James, are you awake?"

"How can I sleep with all this racket?"

"We're going on one hundred percent. I'm moving over to the right about twenty paces."

"What's going on?" His voice became thin and alarmed.

"I wish I knew."

His head swiveled back and forth on his shoulders. "Ray, I don't like it."

"Stay awake." I patted him on the shoulder before I picked up my cartridge belt and pack and paced off twenty steps to his right. The last I saw of him, he pulled his poncho over his head, leaving only his eyes showing while he lit another cigarette.

Thompson went with me to check my new position. I settled down in the grass. It came up around me to the height of my chin. The light wind made whispering sighs in the grass like predators passing in the night. A shiver skittered up my spine and prickled the short hairs on my neck. Folks back in Oklahoma said you got a shiver like that whenever someone walked over your future grave.

"Hildreth," Thompson said, "remember to fire underneath any muzzle flash if anything happens. Then get to the hilltop pronto."

Underneath the muzzle flash was where the largest and most vital area of the firer would be. Why had he thought it necessary to remind me of that? Before I could question him further, he got up and continued his rounds, speaking a few words to each man in the squad.

I waited alone, feeling like the last man on the planet, unable to see anything around me except darkness. The high drone of a jet followed by the crumping detonations of bombs exploding down-valley helped relieve my aloneness. It told me there were people other than the enemy beyond this hill.

It was so quiet afterward that I thought I heard and felt the hill breathing. I gripped my rifle and listened for McKinney. Nothing. I tried to make out his outline for the comfort it might offer, but it was too dark. I kept thinking: *One hundred percent alert, what the fuck?* All I had to do was get through the night. Come morning the choppers would snatch us out of here. An hour later, we would be on stand down at Chu Lai in time for breakfast—powdered eggs, powdered milk, corn flakes in a box, shit on a shingle, hot coffee strong enough to eat out the lining of your stomach. God, that sounded great.

The wind in the grass made me uneasy. But all I could do was wait—and daylight arrived an eternity from now.

34

The north finger stuck out as a rather narrow plateau that banked off on three sides, then rose toward the top of the hill and the Big Rock. Powles and Kosoglow hunkered on the eastern side of the finger, peering cautiously downslope into the near-impenetrable night. Rick Binns and Norman occupied the western side, lying in an old shallow-dug fighting hole. They had been there since nightfall, waiting, listening and looking, hearing nothing but breeze in the grass and occasionally, earlier, artillery rounds exploding in the valley. No one had seen even the ghost lights since shortly after nightfall.

Binns lay on his side propped up on his elbow with his feet downhill. A few minutes ago he thought he detected movement from the corner of his eye, but when he looked straight at it, it disappeared. Imagination under stress did funny things. He kept looking, not convinced it was an illusion or a figment of an overactive mind. He swept his head back and forth slowly to make use of his peripheral night vision.

He hadn't noticed that bush before. About ten feet in

front and downhill. Had he merely overlooked it earlier? He looked directly at it. It disappeared.

He kept his eye on it. Rather, he kept the edge of his eye on it, for any object stared at directly in darkness disappeared.

It moved. It wasn't the wind. It wasn't his imagination.

Slowly, deliberately, almost casually, the lance corporal one-handedly pointed the muzzle of his rifle at the bush. What if he was wrong? One shot and the enemy would certainly know we were up here, if he didn't already. Hesitant now, wanting to make sure, Binns held his fire. He wasn't the type of guy who shot at shadows.

The bush crept from left to right. It made not a sound.

He fired twice in rapid succession, suddenly renting the night apart. Twin muzzle flames speared the darkness. The double report echoed ringing across the valley, alarmingly loud as it shattered the silence.

Bullets smashed into something with a solid sound. The bush pitched backward, thrashing as it rolled downhill.

There was no need for further hush-hush. The enemy was upon us. Binns had just blown their element of surprise. He bolted to his feet, shouting at his watch mates, "Throw a grenade and get up to the hilltop."

Grenades exploded with white strobe flashes, banging further shards of chaos against the night.

2305 Hours

The waiting for something to happen ended when Binns shot the bush that was not a bush. The shots and the grenade explosions cracked through the tension that shrouded Hill 488, presenting themselves hard and clean with the impact of getting mugged in a closet when you thought you were alone. The cheeks of my ass grabbed grass and dirt. I froze in place, unexpectedly and totally scared to death.

I heard scurrying sounds as Binns and his outpost

clawed the sides of the hill in their frenzied dash to reach the Big Rock.

2307 Hours

Jarred awake, still half-asleep, Billy D took a few seconds for the situation to dawn on him. He sat bolt upright as though a spring loosened underneath him. Four Marines scrabbled into view beyond the edge of the Big Rock. Dim shadows, half-crawling and half-running but letting no grass grow beneath their feet. They exchanged urgent words with Sergeant Howard. The corpsman heard "bushes" and "surrounded."

Surrounded?

One of the guys took a knee at the corner of the rock. Still in the open, however, and a silhouette against the cold distant stars. He began chunking 40mm grenades down-range with his M-79. That meant it was Powles, the nice guy with the mild California lisp.

The enemy returned fire. Chicom and Russian-made AK-47s had a heavy accent. A deep throaty rattling sound on full auto. A string of bullets hit nearby, slapping the earth. One of the rounds caught Powles with a meaty, smacking sound that pitched him backward. He screamed with fear and anguish, a scream that seemed to come from hell at the very center of the earth. His body thrashed about in agony, pounding against the ground. The continuous screaming keened into the wind and seemed to freeze there.

Binns dragged the wounded leatherneck behind the Big Rock. *"Corpsman! Corpsman!"*

2308 Hours

Some of the Marines at the Big Rock traded fire with the enemy. A brief violent exchange, broken off first by the attackers. Sergeant Howard barked, "Marines, cease fire!" Such was the hold of discipline he exerted over the platoon that, following a final spatter of rifle fire, shooting ceased from both sides.

2310 Hours

The screaming sounded too otherworldly to come from the throat of a mere human being. It was like the hill itself, a conduit to hell, opened its awful gullet and released a stream of the most horrendous shrieking. It went on for what seemed an eternity but which must have been only two or three minutes at most. It persisted with such raw unnerving intensity that the whole world seemed to stop to listen. It was like both camps took a deep breath, shocked into a momentary fugue state by first blood on both sides.

Oh, Jesus! Oh, Jesus! I prayed. *Please make him stop.*

It was eating me up inside. I felt about to implode. I had never heard a human being make such a sound—and I prayed to God I never would again.

2312 Hours

Billy D fumbled for his aid bag, still not fully comprehending what was going on. The other corpsman, Fitzpatrick, crawled to Powles and began administering emergency aid, feeling the wounds in the dark with his hands. The Californian had caught the round through his left kidney. It entered and exited, leaving a great ragged hole through and through. He was losing a lot of blood. A shot of morphine finally quieted him.

Almost simultaneously, both corpsmen shared a feeling that there would be plenty of work for both before this night was finished.

2313 Hours

Battle was a difficult reality to grasp the first time you experienced it. For radioman Bob Martinez, the thought struck home with: *They're trying to kill me.* His heart pounded like it was trying to jump out of his chest to run away. Sergeant Howard crawled over, grabbed him by the arm and pushed him behind the cover of the rock.

"Stay here—and stay down!" the sergeant snapped.

The radio was our lifeline. It had to be protected. It was more valuable than any individual life.

2314 Hours

Somehow I ended up belly down in the grass hugging the earth. In the silence that followed when the screaming stopped, I was afraid Uncle Ho Chi Minh himself would hear the thumping of my heart and the rattling of my rifle in my trembling hands. I stared intently into the darkness, my eyes desperately searching the hillside below for any telltale sign, any slight movement, anything that looked different than it had before. I strained my ears for sound.

Nothing. There was nothing out there. Maybe I dozed off and had some kind of weird nightmare. Maybe the shooting and the screaming were an aberration of a too-active imagination. It was easy to believe such things because you *wanted* to believe them.

At the same time, you knew this was *real*. It was something with which you had to cope. No amount of avoidance rationalizing was going to turn it into anything else. I searched my mind to extract something from my long hours of Marine Corps training that would save my life. All I came up with on such short order was a single simple phrase: *Shoot and move!*

Shoot at *what?* Move *where?*

Seeing nothing, being virtually blind, was too scary and confusing to endure.

McKinney cried out and fired a burst. His muzzle blast seemed to blossom right in front of my eyes. A grenade detonated at almost the same instant, merging with the gunfire. The strobelike flash of the grenade seared light into the black walls of eternity. I felt the heat; I held my head as a shower of dirt and rock fell on top of me.

Some supernatural, primeval fear of things in the night struck terror in my heart as I listened to the flutter of giant wings in the air, something settling back to earth like a giant dying bat. I thought it would land on me with razor claws extended. I cried out to McKinney as it came to roost only a few feet away.

It took a few moments for me to realize what it was— McKinney's poncho. *Oh, God, no!*

"McKinney! Are you all right?"

No answer.

35

From a time at the beginning when a committee of the Continental Congress met in Philadelphia's Tun Tavern on 10 November 1775 to create a new military force known as the Continental Marines, Marines have looked upon themselves as an elite force. The knife blade, the cutting edge, the first to fight. They assault enemy beaches and die for their country in whatever numbers are required to accomplish a necessary mission. And they never retreat. They make a stand and hold it.

"Marines don't retreat," Marine Corps legend Chesty Puller, among others, was supposed to have said. "We only attack in a different direction."

"When all else fails," goes a Marine matter-of-face assessment of any intolerable situation, "remember we're Marines."

On this philosophy of making a stand, more than two centuries of U.S. Marine Corps history has produced many heroic legends of stands and last stands made by Marines caught in a tight vise at the point of no return. Perhaps the first of these originated during the Revolutionary War after George Washington incorporated a number of Continental Marines into his reorganized army artillery units.

From 22 October to 15 November 1777, Marines participated in the defense of Fort Mufflin on the Delaware River against a superior force of twelve British ships and a number of Hessian artillery batteries. Even though the enemy pounded the fort to rubble, the stubborn defenders held on in a courageous stand that prevented the enemy from relieving and reinforcing his units holding Philadelphia.

U.S. Marines served with the Continental Army in battles at Trenton, Assunpink, Morristown, and Brandywine. They made their first landing on the Bahama Islands in 1776. Although they were disbanded after the Revolutionary War, they were re-created as a military service in 1798 and have been the first to fight in almost every major U.S. war since then, leading to the old saying: "The Marines have landed and the situation is well in hand."

Marines saw action against France in 1798, stormed the Barbary pirates' stronghold at Tripoli in 1805, and valiantly made a stand to defend the capital during the War of 1812. They fought in the Creek and Seminole Wars of 1836, made many landings on both coasts of Mexico and were the first to enter the city gates of Mexico and raise the Stars and Stripes over the National Palace, which later became known as "the halls of Montezuma."

Marines were the first to land in Cuba and the Philippines during the Spanish-American War. They captured John Brown and his followers at Harpers Ferry during the Civil War, and landed in China seventeen times during the late 1800s and early 1900s to protect American interests.

Between 1915 and 1917, Marines developed the institution of the boot camp, with a training program designed to build the toughest fighters and best marksmen in the world, and to weed out anyone not up to Marine standards. A relatively small, elite military force, the Marines desired, as expressed in the slogan, "a few good men" to fill their ranks.

Marines were not used much at first during World War I. It was not until May 1918 when Germans unleashed a major offensive toward Paris that U.S. Marines of the Fourth Brigade were dispatched to breach three large German salients against the line. Marines stamping down the road toward the front encountered large numbers of fleeing French. A French officer advised Captain Lloyd W. Williams to join the retreat. Captain Williams responded with one of the great ripostes of the war.

"Retreat, hell. We just got here."

Establishing defensive positions in the square mile of forest and rock known as Belleau Wood, the Marines, nicknamed "Devil Dogs" by the Germans, fought one of the greatest battles in their history. They opened fire on advancing German units at 800 yards, amazing the enemy who considered fire beyond 200 yards to be ineffective. When the Germans charged, the Marines counterattacked. Sergeant Dan Daly led an attack with the immortal exhortation, "Come on, you sons of bitches. Do you want to live forever?"

It was during this fight that the First Battalion, Sixth Marines, led by Major John A. Hughes, made a valiant last stand by digging into the village of Bouresches and refusing to give up. The Marines took 450 casualties, but it was the Germans who finally withdrew.

One of the great stands of Marine Corps history occurred the same year during German counterattacks at Soissons. Lieutenant C. B. Cates sent a field message back to headquarters: "I am in an old abandoned French trench bordering on road leading out from your CP and 350 yards from an old mill. I have only two men left out of my company and twenty out of other companies. We need support, but it is almost suicide to try to get it here as we are swept by machine gun fire and a constant artillery barrage is upon us. I have no one on my left and only a few on my right. I will hold."

He did.

Marines continued to dismay the Germans with long-range rifle fire and fierce assaults at Saint Mihiel, Blanc Mont Ridge, and the Meuse-Argonne.

During the island fighting of World War II, Marines made scores of such stands. The first of these began the same day as Pearl Harbor when the Japanese also attacked Wake Island.

The three small islands that make up Wake Atoll, site of a Navy patrol plane base, were defended by 449 Marines, a Marine fighter squadron, some 50 army and navy specialists, and about 1,200 civilian construction personnel. Against this small ragtag force, the Japanese attempted an invasion on 10 December 1941 with nine cruisers and destroyers escorting four transports full of infantry. Fierce fighting ended with the invasion fleet limping away, leaving 700 dead troops and two sinking ships behind.

The Marines continued their desperate stand for another thirteen days before, their numbers decimated and with no help on the way, the survivors finally surrendered.

In August 1942, Marines invaded Guadalcanal and launched the first American offensive of the war. Leathernecks (the nickname came from the leather bands early Marines wore around their necks) of the First Marine Division held out on the Tenaru River, the left flank of the American defense line, in one of the bloodiest fights of Marine history. Wave after wave of Japanese swept against Marine rifle, machine gun and artillery fire. When dawn came and the battle ended with the Marines still holding on, the Japanese left more than 800 of their elite soldiers dead on the field.

The heroic stand of 2,000 Marines at Tarawa has been compared to the last stands of the Alamo and the Little Big Horn. Colonel David M. Shoup summed up the situation in five words: "Combat efficiency: We are winning."

The rest of the war saw Marines battling and making heroic stands and last stands all the way to the Philippines. The war ended with the dropping of atomic bombs on Japan. Marines were planning to land on enemy shores when the armistice was signed.

The terrain and the stalemate fighting of the Korean War lent itself to last stands. Marines made countless stands in "The Hill Battles"—Bloody Ridge, Finger Ridge, Heart-break Ridge, Old Baldy, Pork Chop Hill, Bunker Hill where Jimmie Earl Howard made his stand . . . Early in the war, grotesquely outnumbered Marines encircled by the enemy smashed seven North Korean divisions in their winter march south from the Chosin Reservoir. Colonel Raymond Murray told his men, "We will walk out of here as Marines." They did.

The Marine tradition continued with the Suez crisis of 1956, in Lebanon, in the Dominican Republic in 1965, and finally in Vietnam. At 9:03 A.M. on 8 March 1965, Corporal Garry Powers leaped from his amphibious tractor into the knee-deep water at the harbor at Da Nang and splashed ashore. He was the first combat Marine of the first offensive U.S. troops to reach land in the escalating war with the North Vietnamese communists. Tens of thousands more followed—and again U.S. Marines found themselves in situations where they had to make stands.

In boot camp, "boots" were infused with the heroic history and tradition of the Marine Corps. You were a Marine, by God, and, by God, you were expected to fight like a Marine. Division kept encouraging us to find the enemy. Well, we found him. Now exactly who was going to find, fix, and fuck over whom?

36

The Special Forces soldiers were obviously correct in assuming the Main Force VC and NVA they spotted earlier in the evening—*hundreds* of soldiers—were heading somewhere on purpose and meant business. Thanks to them, Vietnamese Reds climbing the hill under cover of darkness, swiftly and silently, weren't going to massacre us in one surprise attack. Still, we were outnumbered, surrounded, unable to use our bug-out plan, and the enemy was getting set up and preparing to attack at any moment. Ominous sounds of movement—rustling, slithering, clanking of weapons, voices—reached our ears. Nerves were on raw edge. The monsters of our imaginations had become real—and they were coming for us.

I had never been so scared in my entire life, not even when the gooks passed by on the trail and I left my rifle with the radio. My tongue felt like a cactus in my mouth. My position had had it. There was no cover here. I had a standing order to pull back into a tight defensive perimeter if anything happened. Still, I felt reluctant to leave McKinney without checking on him.

He had failed to respond when I called out to him. Any further communication would only serve to attract the enemy—and perhaps a grenade—down on me. I lay there longer than I should have, listening for McKinney, hearing nothing else from him. My mind refused to acknowledge that he was probably dead, his body splintered and broken at the same time his poncho took flight. Only a few minutes ago he had been sleeping right next to me, and now— It left a hollow feeling inside.

Further delay would only serve to expose me to the same fate he had already suffered. My guts wrenched, but I knew my duty. Twisting in the grass, dragging my rifle, bandolier and pack with me, I slithered as swiftly as a lizard toward the top of the hill.

"Who's there?" someone challenged.

"Me!"

I kept going. Thompson lay flat in the grass and I couldn't see him, even when I was almost on top of him.

"Me who?"

"Me. Hildreth."

"Damn. You almost got shot. Where's McKinney?"

I told him.

"Sweet Jesus," he exhaled and crawled away to report to Sergeant Howard.

Sergeant Howard was busy making the perimeter tighter, assigning firing positions through his squad and team leaders, and checking on casualties. Two of them already—one seriously wounded and one likely dead—and those in just the first brief exchange.

Thompson came back and positioned me between Mascarenas on my left and Adams on my right. Our area of responsibility lay toward the east and the saddle in the ridgeline below. At the same time, the rest of the platoon also realigned itself in the smaller perimeter, everyone prone and hugging the ground. The defensive three-sixty was no more than twenty paces across, with the Big Rock at its apex. The crown of the hill offered almost no cover, the old VC fighting holes being further down on the slopes. In my mind's eye I saw VC already wriggling into the hole I shared with Mascarenas the two days we were on the hill.

Nothing loud was going on at the moment, which seemed to emphasize the hard urgency in Sergeant Howard's voice as he got on the radio and described the situation to the battalion CP.

"We're under fire, enemy close," he said in a voice remarkably calm and focused. "We need flares. We need the box fired—and we need it *now*."

Artillery batteries commonly preset potential targets on their maps and plotting boards in order to be able to "fire the box" during hours of darkness. A "box" was usually included as part of a unit's defensive measures when it went to the field.

"Hit all around the perimeter to keep 'em off us," the sergeant continued, his voice disembodied in the night. Alerting the world outside this tiny hilltop that Marines were in trouble. "I've got one serious wounded and one missing. Start a medevac . . ."

It was so quiet it was almost like nothing had ever happened. Another still night on a hilltop in Vietnam. I peered down the slope into the darkness, thinking of advice my half-brother Homer gave me before I left for Vietnam.

"Whenever you have the enemy in your sights," he said, "don't hesitate by trying to rationalize right from wrong. Just squeeze the trigger. You'll have time to think about it later."

Knowing that some of your own people were hurt exerted a strong psychological effect on those of us who were not. We were all mature young men who had worked, trained, and striven to reach self-confidence and self-sufficiency, just now beginning to appreciate what we could do and enjoy, and suddenly we were threatened with the possibility that it could all end. Death for men so young and ready to live was a brutal personal affront, an unforgivable insult. Along with our fear came a natural, understandable intensity of rage at those who might take everything away from us. Not a Marine on Nui Vu that night's beginning held a single qualm against killing. When it came down to *them* or *us,* it was going to be *them.*

2318 Hours

We defenders had the advantage of high ground and looking down the enemy's throat when he started up. The enemy had the advantage of the cover of darkness, firepower, and superior numbers. Just how superior in numbers we had yet to realize. It hardly seemed fair to Lance Corporal Bob Martinez as he inched to the end of the Big Rock, next to the shallow sump hole, and squinted into the night. Sergeant Howard was on the radio; Mulvihill's radio had been turned off to save as a spare and for emergencies.

Martinez saw nothing, but he kept looking anyhow. He heard movement all around the hill. Tension clamped his jaws so tight he wasn't sure if he'd ever be able to open his mouth again.

Powles, lying in the safety of the Big Rock, was in bad shape. Morphine hushed his screaming, but instead of euphoria, the drug had produced a type of paranoid schizophrenia that caused the wounded Marine to moan and whimper in fear. While Billy D and Doc Fitz worked on his wound, getting in a spike and administering IV fluids, Binns kept talking to him in a soothing whisper. Lying to him, telling him he was going to be all right, that he'd be going home now with a million-dollar wound. Powles had always looked up to Binns.

2320 Hours

Sergeant Howard crawled around the tiny perimeter on his belly. Touching each one of us, encouraging us, bolstering our spirit. He assured us we'd be backed up by artillery and air support. Assets should be on station and prepared to cover us within the next few minutes. It occurred to me that providing fire cover might be difficult under the circumstances, in the dark with the enemy literally breathing in our faces. I refrained from asking questions, however, because I wanted to believe it could be done. Sometimes, reality came in doses too large to take all at once.

"Hold your fire until you can see them," Sergeant Howard said. "Pick your targets and don't shoot at shadows. Don't waste ammo. Remember, we don't have an unlimited supply."

It seemed on face value that we had sufficient. But before the night ended, even five thousand rounds a man would not seem like enough.

"We need the machine gun," Carlisi murmured. "If Benson hadn't got hurt—"

"A machine gun would do us little good," Sergeant Howard replied. "It's a prime target at close range. So is an automatic weapon. Fire only on semi-auto unless you want to be singled out by every gook on the hill. Good luck, men."

2322 Hours

Earlier that evening of the fifteenth at Chu Lai, Battalion Command Sergeant Major Turner, a wiry career Marine in his forties, attended a briefing with Colonel Arthur Sullivan and other battalion officers and ranking noncoms. Subject matter concerned the seven Recon teams still ensconced around the rim of the Hiep Duc Valley gathering intelligence and providing sightings to the pending second phase of Operation *Kansas*. The Colonel was especially concerned with the status of First Platoon, Charlie Company. Howard's platoon had been inserted the deepest and had reported the most enemy activity. A Special Forces CIDG unit spotted large enemy concentrations moving toward Hill 488 shortly after nightfall. Artillery barrages failed to disperse them.

Colonel Sullivan and his operations officer, Major Jack Cooper, expressed fear that the enemy movement came in response to fire missions Howard had been directing into the valley since the evening of the thirteenth.

"The VC aren't stupid," the Colonel said. "They're going to figure it out. Howard wanted to stay another night. I let him. I want Howard out of there. Jack, you and the Sergeant Major work up an extraction plan."

Turner and Major Cooper took on the task and soon had everything lined up for a pickup of the platoon at first light. It was too late tonight, too dark, and the terrain too imposing. The Sergeant Major had had almost no sleep since Monday when the operation began. He made his way to his cot at about 2200 hours. At that time, Carnival Time still reported everything quiet on its quarter-hourly sitreps.

He had barely fallen asleep when a commotion in the communications tent next door pulled him into awareness. Somebody rapped on his tent.

"I'm awake," he rasped. "This had better be good. What is it?"

It was a corporal from S-2. "Sergeant Major, we got a team in trouble."

Turner immediately launched to his feet and out into the night. All he had to do was slip on his boots. He had been sleeping in his utilities since *Kansas* began. A cool breeze blew in off the South China Sea.

"Which team?" he asked, although he already suspected.

"Sergeant Howard's. You want me to wake the Colonel?"

"I'll get him."

The commo/ops tent became crowded within minutes as the bad news spread: Colonel Sullivan and his executive officer, Major Scotty Harris; operations officer Major Jack Cooper; Charlie Company's commander, Captain Tim Geraghty; staff sergeant Williams, S-2 NCOIC; radio operators; intel personnel; logistics people . . . Banks of radios against the tent walls chattered and crackled unrelentingly as the various support elements of the Marine green machine cranked into action. Aircraft, artillery, ready reaction forces—it seemed everybody jumped on the duty frequency, trying to get a part of the action, volunteering to do whatever they could or was required. Marines were in trouble. It got so crowded on both the working channels and in the tent that Colonel Sullivan had to start kicking nonessential hangers-on off the radio and out of the tent.

2323 Hours

Nothing, I thought, could be as bad as the waiting. And the silence. I was wrong. I almost jumped out of my skin when the first bamboo sticks began clacking. From somewhere down below came a single clickety-clack rhythm echoing eerily out of the darkness. It was like the hill, haunted, stretched and rattled its teeth. Almost before I caught my breath, others took up the signaling until a wave of clicking flowed like a tidal wave around the hilltop and we were completely encircled by the unearthly sounds. It felt almost supernatural. I shivered. My hands trembled with the full realization of our predicament. It was little consolation to know that my comrades were likewise frozen with fear.

I was raised on Saturday afternoon matinees at the old Circle Theater in Tulsa's Brookside area. I knew what happened when the Apache drums stopped beating or natives in the Congo pounded frantically on their hollow logs, then abruptly ceased. The next thing you knew, Randolph Scott was fighting off all the Indians in the world or Van Heflin was preparing for a final stand against painted African savages massed to rid the world of our hero.

I almost jumped out of my skin a second time when the bamboo sticks stopped as suddenly as they began. Something just as terrible and unreal took their place. Whistles blew, shrieking of tormented souls buried inside the hill. There was also a bugle, further down. Either that, or my electrified imagination was running amok and driving me mad. I felt like I was living in a nightmare from hell.

Suddenly, even the whistles stopped. Black objects filled the air against the backdrop of stars. Hailstones the size of fists pelted down on top of the hill out of a stormless sky. I heard them hitting the ground. Like rocks. The crazy bastards were throwing *rocks* at us.

One of the rocks exploded.

Jesus God! Grenades!

Somebody yelled, "Them motherfuckers are coming!"

37

Nui Vu had stirred, clacked its terrible bamboo teeth, shrieked through the whistles, and now it seemed to go ape shit. From a distance, from down in the valley, it must have resembled the site of an amazing Fourth of July celebration or a volcano erupting. Balls of searing lights from grenades popped in random firecracker strings, dusting the black sky with flickering reflection. Strategically placed heavy machine guns lacerated the hill, their streams of bright bluish-green tracers weaving back and forth. AK-47s and M-14s traded savage fire. Men screamed and yelled on both sides. At each other, at themselves, at God. The din of the breaking battle rumbled across the valley, echoing and clapping and reverberating. The ground trembled. Chaos, noise, and confusion reigned.

The attack continued for the next quarter-hour, but it seemed to last forever. Waves of VC charged first one sector, then another, under cover of their grenades, machine guns, and small mortars. Not a mass assault such as the Japanese and Koreans made notorious. These guys fought smart, popping up and down in the grass, probing to find a weak spot to exploit. Firing and maneuvering, cover and assault elements. Crawling right up to our lines and throwing grenades before being hurled back or retreating with their asses blistered. Only to attack again somewhere else.

"Holy shit!" Binns yelled. "This is a big one!"

Pulled back into our tight circle, the platoon fought literally back to back. Defending our tiny perimeter of earth. Counting on each other to work as a team, to become instant combat vets and do the seemingly impossible by throwing back the assault. Sergeant Howard must have had doubts about how his cherry troops would react. I would have, had I been in his place. It was the platoon's first time in major combat. Most of us were young and untried, the first time out for several of us. Outnumbered by more than twenty to one, shocked and confused by the ferocity of the attack and the screams of the wounded.

The situation looked hopeless. We hugged the ground amid the crash of grenades and mortars, below a dark sky spider-webbed with tracer rounds. Giant flashbulbs from grenade explosions winked us in and out of sight of each other, bringing into momentary relief pale, stricken faces. Yet, we fought back out of sheer guts and desperation, this greenhorn Recon platoon. No seasoned outfit could have done better.

A man fighting for his life and for the life of the buddy next to him always failed to see the "Big Picture" of a battle. For him, everything became fragmented with distinct events compressed into comprehensible bites. The whole of his life from now into forever focused on that precise moment and what was happening within the boundary of his own senses gone acute from danger and fear. A battle was like the parts of a puzzle in which each man possessed a single piece. He saw his own piece and that piece differed from how the man next to him saw his. It was said that each warrior fought his own battle within the larger battle. Sort of like life.

Sergeant Howard feared it was "Katy-bar-the-door." Without illumination, he found it difficult to calculate precisely the size of the opposing force. He knew by the volume of fire, however, that it was a large element. He estimated a battalion because of the number and variety of weapons: at least four 50 caliber heavy machine guns chunking away from cross-firing angles; maybe a .51 with its slow cyclic rate of fire that sounded like someone was cranking out rounds with a handle; at least two .30-cal light machine guns; RPD automatic assault rifles; 60mm mortars; Chinese-made "potato masher" grenades with the throwing handles; and a variety of different-sounding small arms. He spotted no webbing fire trails from the use of RPGs (rocket propelled grenades) as of yet—and probably wouldn't. The RPG was an area point weapon, difficult to place on a small target like the top of the hill without endangering your own troops.

The attack seemed to be concentrating on two sides of the hill—on the north where Binns dinged the first soldier and on the more-gentle western slope where the climbing was faster and easier. Some grenades bounced off the Big Rock, rolled back down the slope and blew up among the attackers. A number were duds. Many landed inside the perimeter and whinged shrapnel through the air. Men cried out in surprise and pain.

The sergeant crawled among his men, a reassuring presence as he directed fire or shored up weaknesses in the perimeter. He triggered off rounds at flitting shadows, but he always returned to the radio. The platoon was lost without its lifeline.

"We need flares," he pleaded. "Iron Hand, we need that box bad."

From the Vietnamese point of view, the start of the fight must have seemed to be going well. Green tracers from machine guns streaked toward the Marine positions, pointing the direction for reinforcements assembling in the lower draws. Heavy explosive mortar projectiles arced in from four points of the compass, smashing down and contributing rock splinters to the buzz of metal shrapnel while forcing the defenders to hug the ground. Screaming and shouting, dark figures scrambled up the steep slopes like demons out of hell, firing their weapons as they came, intent on victory at any cost.

It would all be over in short order. From the Vietnamese point of view.

2328 Hours

At Chu Lai, executive officer Scotty Harris in the battalion CP didn't realize how bad things were on Hill 488 until Howard came up on the push requesting, demanding, *pleading* for assistance.

"Two casualties," Sergeant Howard reported. "One critical, one missing. We need medevac if he's going to make it."

"Medevac is in the air, Carnival Time," Colonel Sullivan said. *"He should be arriving over you now."*

It was a decided boost to morale for troops to know they could be evacuated from a firefight and reach a hospital quicker than someone involved in an automobile accident on a highway back in the United States. The average elapsed time between a field injury and surgery was little more than one hundred minutes. Nearly 98 percent of the wounded who reached medical facilities alive managed to survive. Much of the credit belonged to the rapid response and the daring of the dust-off pilots and crews.

The first five medevac UH-1A "Huey" helicopters arrived in Vietnam in April 1962 with the army's 57th Medical Detachment (Helicopter Ambulance). They were soon given the generic name "dust-off" after the call sign of Major Charles Kelly, a famous pilot killed in action in 1964.

In 1966, marines were still using H-34s for medical evacuations, but would soon switch to Hueys.

Air ambulance work was a good way to get killed. Statistics showed that medevac helicopters suffered three times the losses to hostile fire than all other types of helicopter missions. Medevacs made ideal prey for the VC, who knew for sure the unarmed medevacs would come in after or even during a firefight.

When the medevac from Chu Lai reached Hill 488, flying high above it out of range, the crew was astonished at the sound-and-light show going on below. Nonetheless, the pilot raised Carnival Time on the tactical channel and expressed willingness to attempt the pickup.

"It's suicide," Sergeant Howard reluctantly responded. There was no way the chopper could get in and out again under the present conditions; VC gunners would be shooting it at point-blank range. "Abort the mission," Howard said.

The medevac returned to Chu Lai.

2330 Hours

Richard Fitzpatrick, the corpsman on his first combat mission, got hit right away. It seemed to Billy D that everybody got hit at once during the grenade hailstorm and started hollering. A grenade struck Fitz in the face and bounced off before it exploded. Billy D wormed over to him. He lay without moving. The flashing light from a mortar round illuminated his face momentarily. Billy D recoiled. He hardly recognized Fitz. The corpsman's face resembled raw hamburger. A Halloween horror mask with teeth glinting through the sides of his cheeks.

He appeared dead. Billy D dragged him across the ground to the protection of the Big Rock, where he was establishing a collection point for casualties. He left the big man lying next to the comatose Powles.

2332 Hours

Corporal Bob Martinez sprawled at the end of the Big Rock and didn't know what was happening on the other three sides of the hill. He was scared half to death, like everyone else. But also like everyone else, he had trained to react with his natural instincts. React, don't think. That was what it was all about. Don't think of anything. Just go along with events.

He couldn't see shit. He stayed by the rock and the sump hole and kept his head low. Powles moaned in a drug-induced delirium. Binns and Mulvihill lay on their bellies a few feet to his right, shooting down the hill.

In the dark, the enemy squatting down or crawling in the tall grass became nearly invisible. Martinez commanded a certain limited range of vision, perhaps ten or fifteen feet in front, and he pinged away every time a little piece of the night shifted. Those VC who got in that close got dinged. He knew they were coming for him. Even when he couldn't see anything, he kept shooting down into his area of responsibility, one or two rounds at a time. To let them know he was still here. They were going to have to come through steel and lead to get him.

A grenade landed an arm's length away, between him and Binns. Instinct made him roll away from danger. He wrapped his head inside his arms just as it exploded. *Whang!* The blast ruptured his ear drums. His ears rang. Sound, loud as it was, seemed to come from out of a tunnel.

Was he still all in one piece? He felt himself all over for holes or blood. Finding none, he scrambled back into position in time to clobber one of the little attackers who jumped up out of the grass almost on top of him. The guy screamed when the bullet thudded him. He tumbled backward. Martinez heard him whimpering like an injured dog as he tried to get to his feet. He squeezed the trigger twice more at the sound, and then he heard nothing else from that patch of grass.

"Binns?" he whispered. "Binns, are you all right?"

"I got a couple of pieces in my leg. How about you?"

"What? What? Talk louder. I can't hear."

"I said, how about you?"

"I'm okay. How about you, Mulvihill?"

"Jesus God Jesus God Jesus God . . ." the other radioman chanted.

Martinez was trembling all over.

2333 Hours

Bill Norman the Arizona cowboy worked near the northern front of the hill against the main assault. To him, an inveterate chess player and self-taught strategist, it seemed the knights and rooks and pawns suddenly came alive on the chess board and were locked in a throat-to-throat struggle. Bullets ricocheted around him. Shrapnel whizzed. Tracers grazed overhead. There was lots of close shooting. Lots of everything. It was overwhelming.

Somebody hollered that he'd been shot. "A fucking ricochet."

Norman kept shooting into the night. If it moved—if he *thought* it moved—he opened up.

2334 Hours

Private First Class Ignatius Carlisi, maybe the only guy in the world *drafted* into the Marines, got a finger blown off. He started hollering and screaming. "*Corpsman! Corpsman!*"

Billy D crawled to him, dragging his aid bag. The little Italian settled down.

"It's not my trigger finger," Carlisi declared. "I can still shoot."

Only a ragged strip of flesh remained where Carlisi's finger had been. Billy D elbowed up on one arm to give himself room to work. Feeling for things, unable to see, he padded the wound and wrapped the hand in a battle dressing.

Shit was still hitting the fan big time. Something struck the corpsman in the chest. He freaked out and started slapping at the grenade like it was a scorpion or spider dropped down the front of his shirt. The potato masher ended up hissing like a snake between his legs. Both Carlisi and he kicked at it, yelling at each other and at it.

It went off, peppering both men with shrapnel and momentarily blinding them with its flash. By some miracle, both survived. The blast cone of a grenade on the ground was primarily up and out. While anyone standing or kneeling within its radius was dead meat, a prone man lying even a foot away commonly survived, even though stunned and shocked by the explosion.

Billy D's face and upper chest stung from multiple tiny lacerations. He felt blood on his forehead. Carlisi now had both legs seriously mangled to go along with his lost finger.

Ignoring his own wounds, wiping blood from his eyes, the corpsman patched Carlisi's legs. Both men returned to the fray. In this fight, the wounded hadn't the luxury of indulging themselves.

Corpsmen carried M-14 rifles in addition to their standard issue .45 pistols. Billy D crawled over to the edge of the hill and shot a couple of twenty-round rifle magazines at muzzle flashes. They winked and blinked from everywhere, like manic fireflies in swarms. Someone yelled out that he was hit. The corpsman squirmed on his belly back to the Big Rock to see who it was.

2325 Hours

The battle went on for what seemed a long time, maybe five or ten minutes, and I still hadn't fired a round. While the entire hill seemed to be erupting all around me, there I lay hugging the earth, trying to pull the mountain around me, eyeballing my sector for movement. My side of the hill was the steeper aspect down into the saddle and harder for the enemy to climb. There was lots of firing on the north and west but still none where I was.

Grenades exploded near the Big Rock, only fifteen or twenty steps away, with hard, ringing concussions. I dared not raise my head. If shrapnel didn't blast it off, machine guns would. Tracers wove delicate patterns in the black sky above my head. I heard people getting hit, crying out. "*Corpsman!*"

Binns came around, sliding rapidly from man to man. Gutsy Jamaican, not a trace of fear or strain in his voice. Like it was only a training exercise. Checking the perimeter, checking on people, working as platoon sergeant to Howard's platoon leader.

"How're you doing, Hildreth?"

"So far, so good." *But McKinney,* I thought, *McKinney wasn't doing so good.* He was still down there on the side of the hill.

Binns moved on. I heard a thud five feet away. Adams shouted, "Grenade!"

Simultaneously, we rolled over the crest of the hill to get out of the blast radius. I thought the bang was going to shake me off the ground and into the hands of the enemy. Another second or two passed before I convinced myself I remained unscathed. I scrambled back up the hill. I found a shallow depression that offered some minimal cover. I rolled into it.

As I lay there panting, my heart pounding, a piece of the night right in front of my eyes shifted places. I was surprised to actually see him. Probably the same sonofabitch who tossed the grenade. Fury welled up in my throat at finally having one of the little gook bastards within my grasp. Reflexively, I fired three quick rounds. Then, angry or not, I paused to calculate effect. Just like I'd been trained.

No more movement. *I got the son of a bitch.*

2337 Hours

Eighteen-year-old Thomas Glawe, the Chicago kid with attitude, turned out to be a fighting fool. Leaning across the top of the Big Rock with Powles's M-79 grenade launcher, he took a bunch of muzzle flashes under fire. Blooping grenades as fast as he could fire, reload, and fire again, he lay down a belt of flame and exploding steel. The M-79 was a breech-loading, single-shot area weapon like a big sawed-off shotgun. It fired a variety of 40mm grenade rounds, including HE and Willie Pete.

He looked back toward the center and bellowed to no one in particular, "This is bullshit, man. We got to get the hell outa here."

"I'm with you," Corporal Thompson agreed, "but there's nowhere to go."

Glawe hunched down behind the rock. "Sarge, I'm out of M-79 ammo."

Sergeant Howard crawled over a couple of feet to Powles and stripped a bandolier off his body. He tossed the heavy belt to Glawe. "Here. Catch."

"Thanks."

His armory replenished, Glawe returned to the fight. Fighting like he really intended to keep his vow to wipe VC off the face of the globe. Get those medals.

"Fuck you, motherfucker! Come and get it!"

A string of bullets raked over the Big Rock, making slapping sounds and whining off as ricochets. A round drilled Glawe through the head with the impact of a pickax smashing into a pumpkin. It spun him around on his feet and slammed him to the ground.

He was dead when Billy D reached him. Blood poured from the wound in his face and head, spreading out like congealing jelly around his body. It smelled raw and nauseating.

Sergeant Howard scooted over and took the M-79 and the remaining grenades.

38

Time under such circumstances was hard to determine. We might have been fighting for five minutes, five hours, or anything in between. The VC threw everything they had at us, a crescendo as if they opened up with every weapon they owned, laying down a sheet of iron over our heads. Slugs zipped around like lightning strikes. Skirmishers rushed us, but Marines reacted just as savagely. Deadly accurate Marine fire cut through their ranks.

"Heads up and stand fast!" Sergeant Howard yelled. "Use grenades!"

American fragmentation grenades contained twice the blast of Chicom grenades, with more shrapnel effect. We also had the advantage in that the average Marine could throw further and more accurately than the average one hundred ten–pound Vietnamese. Men grunted and yelled as they hurled frags that exploded among the advancing enemy, tearing into flesh and bone. The hill shook as if it were an annoyed dog attempting to get rid of fleas. High-pitched howls and excited jabberings mingled with the explosions. Give the motherfuckers some of their own medicine.

The east side of the hill, my sector, remained relatively untouched. Binns crawled over. "Hildreth, do you have any more grenades?"

I gave him two of my four. They needed them worse over there than we did over here.

We needed help. We needed it fast. Always before, help had been only a radio call away. This time it was different. Sergeant Howard, I thought, should have taken the Colonel's suggestion that we be extracted.

It seemed to take forever to get artillery. I almost cheered when I heard the first low whistling of arriving 105mm howitzer shells. The whistling got louder and louder until they came screaming like jets going over, like compact cars being hurtled through the air at above Mach 1. You got to anticipating where they would land and you hoped they wouldn't land on you.

The first cluster of three splashed down low on the northwestern slope, about five hundred meters away. Someone issued a stream of disappointed profanity, starting with, "Fuck a duck!" The shells landed where the enemy wasn't. Killing dirt and rocks and grass.

Sergeant Howard jumped on the radio, working the horn, calling in adjustment. "The box is no good!" he yelled. "It's five hundred meters to our northwest. Adjust! Adjust!"

Three more rounds landed as he was talking. In the same area.

"No! No! Drop four hundred! Put that box around us. I want everything possible around the hill . . . Need illumination first . . . and fast!"

Flares arrived right over target, popping. Suddenly, three tiny bright suns appeared, swaying and undulating beneath their parachutes as they slowly drifted down, bathing the hill and surrounding draws and saddles in a weird yellowish light like the sodium lights on parking lots. Only not quite as bright. The sway of the parachutes and the flickering of the burning flares created eerie shadows fluttering and leaping about among the hordes of enemy soldiers surrounding us.

In the preceding darkness we had no true picture of what we were up against. As light cast back the darkness, however, it revealed a terrifying scene from an old horror movie in which the living dead were coming to get you. Little evil monsters crawled everywhere, popping up and down in the grass, shooting in volleys. Squads and teams firing and maneuvering. Screaming hellishly. Platoons gathered in reserve on the outskirts of the battle, double-timing in the draws or maneuvering on the ridge opposite the saddle. Exposed by the light like cockroaches caught in a filthy kitchen.

It resembled an ant hill suddenly ripped open. "Oh, my God!" someone squawked in disbelief. It sounded like Norman.

The enemy appeared to be massing to charge in a human wave. The flares arriving in the nick of time betrayed their plan. Rifle fire increased to a spiteful level as Marines on the north and west poured lead down the hill into newly revealed targets. Norman busily shot at men on the ridgeline on the other side of the saddle. VC over there looked as small as bugs from this distance, but they were the only bad guys he could see without sitting up to look over the edge of the hill, thus exposing himself. His sniper training marksmanship allowed him to pick off one or two.

In addition to the flares disclosing what confronted us, unnerving in itself, even more disturbing was what the flares revealed about ourselves. Darkness at least hid the carnage. Now, the horror came into full light.

There was blood everywhere. Pools and globlets on the ground, smeared on the inside of the Big Rock, on men's faces and uniforms. Many already wore bloody, filthy bandages on various parts of their anatomy—arms, legs, head, hands . . . Billy D had been busy. The haze of rifle smoke and explosions swirled in this living graveyard and drifted over the mangled forms of Powles, Fitzpatrick, and Glawe, all lying in a row where the corpsman had dragged them. They appeared dead.

Men looked around with unbelievable shock and fear in their eyes. They looked the way I felt. Victor leaned over the top of the Big Rock next to Bosley, both of them capping rounds downhill. He dropped his rifle and staggered back as a grenade exploded nearby.

"I'm hit!" he screamed.

The sight of his bloodied and dead or dying comrades proved even more of a blow to his system than the shrapnel wounds. He executed a small, wobbling pirouette, swinging his arms wide. Automatic fire cracked and snapped around his head. Always the pessimist, he shrieked, "L-L-Look at 'em out there! Hundreds of 'em!"

He stood in plain view beneath the little suns while every gook on the hill opened up on him.

"G-G-Goddamn, look at 'em all," he exclaimed in awe. He had temporarily lost his bearings.

"Vic!" I yelled, and others took it up. "Get down! Vic, get down."

"There's too many of 'em!" he cried. "Hundreds and hundreds. Let's get out of here."

It must have been Binns who snaked toward the dazed fireteam leader. By now, he had also been wounded. He left a blood trail on the ground.

"Shoot me! Shoot me!" Victor pleaded, throwing up his arms. The gooks were giving it their best shot. Slugs filled the air like furious hornets around a nest.

"Somebody shoot me. D-D-Don't let them get me."

Binns grabbed him by the ankle and yanked him off his feet, then dragged him by the foot to the cover of the Big

Rock. That snapped Victor out of it. He looked around, swallowed and shook his head.

"Vic!" Binns admonished. "Vic! Vic!"

Victor wore the look of a man jerked out of a trance. He calmly retrieved his rifle and rejoined the fight.

I watched all this in cold astonishment. My hands trembled as I turned back to my own sector. The fight still raged to my left, but my section of the perimeter remained calm. I saw a collection of enemy beyond the saddle angling our way, some of whom wore the camouflage uniforms and pith helmets of North Vietnamese Army regulars. I drew bead and cracked a couple of shots, but the range was too great and the lighting uncertain. I held my fire.

Grass waved in the breeze beneath flares that turned everything the same sodium tint. I got to thinking about McKinney, my friend since RIP in Okinawa. He had depended on Moore and me.

The small depression in which I lay offered more psychological protection than it did actual cover. The thought of leaving it filled me with dread. Yet, someone should check on McKinney. He wasn't that far down, only about the distance across the average width of a house. Maybe he wasn't dead after all. Maybe he was only wounded and unconscious. If I could reach him and drag him back into the perimeter with his buddies. . .

"I'm going after McKinney," I shouted to anyone who might be listening.

I didn't wait for an answer. I launched myself on the mission, cradling my M-14 in my elbows. I only made it about eight feet before the sputter of an automatic weapon interrupted progress. Bullets made sharp, cracking sounds as they snapped past my head in the dry grass.

"Hildreth, get back here!" Sergeant Howard shouted. "Stay put."

I scurried back to my depression faster than I left it.

39

We cut down the front lines of enemy skirmishers after the flares presented them to us. Suffering heavy casualties, the attackers failed to gain momentum. Vietnamese in the rear ranks had more sense at the moment than to copy the mistakes of the dead. The enemy had had it for the time being. Whistles and bamboo sticks pulled them away from the crest of the hill to regroup.

During the resulting lull, Sergeant Howard got back on the radio with the battalion CP. Facing overwhelming odds and with our escape route cut off, he kept the message stark and simple: "Skipper, you've got to get us out of here. There are too many of them for my people."

40

Having failed in his first attack, the enemy went to earth and began probing the perimeter to find a weak spot through which the next assault might drive. VC probed one place, withdrew, then probed another. Troops in support opened fire behind the probes while small bands tried to sneak quite close to a Marine, then overwhelm him with a burst of fire or several grenades.

It was nerve-wracking, not knowing when and from where the next strike would be launched. The little suns hissing against the black sky, each set replenished as soon as they fluttered out on the ground, made the job more difficult for enemy commanders, but the tall grass worked to their advantage. It allowed the enemy to get quite close before he suddenly popped up in front of you with startling presence.

Tension, although of a different character, held the battalion CP in Chu Lai in its grip. Whenever somebody got into a fight out in the bush, everybody with a radio tuned in on the tactical net to monitor the outcome. Carnival

Time held center stage tonight. Colonel Arthur Sullivan, his XO Scotty Harris, S-2 Jack Cooper, Captain Tim Geraghty, Sergeant Major Turner—they all crowded around the radios in the common section. If Colonel Sullivan wasn't on the air with Carnival Time, he was talking to Division or on the arty and air nets, trying to shake something loose to relieve his beleaguered platoon on Hill 488. It was frustrating business trying to get the machine moving. The thinning tone of his voice revealed his annoyance.

Even before tonight, Colonel Sullivan was a well-known figure at the Direct Air Support Center (DASC) of the First Marine Division because of his insistence upon detailed preplanning of extraction and fire support contingencies. He couldn't understand the delay now, even though it was explained to him about priority missions and asset commitments. He demanded flare ships, helicopter gunboats, and fixed winged aircraft, not bandying words about it.

"I'm not interested in excuses," he snapped. "My men are in trouble. That's who I'm interested in."

Not just in trouble. *Deep* trouble. Constant firing, the whining shrieks of ricochets, and the bang of grenades filled the Carnival Time frequency. A sudden *Ping!*

"That was a close one!" exclaimed one of the platoon's radiomen.

Sometimes Martinez or Mulvihill came up on the air, but most of the time it was Howard. The younger radiomen were excitable and talking so fast they had to be asked to slow down. Marines in the background could be heard shouting at each other and at the enemy.

"Oh, goddamn! Look at that, *look at that.* That little bastard again with the fifty."

At other times, Carnival Time went chillingly silent. The CP kept calling into open air, afraid the hill was being overrun: *"Carnival Time, this is Iron Hand . . . Carnival Time, this is Iron Hand . . ."*

Howard came up, sounding out of breath. "I'm too god-damned busy to answer you right now."

We were busy people out there.

41

So far, my side of the hill remained relatively inactive while the VC concentrated on taking the shallower northern and western slopes. Arty kept popping two or three flares at a time. Lying there underneath them made me feel almost naked, but I was thankful for them nonetheless. They drove back the terrible night and let us see, and shoot, our foes. The enemy *knew* where we were; we weren't going anywhere. The flares aided us in knowing where *they* were.

Each set of flares lasted about three minutes. They started out bright and high, gradually growing dimmer as they burned out and the little parachutes floated to earth. There were always periods of darkness between the dying flares and new ones come aborning. The dark was even darker, blacker than a serial killer's soul, once you became accustomed to the light. It made you feel more vulnerable and isolated than ever. I lay waiting and listening in the total darkness, praying for the next miniature suns to start going *Pop! Pop! Pop!*

The VC used the darkness to change positions, to regroup and get ready for the next assault. Individual duels broke out as skirmishers searched for soft places in our lines.

"Iron Hand," I overheard Sergeant Howard saying over the radio, "we're being attacked from the west every time the flares burn out. Keep the light on up here."

Please, God, I pleaded. *Please keep the light on.*

At this point, I couldn't be sure who was dead and who alive and still in the fight. Even with the flares, I had myopic vision tunneled straight off the hill into the narrow no man's land between us and them. It wasn't like a PA system announced the score every few minutes.

During a lull, I overheard Binns talking to Powles, even though Powles probably couldn't hear him by now. "Easy, Tom. You'll be all right, kid. You got it made. You're going back to California."

I called out softly to see who was still in the perimeter, to reassure myself that I wasn't alone. Everybody lay flat on the ground, which made it hard to see them and even harder to tell if they were alive or dead.

"Thompson?"

"Yeah?"

"Adams?"

"Okay."

"Mascarenas?"

No answer. Where was Mascarenas? Maybe he couldn't hear me. Our ears all rang from the grenades.

"Mascarenas?"

Still no answer.

"Billy D?"

No response.

"Sergeant Howard?"

"What do you want, Hildreth?"

"Just checking."

I knew we shouldn't have gone northwest.

42

Things were about to heat up in the sector Adams and I covered. Unknown to either of us, two gooks toting a 50-caliber machine gun worked their way around the hilltop to set up on the southeast above the saddle. They went to ground during the flare periods, then jumped up and moved fast when the flares went out. They were now less than thirty meters away, literally at point-blank range, and getting the gun ready to rake the top of the hill.

With the machine gun squad came a security team whose job it was to protect the gunners and prevent interference. Scrambling noises to my front during a dark period announced an alien presence. We were being probed. The thump of a grenade confirmed it.

The grenade fell short. I buried my head against the expected flash. It exploded, and shrapnel buzzed over my head. Immediately after the detonation, while my ears still rang, several VC leaped up in outline against the sky. Not ten feet away.

Adams sprang to his feet and charged, swinging his rifle like a ball bat. All I saw were violent shadows struggling with each other. Three of them—the larger one with the broad-brimmed hat being Adams. There were quick grunts and moans, the meaty sound of wood and steel striking flesh and bone. One shadow went down, then the other.

Adams scrambled back to his position an arm's length away and dived to earth. A third VC appeared, charging directly at us. I dropped him dead in his tracks six feet away.

Hardly had I sucked in a breath of relief than flares burst overhead, bringing light to the darkness. The enemy machine gunners were waiting for it too. The gun opened fire in the fresh illumination.

A 50-caliber was an awesome weapon that took over a battlefield with authority. It spat out projectiles with a deep *Thump! Thump! Thump!* At this close range, it would lacerate the entire hilltop, literally chewing up everything in its path, including flesh and bone. Unless knocked out, First Platoon was done for.

The first tracers lashed out over my head. Heavy slugs pounded against the Big Rock like sledge hammers. Somebody shouted in surprise and terror.

The line of tracers tilted downward. A string of lead slapping ground walked directly over me, gouging holes in the ground and throwing dust and gravel, but miraculously leaving me unscathed.

Adams fared less well. His back exploded in a thick mist of blood that splattered in the light of the flares. The impact slammed Adams over onto his back. He grunted and immediately flipped back onto his belly. In the eerie sodium light I glimpsed the awful wound where his left shoulder blade used to be.

"*I'm hit! I'm hit!*"

"Adams? How bad?"

Stupid question.

Adams's limbs twitched. "Bad. Real . . . bad . . ." Like the bleat of a dying sheep. Last words.

The machine gun serrated the other side of the perimeter, slashing and gouging. I snapped out of shock and kicked around to face the threat with my rifle. The VC must have seen me. The flickering giant blossom of the muzzle swirled back in my direction. Adams, brave man though he was, gave a final gasp as bullets seeking me claimed him, spattering more blood and flesh. Like he had swallowed a grenade just before it went off. His body shielded me as in his dying he saved my life.

I looked directly into the grim faces of the VC machine gunners. Into their dark eyes and into the blazing muzzle of the heavy gun. It became a personal shootout between them and me, a matter of who got who first. Bullets cracked past inches above my head. They couldn't keep missing.

Everything went into slow motion. I lapsed into a momentary trance in which the larger fight no longer existed. My entire concentration focused on getting that gun before it got me. Snipers called it "getting into the bubble." It wasn't difficult shooting, considering the short range, but it could be both tricky and fatal if I lost my nerve. I couldn't blow the shot by rushing it.

All that sniper training in Okinawa was about to pay off. Even I was surprised at how coolly I took aim and squeezed the trigger. The first round turned out to be a tracer; I had retained an old sniper's trick of mixing tracers in my magazines as spotter rounds. The red streak it made seemed to spiral into the enemy gunner's chest, knocking him backwards out of sight. The gun went silent.

Smoothly, still using what I had learned shooting in Okinawa against multiple targets, I switched aim to the assistant gunner, and shot him. He disappeared in the grass.

"I got 'em!" I shouted, exhilarated and excited, as though expecting applause.

There was no one left to applaud. McKinney was dead,

Adams was dead, I didn't know where Mascarenas was. For all I knew, my fireteam was destroyed. Except for me alone defending our sector.

I became aware that the rest of the platoon, those still able, had their hands full with their own individual duels and were probably not even aware that I had knocked out the machine gun that would have ended the fight. The battle hammered away unabated while a hush once more settled over my side of the hill. I lay quietly watching the machine gun in case other dinks tried to take it over.

Night returned as the flares sputtered out. It was almost a blessing when it hid Adams's shredded body. I smelled his fresh blood. It left a nauseating coppery taste in my mouth. In my mind I ticked off the names of comrades I knew or suspected to have already died on this damnable whore of a hill: McKinney, Glawe, Powles, Fitzpatrick, and now Adams. Their loss left me profoundly and perhaps permanently disturbed. I experienced a sudden depth of sadness I had never known before. Life was revealing a nasty side I would rather have never known.

When the lights came back on, I saw that the little sons of bitches had got hold of the machine gun and dragged it to a new location a few meters away from the original site. Two of them were getting ready to man it while a second crew of two men set up a mortar tube. We exchanged startled looks across the distance over Adams' body, a first awareness of each other's awareness.

I recovered first. I picked off three methodically and quickly, starting from left to right since I was a right-hand shooter. They fell one after the other into the grass. The fourth jumped up and bolted down the hillside like a scared rabbit before I could bead in on him.

I decided from then on to squeeze intermittent shots into the nest during the dark times to keep gooks from coming back. I took a savage delight in imagining my bullets ripping into little men whose bullets had ripped into my friends. Nobody returned to the abandoned guns for the rest of the night.

I lay alone surrounded by nothing but death. Adams next to me. McKinney in the grass. And all these fucking wasted gooks. My AOR now expanded to cover the whole of the hill's southeastern blade.

"Mascarenas?" I whispered. Then, louder, "Mascarenas?"

There was no answer.

43

The Reds were mustering their strength and will for a second attack. By now I had figured out their modus operandi. They went down when the lights were on, then popped back up in the short spans of darkness to maneuver, marshal, reposition, get ready and probe our perimeter. I heard shovel work from different places out there. Vietnamese were the digging-est little fuckers. They dug tunnels, holes, and pits wherever they went. They wouldn't be building defense bulwarks since they certainly didn't expect us to counterattack; they had to be digging in, and digging in deep, in anticipation of air attacks, which was our modus operandi. VC were detailed planners. Strict adherence to a plan was both their strength and their weakness. They stuck to a scenario even when things turned to shit.

They planned to wipe us out, and wipe us out they were going to do.

The instant the most recent flares sputtered out, whistles began blowing, bamboo clacking. Figures downslope sprang to their feet and raced up the sides of the hill. The 50s opened up with their contrapuntal *Chut! Chut! Chut!*

"Get ready, men!" Sergeant Howard shouted. "The little bastards are coming again."

The battle rejoined at point-blank range. It continued right through the next sets of flares, the fighting persisting through light and through darkness. An NVA soldier in pith helmet jumped up right in front of Bill Norman, spraying a burst of fire from his AK-47 over the heads of the defenders in his excitement. It happened so fast that he was gone again before Norman could get off a shot. Norman kept his rifle trained on that spot for a while, waiting for him to jump up again, but he never did.

Carlisi might not have looked like a typical Marine, but he stood his ground and fought like one. A grenade exploding near him stitched his legs and back with shrapnel. Stunned and hurt, he slid back from the edge of the hill, shook himself, then returned to the defense and kept firing. He fought on for several minutes before the shock wore off and pain caught up with him. He screamed in agony.

Victor dragged him behind the Big Rock and shouted for the corpsman. Billy D, wounded himself several times, moved around the perimeter, checking injuries, patching up arms and legs and heads and hands. Crawling from place to place beneath the flying steel, a canvas aid bag in one hand and a rifle in the other. Getting low on supplies. He responded to Victor's call for help.

While he was patching up the little New York draftee, another grenade banged near them. Billy D threw himself across his patient's body to shield him from the blast, sustaining additional wounds in the process. He groaned, but finished the job on Carlisi. Carlisi pulled himself back on line with his fresh bandage and his rifle. Valor was indeed common on that hilltop that night.

I suspected the VC must have zeroed in on me, because of my work against the machine gun and mortar. I called out to Mascarenas to let him know I was shifting positions to my right, past Adams's body. He stilled failed to respond. I didn't know if he was hurt or what. I figured I was probably the only one in defense of this sector of our perimeter.

I squirmed past Adams, inadvertently brushing up against his body. I recoiled at the contact. He felt like he was already getting stiff. I crawled through his gore and tried not to think about it. There would be plenty of time for that later. If there was a later.

At my new location, only ten feet or so from the old, I remained scanning my sector, hunting for targets and keeping a wary eye on the abandoned machine gun. Just in case. As an afterthought, I unsheathed my Ka-bar and jabbed its blade into the ground near at reach and handy as a last resort. A few minutes later, grenades discharged all around in murderous blossoms of flame. I rolled downhill to avoid them. I couldn't find my Ka-bar when I crawled back up. I felt all around for it but couldn't find it. Another of life's little mysteries. It was almost like the hill, a live thing itself, had stolen it from me.

Binns scooted around the perimeter collecting ammo from the dead and badly wounded and redistributing it. A bullet creased his head. Another dug a gash across his back. More grenade shrapnel sliced into his arm, his upper lip and his eyebrow. He kept moving, shooting, yelling, calling for more grenades to throw.

"Nice shooting, jarheads. That's the way. Who needs more ammo?"

Sergeant Howard fired Powles's M-79 with deadly effect until he ran out of grenades and tossed the useless weapon aside. It wasn't long enough to use as an effective club.

"Stay alert, Marines," he roared. "We're gonna walk out of here."

Combat discipline held. Marines threw grenades and fired semi-auto, relying on accuracy to suppress the enemy's volume, constantly repositioning to get better fields of fire or fill in gaps. All we had to do was hold out till first light when commies turned from ants to cockroaches and faded back into the hills and jungles.

The undaunted spirit Sergeant Howard displayed in front of the platoon revealed an occasional crack when he was on the radio with Colonel Sullivan. I overheard him stressing the desperation of our circumstances.

"Colonel, my boys can't hold out much longer without support."

"Jim, you must hold on." It sounded like an order, a plea, a prayer, all in one sentence.

0045 Hours

On the opposite side of the perimeter from me, Corporal Jerald Thompson, First Squad Leader, rapidly burned up magazines. His was a hot place in the line. A grenade peppered him with shrapnel. Shock and acute pain jarred him enough that he got to his knees. A pair of hands reached out of the grass and grabbed him, pulling him down. He and the VC tumbled over the edge of the hill locked in a deadly embrace.

Thompson managed to whip out his knife as they rolled. He buried the blade to the hilt in his skinny foe's back, jabbing it deeper and ripping as he cut vitals and severed the spine. The VC stiffened, then began thrashing and whipping about in his death throes, spraying blood.

The corporal scrambled back to the top. "Corpsman! I've been hit," he called out in pain.

Billy D was up by the Big Rock with Bosley, Victor, Mulvihill, and Martinez, all of whom were unleashing volley after volley into the advancing hordes. I overheard Thompson's cry for aid and turned my head to watch Billy D under flare light bellying slowly across the ground. Thompson was only about twelve feet away, but it seemed to take the corpsman forever to reach him. Billy D suffered from a number of untreated wounds. He looked so bloody and so pitiful and so . . . so *brave* that my heart went out to him.

Billy D never reached Thompson. A grenade went off between them. Both lay still in the aftermath as the lights went out, plunging the hill once more into deepest darkness. I thought at that moment, seeing that, that it was all over. Help would never get here in time.

"Doc? *Doc?*" I howled in anguish.

Nothing.

"*Thompson?*"

Nothing.

Most of the frag blasted into Thompson, but the concussion knocked Billy unconscious. He lay in total darkness when he revived. Spasms of pain throbbed the length of his body. His hands and his face felt warm and wet and sticky. Yet he couldn't move, couldn't shake the fog from his brain. It was like one of those nightmares in which the monsters were coming but you couldn't move to get away from them.

In a daze he watched Thompson being dragged off the top of the hill. Two VC on their bellies had him by the head and were pulling him away from the perimeter. Then, to Billy D's growing horror, he felt hands touching him. Somebody grabbed him by the collar and started pulling *him* down the hill. Helpless, he hadn't the strength or the sentience to resist. All he could do was lie there on his back and be dragged across the ground, staring up into that Oriental face so close to his, smelling *nuc mam* sour and sweaty so that his stomach revolted at the stench.

Oddly, the thing that went through his mind was: *Who's gonna get my insurance money; what're they gonna do with all that insurance money?* There was no accounting for last thoughts when you expected death. Even more oddly, in the gallows humor so typical of grunts in a combat zone, he heard a revised stanza from Barry Saddler's song, "Ballad

Of The Green Berets," run through his mind. He found it bizarrely amusing under the circumstances. It went:

> *Back at home a young wife waits,*
> *Doing the Dog with six or eight.*
> *Ten thousand bucks she got to play,*
> *'Cause Charlie done greased her Marine today.*

The Dog was a popular dance at Annex 8, a dance spot in Fayetteville, near Fort Bragg.

It was so dark that from my vantage point all I saw was a figure silhouetted against the sky and hovering over Billy D, tugging at him, pulling him *off* the hill. I couldn't tell if it was Thompson or not. I yelled, "Thompson?"

I was frantic trying to determine what was going on. "Thompson?" Much louder.

Still there was no response. Thompson surely would have said something. In another second or so Billy D would be gone. I had to do something quick. God help me. I twisted on the ground, took aim at the outline that *had* to be a VC, and fired. Again, training came into play. A few inches one way or another and I either missed completely or hit the corpsman.

Billy D was staring up into the Viet's face when it exploded in front of his eyes, splattering him with bone fragments, blood, and brain tissue. The VC's hands flew to his face reflexively as the bullet knocked him on his side away from the Marine.

A moment later, under the light of new flares, I saw Billy D painfully dragging himself in slow motion across the ground toward the safety of the Big Rock. Thompson was nowhere in sight.

44

Marines continued to fall and defenses on the hill weakened and thinned. Every weapon was needed. Martinez and Mulvihill were by necessity no longer radiomen but riflemen instead. Martinez in his sump hole depression pumped 7.62 lead into the masses of enemy mobbing the defensive perimeter. VC went down for keeps. All around the hill, but mostly still on the north and the west. Two or three, then four or five. Yelling and shrieking and dropping, the poor bastards. To Martinez, watching them die in the heat of battle was exhilarating. Every one he zapped meant fewer to scavenge over their corpses when the platoon finally fell. It wasn't a fatalistic thought. It was simply being realistic.

"Beautiful! Beautiful!" Martinez recited, heating up his rifle barrel.

Even though Sergeant Howard and Binns warned the platoon to fire semi-auto and make every shot count, we still burned up ammo at an alarming rate. Martinez scooted behind the Big Rock to reload and recoup. Empty rifle magazines clattered underneath his movement. He lay on an uncomfortable carpet of spent cartridge casings while other expended hulls rained down on his patrol cap from the rifles of those popping away over the top of the rock.

Recharged, he elbowed back to his old position where he could effectively fire downslope. Automatic rifle fire seared a blue-green line into his front, geysering dirt. He ducked. Slugs spanged and ricocheted off the boulder.

Where the hell did that come from? That guy wasn't there a minute ago. He made the mistake of rising out of the grass to take better aim. Martinez beaded on him and fired. The VC reacted as though he'd been thumped with a baseball bat.

"Beautiful! Beautiful!"

0105 Hours

Binns moved Norman on the other side of Kosoglow and spread Mulvihill in my direction to cover the gap left by Mascarenas. Mascarenas had a good reason for not answering those times I called out to him, other than his being a quiet little man from New Mexico. Apparently, grenade fragments hit him in the head and took him out of commission almost at the beginning of the action. He lay unconscious on the ground all that time. The only way anyone knew he still lived was by the gurgling and gasping noises he made when he breathed. Even those sounds seemed to be growing weaker. How characteristic of him, I thought in a wave of sadness, that he was dying the same way he lived, with hardly a word to draw attention to himself.

0106 Hours

A grenade sailed over the Big Rock and landed next to Sergeant Howard. Howard was busy on the radio and failed to notice. Kosoglow threw himself at it and kicked it away just as it exploded. He took most of the shrapnel meant for the sergeant.

"You okay, Joe?" Binns asked.

Kosoglow retained his dry humor in spite of the pain. "I'd rather be fishing," he wheezed.

We can't let anything happen to the sergeant, he thought to himself, *else we'd really be up shit creek.*

0108 Hours

Charles Bosley was also giving a good accounting of himself. He braced himself behind the Big Rock with Victor and Carlisi to his left. The wounded men lay on the ground slightly behind him. Sometime during the fight, the gas cylinder cap on his rifle vibrated loose and fell off. Uncomplaining as always, he kept firing but had to manually eject each cartridge casing and reload one round at a time.

Carlisi, the platoon's draftee and most unlikely Marine, didn't even notice. He was so shot up by this time that he could hardly remain erect without the rock to support him. He had a bullet hole in the left calf, another in the left foot, and his finger was shot off. Shrapnel wounds added to his misery. He propped his rifle across the top of the rock in order to fire it one-handed, the other hand being heavily padded to stop the bleeding.

A grenade landed behind him and Victor. He was unable to get away from it because of his wounds. The concussion knocked him down on top of the comatose Powles. Powles didn't move. Moaning in pain, the new guy crawled over to where Binns was fighting, as though seeking psychological comfort. Binns checked for a pulse the next time he had a chance. There was none. Carlisi would never go back to New York.

Victor attempted to escape the explosion that got Carlisi by diving right and to the ground. The blast caught him in midair and slammed him against the side of the rock.

Wincing in pain, he pulled himself into a sitting position and tenderly rubbed his mangled legs. There was almost no feeling in them. He leaned the back of his head against the cold stone and closed his eyes and for a brief, blissful moment blocked out the war. It was a well-deserved respite.

After that, he felt around for his rifle, found it, and staggered to his knees. He noticed Carlisi was gone. Bosley had dived for the earth in time to escape the grenade, and had now returned to the fight, still cranking out one round at a time.

Moments later, a second grenade got both of them. It only peppered Bosley, but steel fragments buried themselves deep into Victor's back and knocked him breathless to the ground. Billy D saw him fall. He tried to crawl to the wounded men, but he moved pretty slowly himself because of his own trauma.

"S-S-Stay where you are, Doc," Victor managed. "I'll be all right."

Victor the pessimist and fatalist sounded more resolved and determined than in his entire life, or at least since he had been with the platoon. He hadn't the strength to regain his feet. He fully expected to die. He dragged himself with heartbreaking doggedness to the end of the Big Rock where he could lie on his injured side and operate his weapon with his good arm. He fought on.

At some point he passed out. Billy D crawled over and, after a number of attempts, dragged him behind the Big Rock and treated his wounds. Victor regained awareness when the Doc left to tend to another hurt Marine and crept back into his defensive position.

45

Colonel Arthur J. Sullivan at Chu Lai listened to Howard's deep, precise voice over the radio.

"Skipper, do you have a reactionary force or something? We're getting low on ammo. I don't care about myself, but I got good goddamn men out here. I'd like to get them out."

Everyone, it seemed, was eavesdropping on Carnival Time's tactical channel—high-ranking officers of the First Marine Division; battalion and company officers and NCOs; the Special Forces soldiers Howard mistakenly called "Stiff Balls"; other Recons in the field; even aircraft within range of the radio waves. VC may even have been listening in. It was the most suspenseful show going on at the time in I Corps.

"Skipper, just in case . . ." Sergeant Howard's voice broke. Things must be really going to hell, judging from battle sounds in the background. *"Skipper . . . tell my wife I love her."*

Everyone heard the sharp scream of a ricochet that followed the sergeant's somber request. They flinched and jumped back, the bullet sounding as though it were coming through the radio at them. Howard gave a loud cry of shock and pain.

"*I'm hit! Oh, my balls. I'm hit. My balls. Oh!*"

The radio went dead, fostering an immediate assumption at the CP that Sergeant Howard had been killed and the platoon was finally about to be overrun. Looking desperate and stricken, Colonel Sullivan shouted into his handset.

"Jim? Talk to me, Jimmie."

Nothing but more dead air, leaving the outcome of the fight on Hill 488 to the imaginations of those gathered around distant radios.

"Get me Division," Colonel Sullivan snapped at his radioman.

The battalion commander minced no words when Division came up.

"Damn it, my men need fire support now. They've gone off the radio. What do you have available?"

"*Colonel, we've got A-4s on station now with rockets and 250-pound bombs. What do we tell them?*"

"Tell them to dump everything on the north and west slopes of the hill. Where's my flare ship?"

"*It's waiting for the A-4s to clear the area.*"

"Damnit, hurry."

He switched back to Carnival Time. "Carnival Time? Carnival Time, this is Iron Hand . . . Jim, are you there? Is *anybody* there?"

More dead air.

46

To an outsider, the men who piloted UH-1 "Huey" gun-ships seemed a rather rebellious, devil-may-care, anti-authority breed. That was true of most fliers who went to war. War was a hazardous occupation which, for your own peace of mind, must not be dwelt upon. Pilots therefore cultivated the image through rough braggadocio, dark humor—"If you get shot down, can I have your stereo?"—and whimsical songs they made up.

> *If I die in Vietnam,*
> *Send a letter to my mom.*
> *Tell her I died with a grin,*
> *Putting smoke on Ho Chi Minh.*

That was as true of the Marine pilots at Chu Lai as it was of army pilots with the First Air Cavalry Division or any of the other outfits of airmen.

> *O' Chu Lai, O' Chu Lai's a hell of a place,*
> *The organization's a fucking disgrace.*

There are captains and majors and light colonels too,
With thumbs up their asses and nothing to do.
They sit on the runway, they scream and they shout
About many things they know nothing about.
For all of their worth they might as well be
Shoveling shit on the South China Sea.

Most gunship pilots were not much older than the grunts on the ground. The flight crews were even younger than the pilots. For all the image of recklessness and derring-do, however, Marine pilots proved to be thorough professionals at the game of war who risked their lives almost daily in support of their comrades in the bush. Like cops on patrol in big cities back in the States, they were always ready to respond to a trouble call.

Marine Captain Jim Perryman was flying his second Vietnam tour with MAG-36 (Marine Air Group-36), assigned to VMO-6 squadron as a gunship to cover helicopter medical evacuations. Shortly after midnight of 15 June, he flew routine shotgun escort for an H-34 medevac that made a run to pick up a leatherneck wounded in a night ambush southwest of Chu Lai. There had been no action at the pickup point, none expected, so Perryman's chopper was still fully armed.

It was a dark night. Perryman used his running lights on the way back to Chu Lai. He and his copilot anticipated hitting the rack again as they returned along the coastline with the medevac. They were not to make it, not tonight.

The controller at MAG-36 broke UHF radio silence: *"Klondike Zero-Three, this is Klondike One, over."*

"Klondike, this is Zero-Three, over."

"Klondike Zero-Three, divert to BT 135203, Hill 488. Carnival Time needs help. Be advised, the unit has lost radio contact, over."

"Roger, One. This is Zero-Three, out."

With a grin and a word to his crew through the inter-com—"Forget about sleep"—Perryman broke off from the medevac at five thousand feet and soared northwest alone into the entrance of the Que Son/Hiep Duc Valley. The valley and its surrounding ridges and peaks lay cloaked in near-total darkness. Once Chu Lai lay behind his tail rotor, hardly a pinprick of light penetrated the darkness. Viet-namese farmers went to bed early while the VC went out to play overnight.

Gunships normally operated in pairs. Lieutenant Mark Shields came up on the air to advise he had scrambled a second gunboat and was on his way.

"I wouldn't want you to get all the glory, Zero-Three," he said.

A Huey gunship, heavily armed for a small helicopter, was a virtual flying armory. It was equipped with fourteen 2.75-inch–diameter folding fin air-to-ground rockets, each with a nine pound high explosive warhead. Fixed-mounted for forward firing were four 7.62mm M-60 ma-chine guns. Every fourth round was a tracer. At night, the tracers when fired made a beam of red light shining from the bird to the ground.

Four fliers made up a gunship crew—two pilots and two crewmen who acted as door gunners. Each open door con-tained an M60 machine gun either mounted on a pintle or suspended on a rubber bungee cord which allowed the gunners to shoot in any direction. They could stand out on the skids or rocket pods and shoot underneath the helicop-ter. They always carried two more extra barrels and an as-bestos glove in order to take out hot barrels and replace them with cool. Crew sometimes shot until, at night, the barrels glowed white hot.

It was about a twenty-minute flight from Chu Lai to Nui Vu. The hill was the highest point in the area and therefore a landmark for airmen. Perryman knew the terrain well. He followed the crook of the valley as it twisted back toward the southwest. Ahead lay the Nui Vu hill mass.

It seemed to be celebrating the Fourth of July. Green enemy tracers crisscrossed in an amazing spider's labyrinth, punctuated by quick white-light explosions. Marines on top of the hill were still putting up one hell of a fight.

Perryman soared lower over the peak to take a closer look, but stayed out of gunfire or RPG range. He noted two crucial factors: there was no way helicopters could land in that melee; the fight was so closely joined it was impossible to distinguish the Marine perimeter.

"Klondike One, Klondike Zero-Three. Be advised the unit is still fighting and has not been overrun."

47

Sergeant Howard lay wounded and dazed, almost unconscious. Binns crawled to him to take over. He attempted to
tug the radio handset from the sergeant's death grip. Howard
resisted. Binns jerked it free. Sergeant Howard shook himself
to clear his head. He snatched back the handset.

"Goddamnit, Binns," he growled. "I'm not done for yet."

The bullet had gone through his lower back and his legs
were paralyzed, permanently or temporarily he didn't have
time to consider now. He grunted in pain as he shifted to a
less-uncomfortable position.

"How long was I out?" he asked.

"A minute or two," Binns said.

"How are we doing?"

"Hanging tough, but—"

There was no need for Binns to finish the sentence. It
was the low point of the night and the fight. Word went
around the perimeter that Sergeant Howard was hit and
blood froze in our veins. Howard was our rock. We depended on him for guidance and strength.

Although we had beaten back the attack, shooting continued, unabated, rolling back and forth across the perimeter. Long bursts of machine gun and automatic weapons fire raked the hilltop, rattling for a minute or two at a time. Somebody would see something and things started up heavy again.

Every Marine on the hill had to be thinking the same thing. We were merely waiting for the other shoe to drop. We could never repel a third massed charge by an enemy determined to eradicate us. We would all die in the next assault. All you had to do was look around to understand that.

Eerie illumination from the flares revealed the bloody wreckage of a platoon literally making a last stand. Like General Custer at the Little Big Horn, Colonel Davy Crockett and James Bowie at the Alamo, Marines on Wake Island . . . I had been scared all night, but now I was *really* scared. I couldn't help it, and I knew it was the same with the others. A sense of despair, of impending doom and certain death settled over the battered survivors of First Platoon. A boiling kettle of mixed feelings that included a deep sense of anguish and loss, of the natural rage young adults experienced as we were about to die prematurely. For the first time since the battle began, I knew we all felt like giving up.

We mustn't give up to the VC. We couldn't let the enemy take us alive. We had all heard too many accounts of the atrocities the VC inflicted upon any Marine unfortunate enough to be taken prisoner. Such as the one about a platoon of the Ninth Marines who lost one of their guys to the VC. All night long the VC tortured him within hearing distance of the dug-in platoon. His screams of agony shredded the night, but there was nothing anyone could do.

The next morning, his buddies found his naked body painted red with blood and strung up in a tree by his heels. Pieces of flesh were hacked out of his belly and legs and arms. He was scalped and his entrails strung out on the ground. His privates were cut off and rammed into his rectum while he was alive. The tongue was saved for last because the gooks wanted him to scream until the last minute.

Or the one about the mamasan who tied up a captured American soldier, put a basket around his neck, filled the basket with rats and sewed a lid over the top of his head to make sure the rats stayed around his face and got good and hungry.

Better a quick death than that. And better to take some of them with us. It was hopeless otherwise. I simply lost heart. I turned my head toward the Big Rock and shouted a shrill, desperate cry.

"Sergeant Howard, don't let them get us. Please? Call a fire mission in on our position."

Erase our colored grease pencil off the map. Turn it black. Whatever.

Norman and Kosoglow, among others, took up the plea.

"Have mercy on us, Sarge," Kosoglow begged. "Let's take 'em with us."

Now seriously wounded, Sergeant Howard must have also glimpsed the abyss. His state of mind was in such temporary disrepair that, coughing, in severe pain, he got back on the horn and requested artillery be dropped on coordinates BT 135203. "And keep 'em coming," he added.

The puzzled FDC came back with, "*Carnival Time, say again. Say again coordinates.*"

Sergeant Howard did.

Still believing the request to blow off the top of the hill an error, arty responded that the mission was not authorized. Before the exchange could go further, Colonel Sullivan interrupted.

"*Carnival Time? Carnival Time? Jim, is that you? Are you still there?*"

Sergeant Howard composed himself. Almost as quickly as he vanished, the old hard-core sergeant returned. There would be no other suggestions given or taken that we blow up ourselves and take them with us. He came back up on the radio to Colonel Sullivan, his voice intentionally falsetto high and lilting, loud enough that we could all hear. The message was really meant for the platoon.

"Yes, sir, Colonel. I'm here. If my voice has changed, you'll know where I've been hit."

"Jim, thank God. Hold on out there, son. TacAir is on the way."

Sergeant Howard's response had its intended outcome in a resurgence of morale. Kosoglow even chuckled. Billy D crept over and offered to administer morphine for the sergeant's pain.

"Are you taking it, Doc?" Sergeant Howard asked, turning down the painkiller.

"No."

"Why?"

"The men need it worse."

The sergeant nodded. "I have to stay alert. This fight's not over yet, not by a long shot."

48

How long had the fighting gone on? Two hours? Three? A week? A month? Time lost all meaning.

Having been badly mauled twice, the VC would be lis tening for signs to indicate we were shattered or demoral ized before they stormed the hill a third time. They reverted to psychological warfare during a lull in which virtually all firing ceased for quite long periods. They must have watched the same old Wallace Beery movie I had, in which the Japanese surrounded the American heroes and started bellowing taunts in high-pitched accented English: "Ameli-cans, you die!" Insults Marines had heard in other places, in other wars, floated up the slopes in high, sing-song voices.

"Marines—you die tonight. Marines, you die in one hour!"

Voices screeched from a number of different places out of the darkness. Instead of being intimidated, however, we reacted with rage.

"Motherfuckers!" Kosoglow snarled. "Sarge, can we yell back at them?"

"Go ahead. Yell anything you want. Tell them what we think of them."

Thus inspired and given the official go-ahead, the surviving Marines of Hill 488 enthusiastically responded with all the curses and invective we could muster from our inventive collective repertoire mastered in a world without the gentling influence of women. It felt even better than shooting at them. From all over the hill, badly wounded Marines, Marines unable to walk but who could still pull a trigger, Marines weakening from loss of blood—we all found a voice and hurled back what they threw at us and even worse. I yelled at them until my throat went scratchy, venting my fury and sense of helplessness.

"Fuck you! You motherfuckers haven't got us yet."

"Come on up here, you pussies, and eat shit."

"Stuff it up your asses."

"Here's one for your mother, cocksuckers!" Somebody fired off a burst.

God, it felt good. Screaming and letting it all out. *Cram it, ram it, rotate it, you little cocksucking sons of bitches.*

The gooks soon ran out of English. How many ways could they say *Marine, you die* with the same impact? They resorted to their native language. We roared back and forth at each other. It wasn't necessary to understand the words, we understood the meaning. Some of them started shooting again out of frustration.

"Hey, Top Notch," Binns said. "Ain't that a laugh."

"Yeah, ain't it?" Howard said.

Then an idea struck him—the opportunity to deliver a master stroke in psychological one-upmanship. In a low voice, he said, "That's right, it is a laugh. All right, Marines, give 'em the old horse laugh. All together now. Ready? When I count to three . . ."

There can be few moments in the annals of combat to compare in sheer audacity to that one. The handful of us, beleaguered, outnumbered, and apparently hopelessly trapped, seemed to infect each other with a kind of gleeful exhilaration.

The situation wasn't funny, not a bit, but suddenly it *was* funny. The more we laughed, the funnier it became. The laughter was loud, genuine, rollicking, contagious—and it went on and on. Laughing in the faces of the enemy. I could almost see the gooks out there with their eyes bugged out and their jaws dropped. They must have thought we were going insane.

Whatever they thought, it temporarily silenced them. Months later, captured enemy troops admitted the moment had a shattering psychological impact on them. It was the turning point in the fight. Whereas a few minutes before we had been at our lowest ebb, we were now soaring. We were going to beat these sons of bitches.

Sergeant Howard keyed his mike because he wanted the CP to hear. Colonel Sullivan had fought in three wars, but he could recall nothing to match it. He looked stunned as laughter poured out of the radio like a freshet of water. Sergeant Major Turner blinked and slowly allowed himself a guilty grin. Some of the others in the commo tent started to laugh along with the trapped Marines.

"Those crazy, magnificent bastards," Colonel Sullivan exclaimed, expressing the sentiment of everyone listening.

Everything got better fast. Out of the ensuing silence at the end of the laughter crackled a voice from an Air Force C-47 pilot with the poetic call sign of Smoky Gold.

"Carnival Time, this is Smoky Gold. We're on-station overhead. Where do you want these flares, over?"

As if in echo from heaven came other voices. An A-4 Skyhawk flight leader radioed, *"Carnival Time, we're approaching your position now."*

Helicopter gunships circled overhead. *"Carnival Time, this is Klondike Zero-Three. Do you read? We have some special delivery for your guests."*

The cavalry was coming. Just like in the movies. God, it was a good feeling. Maybe we had a chance after all.

But daylight was still a long way off.

49

With TacAir arrived a renewed hope for survival. Sporadic firing resumed. More grenades sailed in. I looked for my Ka-bar again, but still couldn't find it. I strained my ears listening for rustling in the grass, scanned the tops of the grass as it rippled in the breezes, looking for movement to give *them* away. Occasionally, nursing my dwindling supply of ammo, having already twice shared my basic load with the platoon, I fired a round or two down the hillside to discourage approach.

I looked up at the sky, waiting for TacAir to start making runs. Red and green running lights from the circling helicopters blinked against distant cold stars. I didn't see the jets, but Smoky Gold was up there. I could hear him. He kicked out flares, and they lit up the world, blinding me so that the suns were all I saw and the aircraft were hidden behind them.

Sergeant Howard pulled in the perimeter even tighter since we had lost so many defenders. The diameter of the defense from the Big Rock on the north to me on the southeast was only about ten steps. I now lay prone a few feet away from Mascarenas on my left and Adams to my right. Mascarenas hadn't moved at all in at least two hours. The only way I knew he was alive was when I heard him sucking air. He would suck in with a gurgling sound—Cheyne-Stokes breathing—and then lay without catching his breath for long minutes at a time, or so it seemed.

I looked toward him underneath the flares, my face on a level with his on the ground. We were only about eight or ten feet apart. His head lay turned to his right pointing down the slope.

Each time he breathed the gurgling sound, it cut deep into my heart. I felt a combination of guilt and remorse. It's hard to explain. I actually felt *guilty* because I alone, out of an eighteen-man platoon, remained the only man not wounded or not dead. Of my four-man fireteam, McKinney and Adams were dead and Mascarenas was almost dead. My squad leader, Corporal Thompson, was dead. Everyone had at least one wound—except me.

Strange, frightening thoughts ran through my head. *My God, what is the matter with me? Why haven't I been wounded yet? Why are my friends dying while I'm still alive? What are You saving me for, God? Something even more terrifying than what we've already seen?*

Each time I breathed in air I drew in the sickly stench of coagulating and fresh blood, cordite, smoke, and human fear. And now I felt guilty because my blood wasn't mixed with all the others'.

I was one sick, confused Marine. Fucked up from the shock and horror.

To me, in my present state of tumult, it seemed I actually *willed* myself to get hit. I spotted a form downhill in the shadows and popped off a couple of quick rounds. A few minutes later, a burst of light machine gun fire—it sounded like a BAR, Browning automatic rifle—spanged a string of steel off the Big Rock. A ricochet thumped me hard in the ribs, like a piece of the night doubled its fist and hit me with everything it had. The blow actually shoved me two or three inches across the ground and knocked the breath out of me.

"I'm hit! I'm hit!" I gasped as soon as I was able.

It was a call for help. At the same time it was an expression of relief. With that wound, I became a member of First Platoon once more in good standing. We were *all* wounded now. We were all *really* in this together.

I was also scared half to death because I didn't know how badly I was hit. I unbuttoned my utility shirt and felt the tender welt and cut skin. It didn't seem too bad.

Billy D showed up in response to my cry. Like a man obsessed with duty, he refused to quit until he literally couldn't drag himself across the ground. He was a lot worse off than I.

"Where are you hit?" Billy D asked, his voice stretched as thin and tight as a guitar string.

It's my side. I think I'm all right." I don't feel any blood." I couldn't tell him I was glad it happened.

"Let us have a look."

"I'm okay."

I dared not roll onto my side and provide an inch or two more of myself as a target. Doc took my word for it and crawled away to assist other wounded. Binns scooted over to check on me.

"You all right, Hildreth?"

"Yeah."

It was a good feeling having them check on me.

Binns returned to the Big Rock. My side hurt like hell, like I had been kicked by an Oklahoma mule. Nonetheless, I peered down the hillside with new resolve, feeling better now and more settled. I no longer felt guilty.

50

For some reason we found inexcusable, which even Colonel Sullivan couldn't understand and because of which he was almost livid with anger, it had taken more than two hours to get tactical air overhead. Later, it was explained that the problem wasn't so much in getting aircraft as it was in trying to figure out how to aid us in the dark with the enemy so near our lines actually merged. At the best of times, TacAir was not the asset of choice for real close-in support. To even contemplate using it in the dark, with all the smoke and confusion on the ground, bordered on criminal lunacy.

But something had to be done. Artillery barrages had proved ineffective, the rounds exploding too far away from where they were needed to do much good. To be fair, the hilltop was one small geographical feature. To get HE on that feature within a few feet of the Marines without actually putting it square on top and wiping *us* out was an almost impossible task. I suppose Division brass, goaded by Colonel Sullivan, probably decided we were gone anyhow—so they might as well give TacAir a chance.

From Captain Jim Perryman's point of view, overhead in

his attack chopper, the question was a simple one of not *whether* to strike but rather *how* to strike in the dark, in a battle so closely joined, without killing Marines. Looking down, he saw the objective as a black pool with the hulking shape of a mountain barely visible in that pool. Muzzle flashes strobed and tracers zipped, but they did little to differentiate between who was who down there. Perryman could not even imagine what those trapped Marines must be going through.

It was difficult to distinguish lines drawn between friendlies and foes even when Smoky Gold popped flares, illuminating Nui Vu and surrounding terrain. The lines formed a confusing labyrinth that appeared to be fused together, at least that was the way it looked from the air.

"My God!" exclaimed Smoky Gold. *"Look at them all. All over the hillside. It looks like an anthill ripped open."*

The analogy had been used before.

Sergeant Howard shouted over the radio in his exhilaration and anxiousness, "Klondike, they're coming for us. Why aren't you firing?"

"We can't determine your position, Carnival Time," Perryman responded. *"We can't see anything except weapons fire. We might strike you."*

"Spray the area, Klondike. Everything within twenty meters around the top of the hill."

"Stand by, Carnival Time."

The strikes required superb coordination and cooperation. For one thing, it wouldn't do to have an A-4 suck one of Smoky Gold's parachute flares into its jet intake. That would ruin your night. The helicopters had to stay out of the way of the jets and the Skyhawks had to watch out for Smoky Gold and the two Klondikes now on-station. Together, bunching on the same tactical channel, the various pilots came up with a plan of action.

The gunships and the A-4s would alternate in their initial attacks. Perryman and Mike Shields in their respective Hueys would perform a secondary role as TACs, Tactical Air Controllers, by marking and directing jet bombing runs. They would fly in the dark while the jets timed their approaches either underneath the high flares or immediately after the flares extinguished. To mark specific targets, the Klondikes directed Smoky Gold to drop flares on the ground as signal lights. Communications over the tactical frequencies crackled with excitement and urgency.

"Skipper, if you can keep 'em from coming up the hill," Sergeant Howard radioed Iron Hand, "we'll fight 'em off our backs up here."

"All right, Jim, you got it," Colonel Sullivan replied.

The first order of business was to coordinate air with ground.

"Carnival Time, we're going to make a pass," Perryman radioed. *"Do not fire. I say again, hold your fire."*

He waited for the flares to extinguish—no sense making a more visible target of himself—and kept his external red and green beacons lit so Carnival Time could see the helicopter and make adjustment. The Huey came in low and fast through the saddle opening in the ridge and skimming the hill's northeastern face. The VC were brave and disciplined. They held their ground and tried to shoot the helicopter down. Green tracers weaved webs around it.

The gunship made its low pass, whooped up and out.

"You're close, but that looked pretty good," Sergeant Howard complimented him.

"Roger that, Carnival Time. Keep your heads down. We're gonna get closer."

On his next pass, while Shields's bird hung fire in the air, Perryman came in low and released rockets. Both door gunners blistered the enemy. The pass brought an immediate response from Carnival Time.

"No, no! Jesus Christ, you're shooting at us. Back off! Back off!"

Perryman pulled into a steep climb out of the cauldron before he did damage to us. *"Carnival Time, be advised we cannot tell you from Victor Charlie. We see people everywhere. We need you to mark your position, over."*

"Gunboat, we're out of flares. The only thing I have is a flashlight with a red filtered lens. Can you home in on that?"

"Roger, Carnival Time. We'll take a stab at it. Give us your red light."

Klondike 03 circled Nui Vu searching for the red light in all that flashing and flickering and streaking. He had a difficult time. Finally, he located it.

"Gotcha, Carnival Time. Now where do you want our ordnance?"

"Fire everywhere outside a twenty-meter radius of the red light. Lay it any closer and you'll really cream us."

"Roger, Carnival Time."

Perryman prepped his crew, made sure his gunners and copilot understood the parameters. "Be careful," he told them. "We're going in."

The chopper veered into a dive to attack a large concentration of VC advancing up the north slope. Tracer red from the Huey's fixed forward firing machine guns and door guns stomped across the slope, chewing up everything in its path. Fire whipped down from the bird. It was like watching a big red snake cracking out of the sky like lightning. Rockets left contrails from the helicopter's pods, creating bright explosions that rattled the countryside and echoed in relays down the valley.

We were gaining fire superiority in a big way.

Skyhawks burned fuel at an amazing rate and therefore had limited time over target. They made their passes, guiding on terrain marked by the helicopters. On the ground, we heard the roar of their engines coming out of the black sky for what seemed like hours before they actually arrived, but arriving silently, outrunning their sounds. They rolled in and almost directly overhead in the ghastly light of the three-million-candlepower flares popped at 3,000 feet and swaying underneath their tiny parachutes. Flying between the flares and the ground, putting iron on the target with 250-pound bombs.

The first bomb felt like it landed ten feet away. The fierce little fighter dumped its load and was gone all in an instant. The tremendous concussion of the bomb and the delayed roar of the jet engine coalesced in a crack that seemed to open a hole through the universe. I felt like standing up and cheering, except I couldn't have stood up had I been so foolish as to try. The ground shook like from an earthquake. That damnable hill was being smashed into submission.

While maintaining vigilance over my TAOR, I watched the jets with mixed fascination, horror, and numbness, gripping the soil to keep from being thrown off the planet as the warbirds streaked over us one after the other. Each one seemed to come in lower than the previous, and closer to our perimeter. It seemed the pilots meant to land, get out on foot and fight. How could they be so accurate and so close without dropping a bomb right on top of us?

They concentrated on the approaches to Nui Vu as well as on the hill itself, laying their ordnance in downhill directions so shrapnel burst away from the hilltop. Making pass after pass, grim pilots in the cockpits performing the precision close support bombing for which they were becoming famous. Mushroom explosions only a few yards away from our outpost tore up the VC and jostled us with the impact, sometimes bouncing us two feet off the ground. Smoke and fire writhed downward like boiling lava. The hill was what pilots called a target-rich environment. The acrid smell of cordite mixed sharply with the stench of jet fuel, blast haze, and blood.

It was terrible. It was *wonderful.*

As quickly as the jets were out of the way, the gunships returned, fast and dangerous, picking off stragglers, surveying the damage and directing more runs. Whooping and thumping and scouring the hillsides with machine gun and rocket fire. Like miniature storm clouds hurling lightning bolts. Flying at altitudes as low as twenty feet above the grass and bushes.

Whereas the A-4s made their appearances on-stage, then had to zip back to Chu Lai to recoup, one or another of the gunships remained over us like a guardian angel, one staying while the other scooted back to Chu Lai to refuel and rearm.

"We're heading back to rearm," Perryman in Klondike 03 might say. *"Be back most skosh."*

"Klondike," Sergeant Howard said quickly, "can you get that little motherfucker with the machine gun northwest of us before you go?"

Captain Shields came on the air. *"Carnival Time, this is Klondike Zero-Four. I'll be your pilot, over."*

"Roger that. Glad you're here. Can you see my red light?"

"Roger back. Now where's that little motherfucker you want us to burn?"

The gun ships kept switching back and forth like that. Sergeant Howard always had a job for them.

"Keep 'em coming, Klondike," Howard cheered. "Lay 'em right in our back pockets. It's the only way to stop the fuckers. We still have automatic weapons firing at us."

Perryman was back. *"Carnival Time, I can't see the auto weapon."*

Mulvilhill stood up. "I can see him," he shouted to Sergeant Howard.

He cranked off four rounds. That elicited instant feedback from the hidden gun. As Mulvihill intended, blue-green tracers gave away the VC's position.

"*I see him now, Carnival Time,*" Perryman said, and a moment later knocked out the machine gun. He drew fire in the process.

"Klondike, you got two 50s firing at you," Sergeant Howard warned.

Mulvihill opened up on the nearest heavy machine gun. A grenade from a different source exploded next to him. He fell, painfully wounded for the second or third time. He soon recovered and pulled himself back into position to continue the fight.

Support coming as it did just in the nick of time provided motivation and reawakened courage in those of us on Nui Vu Hill who had all but resigned ourselves to our fate. We might still be out here in the middle of the night with enemy all around, but the break in odds provided a new chance and possibly changed the outcome of the battle. Colonel Sullivan was coming through for us. Hope returned to Sergeant Howard's voice.

"Beautiful," he radioed Smoky Gold. "Keep them flares coming."

To Klondike, he added, "Good job. Do it again. Can you get the machine gun northwest of us?"

"*Roger.*"

Ultimately, jets and helicopters expended over 200 2.75-inch rockets, 23,000 rounds of M60 machine gun ammo, 1,750 rounds of 20mm cannon, 44 bombs, and sixteen Zuni rockets in defense of Hill 488. Although we hoped, *prayed,* that the VC would withdraw, we could have saved our energy. They still weren't ready to quit, even though they appeared frightened by the aircraft and their attacks subsided for a short period. They stayed, perhaps, because they had been ordered to wipe out the Marines at any costs. They stayed, perhaps, because their commanding officers had been killed and subordinates continued to follow dead orders. They stayed, perhaps, because they thought victory was still attainable. The VC knew how to stick to a plan, come shit or high water.

That artillery fire and TacAir could blow an area to smithereens until not a blade of grass remained standing and the VC survive was testimony to their amazing shovel work. All that digging we heard down there must have resulted in some awfully deep holes and bunkers.

Pilots fearful of hitting us had to leave a narrow space around our perimeter untouched and still growing tall grass. Into those spaces crawled the Vietnamese where they hugged the line closely, making it difficult for artillery and aircraft to get them. Every time the flares went out, the enemy jumped up in that "safe zone," determined to take the hill at any cost, pounding us while they in turn were pounded. Savage point-blank fighting continued. Fighting remained so intense that neither Colonel Sullivan nor Sergeant Howard could ask choppers to try to rescue us. We would simply have lost aircraft and more good men.

"Jim, you'll have to hold on 'til morning," Colonel Sullivan reluctantly informed his battered platoon leader.

Jesus God. Dawn was still over three hours away.

51

What should have been a dispirited force threw its weight first against one side of the tiny Marine perimeter atop Hill 488, then against the other. The VC and NVA were well-trained and demonstrated good fire discipline; they were not a local yokel outfit. They had a lot of ammo to burn on us.

Although badly mauled, the bad guys still had us ringed in. Fortunately, they no longer attempted to mass for a big rush. Each time they had been bounced back with heavy losses. Plus, TacAir dealt them so many casualties they were afraid to mass. Knowing what the jets and Hueys and artillery and our sharpshooting did to them further down on the slopes, they hugged the perimeter, dug in not thirty meters away, and tried to cut down any Marine who raised up and silhouetted himself against flares or the skyline.

Two of the enemy battalion's four original 50-caliber machine guns survived to lace the hill in a net of green tracers. A light machine gun, a BAR or RPD, positioned itself downslope on the north. Instead of waiting for targets, its gunners began bouncing bullets off the Big Rock in hopes of catching some of us with deadly ricochets. Sure enough, one of them got Martinez.

Throughout the fight, the radioman from Kansas battled from the same place—next to the sump hole near the Big Rock. The sump hole, Martinez saw by flare light, now contained several Chicom grenades that failed to go off. He avoided them with great care. He crawled around the outside of the depression to the edge of the hill, checked the area and fired off rounds when he spotted movement, then wriggled back around the edge of the depression to his alternate position at the rock. He was on his way back to the rock with ricocheting bullets and tracers buzzing overhead when one of them caught him in the back.

Like someone hit him with a fist and knocked the wind out of him. He already had grenade fragments in his legs.

"I'm hit," he groaned when he caught his breath. He gestured at Mulvihill. "Check me out, Dan."

Mulvihill slid over to him. Billy D was busy elsewhere. Martinez kept his weapon ready.

"You're really hit hard in the back," the Chicago radioman determined. "It's right next to your spine, but I can't tell. Can you move your legs?"

Martinez tried. "Yeah," he said. "Go ahead and patch me up."

It would have been a disabling wound at any other time. But tonight, anyone who could still move and fire a weapon wasn't considered disabled. Both men returned to their battle positions. Martinez wasn't in a great deal of pain yet.

"Dan?"

"Yeah, Martinez."

"Thanks."

Nearby, a grenade landed next to Bill Norman. He rolled away from it and buried his face in the dirt underneath his arms. He waited and waited, but the grenade never went off.

First Platoon along with artillery and air assets extracted

a fearsome price from the enemy. We had also paid, and paid dearly. I overheard Sergeant Howard on the radio during a lull delivering our casualty report: seven wounded so severely they were either unconscious or conscious and unable to move (even though they fought on); six more wounded but still fighting; at least five dead.

"This is one hell of a bunch of men," the sergeant relayed to Colonel Sullivan during a slow period. "The Good Lord never put a better crew on this earth. These men are doing more to get the job done than anybody can ever expect of them. Skipper, I don't want to see any more of them die."

Colonel Sullivan sounded like he had something in his throat. "Neither do I, Jim. Neither do I."

Although I occasionally saw bad guys flitting from place to place, most of the activity was happening on the other side of the hill from me. I lay on the top barely able to see down over the crest into the tall grass where McKinney lay. It seemed like a year ago, a decade, since McKinney's poncho fluttered down almost on top of me. Yesterday and the day before when we hung loose up here, reading and basking in the sunshine like a bunch of tourists, had to have been at least a lifetime ago.

Tonight was the longest night I could ever remember.

Why would anyone want this hill so badly, I wondered, that he would sacrifice so many lives to take it? It was a worthless hunk of real estate. It wasn't a big hill, as far as mountains went, nor was it a productive hill. It wasn't even much for looks. As far as I could tell, rainwater washed right off and left it so dry it grew nothing except brown-looking grass, a few shrubs, some weeds, and rocks. There were no obvious minerals. Nobody could live up here. It had a feel of evil about it, especially after tonight. And especially after tonight it was sure to be haunted by the restless spirits of the dead, ghosts the Vietnamese called *pratas*.

We didn't want the hill. Neither did the Viet Cong. If we succeeded in holding it, tomorrow the helicopters came for us, we abandoned it and went away. If the VC seized it, tomorrow they abandoned it and climbed back down. What sense did it make to fight over something nobody wanted?

We Marines weren't fighting for this damnable hill, I realized. We fought because we had no other choice, and we fought so fiercely because we fought for our lives and for *each other*. It was no more complicated than that. Life on the hill that night returned to simple basics. Tooth and claw. Survival for the clan.

The night was not our friend; it was the enemy's friend. Our survival depended on holding out until daybreak. My eyes anxiously and longingly scanned the eastern horizon in the direction of Chu Lai. This must be the darkness before the dawn.

"Sarge, I'm really low on ammo," someone whispered.

"Me, too," came an echo that relayed itself around the perimeter.

Billy D had two magazines of ammunition left. He gave one of them to Victor, who had only ten rounds remaining. Mulvihill had fewer cartridges left than Victor. Bosley gave them each one of his magazines, because he had been firing single action the entire night due to his missing gas cylinder cap.

None of us had grenades left. I still had two mags remaining and a partial in my M-14. Sergeant Howard ordered redistribution, followed by the admonition to fire only at identifiable targets—and then only one shot at a time. It didn't take a math professor to calculate how precarious times were becoming.

I crawled over to Adams's body to retrieve any ammunition he may have had left. I felt queasy robbing a dead man, but I knew he wouldn't have minded under the circumstances. He lay in a thick pool of sour, congealing blood. I found two magazines in his magazine holder.

Unbelievably, Mascarenas still lived. Rasping breaths hissed through his teeth in quick gasps followed by long pauses. I removed two more magazines from him.

Even though he was wounded and in severe pain, Sergeant Howard never ceased to encourage the battered platoon, reminding us that more Marines were ready to come in at daylight to get us out.

Daylight? I hardly remembered what daylight was like.

Enemy soldiers pushed their way through the close-in grass in another probe. Sergeant Howard, relying on cunning, issued what surely had to be one of the most unusual combat orders in recent history.

"Throw some rocks," he whispered.

What? Had it come down to that—rock throwing? Primitive survival in its most fundamental evolutionary step?

"They'll think we have grenades," he explained. "When they jump out of the way, we'll zap 'em."

As incredible as it sounded, it worked. Again and again. As Powles might have said were he able, "Them goddamned gookth will never learn." I felt around on the ground until I found a couple of fist-sized stones. Every time I heard a sound, I hurled one of the rocks and waited ready with my rifle.

Attackers instinctively sprang away from the *Thunk* of the "grenades," exposing themselves and allowing us to make every shot count. Just like squirrels back in the woods of Oklahoma, they couldn't keep their heads down. The range was generally less than thirty feet. A lot of gooks ended up with holes in their foreheads.

It was becoming a crazy fight. The enemy fired automatic weapons; we replied with single shots. The enemy tossed grenades; we threw back rocks. Victor the Mormon threw his empty canteen and scored with it. Pessimist though he was, he rallied and became a funny kid under the circumstances. He started slinging C rat cans, commenting that the rations were deadly if we could get the dinks to eat them.

Finally came the desperate report everyone dreaded: "I'm out of ammo."

And an echo just as chilling: "So am I."

Air cover and artillery kept the hillsides cleared, but it was up to us to either kick Charlie back from the crest or go down beneath the onslaught. Soon now it would be rocks, knives, rifle butts, teeth, and claws. We waited anticipating the final assault. I still couldn't find my Ka-bar.

52

Thick, heavy fog settled in on the seacoast at Chu Lai while on Hill 488 we waited for the enemy's final assault. Colonel Sullivan rotated from battalion to Division CP to the helo pads. Tense, dead tired, and anxious. At Division, he bulled his way in to see the Division Chief of Staff and his G-2 in operations. Operations assured him that Charlie Company, First Battalion, Fifth Marine Regiment was prepared to fly to the rescue as soon as fog permitted takeoff for the flight of waiting CH-47 Chinook heavy troop helicopters.

"Get them birds up. Get them out there," the Colonel prodded.

"They'll have to wait a little longer because of the fog," the G-2 said.

"Wait? My boys out there on that hill have been waiting all night. I don't know how much longer they can wait."

53

Almost imperceptibly, the darkness began to lift. The band of gray toward Chu Lai widened inch by slow inch. We anxiously awaited the sunrise. Our spirits rose with it. Each man at some point had given up in despair at ever living through the night. Some of us hadn't lived. But here the night was almost over.

A probe came with the first gray streaks, but it was half-hearted and broke off quickly. Captain Perryman and Captain Shields in their gunships, our guardian angels, helped smash it. Norman fired his remaining rounds. So did several others. I had three bullets left. Firing slacked off into a lull.

"*Pst! Pst!* Norman?" Joe Kosoglow hissed. "You got any water left?"

"A little."

Norman tossed his canteen. It struck Kosoglow's injured foot. He let out a yelp.

"Sorry, Joe."

" 'S all right. I think anywhere it landed would have hurt."

I was spent, exhausted, deep-down bone weary. Like everyone else. Our wounds and injuries hurt like hell. The air tasted fresh and moist, even laden as it was with the scorched scents of battle and death. Dew settled on our clothing, pushing in the morning chill. My head throbbed from the reverberations of explosions and hours of almost constant gunfire.

For all the light they provided, flares distorted as many details as they revealed. Gradually, as daylight approached, things began to take shape that I hadn't seen clearly since nightfall. Farther down off the top of the hill, inky blackness still reigned where the VC were, but here I saw things beginning to outline. I lifted my head tentatively off the ground, surprised that no one took a pot shot at me.

The bipods of a light machine gun—the gun itself missing—lay about twenty feet to my front. Beside it sprawled a dead NVA soldier. So close! I must have got him sometime during the night. Farther down and to the right was the 50-cal machine gun I silenced early in the battle. It was barely visible in the still-dark time. I barely made out the mashed-down grass where the gunners lay next to it. Motherfuckers shot Adams. I paid them back.

Much nearer, unsettlingly nearer, looking like bloody bundles of discarded clothing, lay the two men Adams killed in hand-to-hand. Looking at them and thinking of Adams made me shift my eyes toward where he slowly seemed to be sinking into the earth. Adams and I hadn't been the best of friends, but out here every Marine was a brother. The top of his shoulder had a gaping hole in it that extended past his shoulder blade.

I jerked my eyes away.

I heard Mascarenas gasping for breath. *Please, God*, I prayed, *make the helicopters come soon*. I searched the pale gray of coming dawn above Chu Lai, hoping to spot them.

Maybe they weren't coming.

They'd come. Marines always came if they could.

Sergeant Howard looked at his watch at 0525. I saw him glance impishly around the perimeter at us bloodied and tattered Marines. Then he yelled out in a strong voice to make sure the enemy heard, pulling off another coup in one-upmanship psyops. It was almost as good as the laughing.

"Hang on, you Marines! Reveille goes in thirty-five minutes."

I hoped enough English-speaking gooks remained alive down there to translate that audacious announcement for all the rest. It sounded as though we took their continued presence so lightly that we were all sleeping.

Whether it was the final demoralizing effect of Sergeant Howard's broadcast or merely the coming light, it was enough, finally, for the VC commanders to admit defeat and cancel plans to wipe us out at all costs. Bamboo sticks and whistles sounded. The enemy began to withdraw under cover of the remaining darkness, like cockroaches scurrying away, lugging the bodies of their dead and wounded with them, which in and of itself must have been a considerable task. They rapidly faded into the shrubbery and jungles of the lowlands, dispersing in order to elude harassment by aircraft and pursuit by fresh Marines.

Not all of them pulled out, however. At least some stayed behind to delay pursuit. A gunner with an RPD light machine gun dug in on the northern point where Binns initially set up his OP/LP and dich'd the platoon's first kill when the fight started. He pinged away, at anything that moved on the hilltop. Not that we were moving that much. Some of us *couldn't* move.

There might have been others for all we could tell. We were still pinned down.

At 0600 on the button, the usual time for rising when we were not in the field, Sergeant Howard sounded off again.

"Reveille! Reveille! Time to get up. Reveille!"

Victor was one tired leatherneck. Groaning in mock slumber, he chided, "Chickenshit t-t-to the end."

Bosley grinned and whispered back, "Uh huh. But we're still alive."

The VC with the machine gun thumped in a couple of rounds to let us know that the fight wasn't over as long as some of us were alive and some of them remained on the hill.

Part III

"There is still one sentence, dear master,
that we haven't written down."
And he said, "Write it." After a little while
the boy said, "There, now it is Written."
"Good," he replied. "It is finished,
you have spoken the truth."

CUTHBERT'S LETTER TO CUTHWIN ON THE DEATH OF BEDE

54

When you were involved in something as personally intense and telescoped to a particular time and place as we were on Hill 488 that June night, it was impossible to think of, to even *believe* in, a world outside. For many of us, life indeed ended that night, and there was no other world anywhere, forever. For the rest of us, the survivors, life became compressed and condensed so that the entire world represented itself to us only in the top of a hill about twenty meters in diameter. It was hard to believe that life went on more or less normally for the majority of the people on the planet.

Back in the United States, people set their alarm clocks, got up and went to work or school, had hamburgers and Cokes for lunch, and battled the traffic rush to get home in time for dinner. They dutifully attended their kids' piano recitals, fell in love, got married, and had more kids. They sneaked around on their wives and husbands, paid bills, bought new cars, protested the rise in taxes, and damned the government.

They thought of Vietnam only because it was the world's first television war. Night after night, it was Vietnam *live* on TV following *Gunsmoke* or *I Love Lucy* reruns. The horror of modern warfare running like a macabre soap opera accompanied Americans to their dinner tables via the six o'clock news with Walter Cronkite or Huntley and Brinkley.

"Oh, my God! Did you see that? They killed him right on camera. Will you please pass the potatoes? I was saying to Mr. Snodgrass only today that—Oh, Jesus, Jesus! Look at that!"

The black ghettos in Watts blew up last year, and the Black Panthers were threatening a race war. Antiwar demonstrators and "peaceniks" took over college campuses and snake-danced in city streets to protest about everything imaginable, including the "establishment" and the Vietnam war. Hippies painted flower petals on their old vans and migrated to California and Haight-Ashbury to smoke dope, avoid the draft, and "make love, not war." College professors and Dr. Spock were saying how "our children are trying to tell us something. Listen to them." And, of course, you couldn't trust anyone over thirty.

The month I enlisted in the Marine Corps, 25,000 antiwar demonstrators took to the streets of Washington, D.C. The 173d Airborne Brigade now operating in War Zone D northwest of Saigon saw action before it ever got to Vietnam—against protestors who attempted to block the troop train. Even while McKinney, Adams, Carlisi, and my other fellow Marines were being killed on a nondescript hill in Vietnam, many of those who stayed behind sucked weed and chanted, "Hey, hey, LBJ. How many kids did you kill today?"

They didn't mean kids like Glawe and McKinney; they meant Vietnamese kids we "baby killers" in uniform, like Glawe and McKinney, were supposedly shooting.

Burning draft cards was big. Young men evaded the draft by going to college, getting married, feigning homosexuality, or faking medical conditions. Some took drugs to raise their blood pressures. Others punctured their arms to simulate an addict's needle tracks. Doctors were often sympathetic. "I save lives by keeping people out of the army," said one, not realizing that someone else went in the place of the one he "saved." Thousands fled to Canada, leaving behind signs on walls like *Where is Lee Harvey Oswald when you really need him?* A future president of the United States was conspiring to evade the draft rather than go to Vietnam and fight.

Also that June back home, the unmanned Surveyor I successfully landed on the moon. A sniper wounded James Meredith in Mississippi, leading to mass demonstrations in the "March Against Fear." Congress raised the hourly minimum wage to $1.40, and the Supreme Court ruled in the Miranda case that suspects must be advised of their Constitutional rights.

The Rolling Stones rose on the charts with "Paint It Black." A *Time* magazine cover asked *Is God Dead?* Abbie Hoffman was creating the Youth International Party (Yippies), LBJ continued to pursue "The Great Society," and comedian Lenny Bruce talked dirty for fun and profit.

Many of us in Vietnam wouldn't have recognized the new America as the same one we left.

Life went on "normal" back home, while in Vietnam that week of 16 June, 142 Americans were killed and 941 wounded, including those of us on Hill 488. That was an increase over the previous week when 109 were killed and 636 wounded. We were still winning though. The Reds lost 1,240 killed that week, up from 902 the previous week. So far, the toll of combat American deaths in Vietnam since 1961 stood at 3,804.

The only thing we survivors on Hill 488 cared about at the moment was that the sun rose for us one more time.

55

Vivid reds and oranges and pinks and hope streaked the sky as the sun burned through the morning haze and fog on the seacoast. First rays touched the lacerated face of Nui Vu. I thought it the most beautiful sunrise of my life, all the more striking for the salvation it promised. There was an emotional release when the sun came up, a time to let go of pent-up feelings. Morning tears came. My God, we made it. We hadn't turned to black on the maps after all.

I still lay flat on the ground in what had turned into a waiting game between us and the machine gun sniper and whatever other number of his comrades remained while warm tears of combined relief and sadness slowly rolled down my grimy cheeks. Relief because I felt surprised to have lived through the night when many times I thought it was all over, when I thought, *So this is what it's like to die.* And sadness because of the price we paid in the lives of our friends. This was no Wallace Beery movie. One look at those maimed and savaged corpses told you they weren't coming back for the next film.

"I see a pretty sight coming up over the hill," Sergeant

Howard commented to Colonel Sullivan on the PRC-25 as he turned his face toward the sun. "Papasan, you don't happen to have a cold beer and a cigar, do you?"

"I hope you have a match to light it with, boysan."

"It's smoking, buddy, it's smoking. Papasan, after this night I'm older than you."

"Not by much, pardner, not by much."

"Colonel, we'll need help for all my people on extraction. The only way we can get out is with troops. I have three able to walk, but everyone, even those three, are wounded."

"You've heard it before, Jim, but this time they are in the air."

"Skipper, we're out of ammo." A total of *eight* rounds of live ammunition remained on top of the hill. Billy D had even fired up all the .45s he and Fitzpatrick carried. "We're dead if these snipers decide to come up the hill. I've only got seven men left that can pull a trigger."

I had three rounds left.

An unarmed H-34 medevac circled the hill out of ground fire range, waiting to come in for the wounded. The two Huey gunships initially piloted by Perryman and Shields remained over target. Toward morning, an exhausted Mike Shields had finally relinquished his bird to his VMO-6 squadron commander, Major William J. Goodsell. A young first lieutenant named Stephen Butler flew with Goodsell. The hill remained so deceptively quiet after sunrise that the Huey jocks thought they might be able to get medevac in to pick up First Platoon's wounded while they flew shotgun for it.

After all, the enemy had tried unsuccessfully all night long to shoot down the fleet helicopters as they darted dauntlessly about hammering the sides of the hill with rockets and machine guns, exposing themselves in order to aid us. The risk of getting in a medevac now seemed acceptable. Most of the bad guys had packed up their toys and gone home.

The Hueys tested the water. One hovered high and off to the side, prepared to unleash its deadly fire on any enemy movement. The ground around the hill was so cut up and furrowed that it was impossible to tell where VC might be hiding. The second helicopter made a couple of low passes from east to west in a deliberate attempt to draw fire. Nothing happened.

"*Carnival Time, this is Klondike,*" Major Goodsell radioed. "*We're bringing in a medevac. Can you get your whiskeys [wounded] to us?*"

"Roger that, Klondike." Sergeant Howard hesitated. By some miracle, the more seriously wounded—Powles, Fitzpatrick, and Mascarenas—had managed to hold on. They might make it yet if they could get to surgery. But was the gamble with the lives of the airmen worth it?

"Maybe you should wave off," Sergeant Howard offered. "It's too risky."

"*We're coming in, Carnival Time.*"

Major Goodsell's Huey fluttered down over the peak and hovered no more than twenty feet off the top, creating a blade wash typhoon that stung us with grit and snatched at our clothing. Nonetheless, it was a welcome event. Deliverance was so close, *so close.* I turned my head, shielding my eyes from rotor wind, and looked up at the green belly and the machine gunner in the door. Lieutenant Butler opened his side window and dropped yellow smoke in the small opening of our perimeter in order to mark the spot for the medevac. He stuck his head out the window, smiled and gave us a thumbs up.

As yellow smoke boiled into a cloud, Major Goodsell waved at Sergeant Howard. The Huey put down its nose and skimmed north over the forward slope, only ten feet above the ground. Perryman followed in his gunship, but higher up where he could keep better watch.

It happened all at once. Frustrated all night at his inability to retaliate against the helicopters, the VC machine gunner unexpectedly found himself with a low, almost stationary target. The rapid thumping of the RPD machine gun punctuated itself against the sound of chopper engines and blades. Balls of blue-green tracer converged on the bird, delivering sledge hammer blows and sparking like firecrackers against its steel underbelly.

Goodsell's face contorted in pain. One round busted the chin bubble and passed through the major's right leg and the radio console, ricocheting off his control stick. Smoke filled the cockpit, and his radio went dead. The bird rocked in the air in sort of a wingshot dove flutter. Barely staying in the air, it made a hard right bank and slid off zigzagging almost out of control down the side of the hill toward the valley, trailing smoke and spewing hydraulic fluids. Butler grabbed the stick to take over, but there was little he could do to keep the bird aloft. He was along simply for the ride.

At the bottom of the hill, the aircraft yawed hard left. The toe of the left skid hit first, rolling the chopper 360 degrees to the left. The transmission and attached parts exploded from their mounts as the main rotor blade hit the ground. Metal crumpled. What was left of the Huey came to rest setting upright in a cloud of red dust. None of the crew was seriously injured in the crash.

Captain Perryman's ship remained flyable, although it also took hits. He trailed his wingman into the valley and set down next to the crash site. Crew from both helicopters extracted Goodsell and carried him to the good aircraft. Perryman took off and poured the coal to his bird. Major Goodsell died before he reached Chu Lai and medical help. The bullet had clipped the artery in his leg and he bled to death. He had commanded VMO-6 for less than one week.

Medevac was still game to try the pickup. It dropped down over the yellow smoke. Sergeant Howard and the rest of us frantically waved it off as machine gun bullets clanged against its underplating. It veered erratically to one side and turned sharply toward the east from which it came. Yellow smoke that would have guided in deliverance slowly dissipated in the morning breeze. The hill had claimed still another American life.

56

Like other aspects of the war in Vietnam, the air war began gradually and in incremental stages. Several hundred U.S. Air Force personnel were stationed in Vietnam on the eve of the French defeat in Indochina in 1954, their job to help maintain a fleet of C-47 transport aircraft for French forces. They remained in South Vietnam to work with its air force when the country divided. By 1961, their advisory role was extended to include a special U.S. training squadron known as Farm Gate, whose duty was to instruct South Vietnamese pilots in combat flying skills. A year later, American pilots actually flew combat missions when the Viet pilots proved unable to cope.

The full force of American airpower was unleashed after the Gulf of Tonkin incident of August 1964. Carrier-based aircraft of the U.S. Seventh Fleet launched retaliatory air strikes against North Vietnam coastal targets. More raids followed after deployment of U.S. fighters and bombers to bases in Thailand and South Vietnam. March 1965 saw American activity increasing even further, as U.S. warplanes began a sustained bombing campaign against the North called Operation Rolling Thunder. U.S. aircraft, including Marine and Navy warplanes stationed at Da Nang and Chu Lai, also began flying close air support missions for troops on the battlefield and attacked convoys of enemy troops and supplies coming down the Ho Chi Minh Trail network. By 1966, the sledgehammer of U.S. air power was in full swing.

The air war was particularly busy that week of 16 June 1966. In addition to supporting ground troops and hitting tactical enemy targets in the four Corps War Zones, U.S. pilots struck supply routes and storage areas in 66 raids over North Vietnam. Navy pilots dodged nine Russian-built surface-to-air (SAM) missiles in attacks on barges, junks, bridges, buildings, and conventional anti-aircraft sites. Although no U.S. aircraft were lost to "flying telephone poles," hostile AA fire brought down a Navy A-4 Skyhawk and an Air Force F-105 Thunderchief. The Skyhawk pilot was listed as missing in action. Rescue helicopters plucked the Thunderchief pilot to safety.

The loss of the two jets brought the total number of U.S. planes shot down over North Vietnam to 265. The number shot down over South Vietnam, where helicopters proved the main targets, was far lower.

After the downing of the Huey gunship at Hill 488, a flight of A-4 Skyhawks scrambled from Chu Lai to deal with the matter once and for all. The Skyhawks carried 250-pound bombs and were armed with 20mm Vulcan cannon. Marine Captain Bill Luplow took command of the flight after the squadron commander, a major somewhat older than the other pilots, reported radio trouble and turned back. It was no surprise to Luplow. The commander enjoyed a reputation for experiencing "radio problems" in order to avoid potentially hairy missions.

He often impugned his men while playing hero to his wife back in the United States, a pattern that came back to bite him in the ass. In a most recent letter to her, he wrote that "all these young pilots are so scared they wear their steel pots (helmets) in the shower." One of the fastest ways to dispense information or start a rumor around a military base was to divulge a confidence to a wife. It wasn't long before the contents of the letter reached other wives, who, in turn, informed their husbands in Vietnam.

Sure enough, one evening the previous week, all the pilots in the squadron showed up in the showers when they were sure the commander was there engaged in his ablutions. They solemnly marched into the open showers one at a time, each stark naked except for the steel pot he wore. The commander grew red in the face and stormed out. The incident still failed to prevent his "radio problems."

As Luplow and his angry jets streaked toward Nui Vu Hill, he heard the Marine sergeant radioing from the ground: *"You've gotta get this guy in the crater because he's hurting my boys."*

A FAC Bird Dog flying his little fixed-wing silver Cessna preceded the fast-movers to spot for them, a job the gunships had accomplished during the night. Targets were too close to friendlies and the jets flew too fast to select their own marks. Bird Dog zipped in low and relatively slow and lay smoke rockets on suspicious holes and craters. The jets followed him in.

They worked over the hillsides yet again, firing 20mm exploding rounds that literally chewed swaths in wide strips out of the mountain. They crisscrossed the slopes, hammering them. The hill shook with the fury of the attack.

"Oh, my God. You're into friendlies!" Bird Dog cried.

Sergeant Howard's voice shot back over the net. *"Hell, no. We're deaf, but bring it right back in there. The A-4s are doing a good job."*

Howard helped direct the strikes.

"How're we doing, Carnival Time?" radioed Luplow, whose call sign was Red Hog.

"They're in the holes, Red Hog. Can you see them?"

The Skyhawks flew lower on each pass in their attempt to knock out the dug-in machine gun.

"Come down and get 'em," Sergeant Howard encouraged. *"They got that machine gun on us. It's right on the north finger with the rocks on it."*

The jets flew so low they kicked up dust storms.

"He's still there firing at us," the Marines reported.

The A-4s threw and dropped everything they had at the elusive gook with the RPD. As soon as they were gone, he came right back. He was like a prairie dog who popped in and out of his deep tunnel. He was there to stay until someone on the ground went in to dig him out. Stubborn, gutsy little bastard who remained dangerous to both ground troops and helicopters.

57

The Marine Corps honors tested traditions: It will never leave on the field of battle one of its fighting men, whether he be alive or dead. It will go to fantastic lengths and commit scores of men to aid and protect a few.

"*Hang on, Jim,*" Colonel Sullivan radioed. "*We've got three hundred men headed your way.*"

I watched UH-34s, twenty or thirty of them plus gunships, rise above Chu Lai as the fog lifted. They resembled a swarm of disciplined bees against the red sky of the sunrise as they headed our way, barely seeming to move because of the distortion of distance. No cheering came from the hill, no visible reaction. We merely watched like zombies caught in headlights, by this time too stunned and drained to show emotion. My only thought, my only acknowledgement, was a simple: *It's almost over.*

McKinney, if he were still alive, might have thought the occasion deserved a musical score. Something stirring to announce cavalry coming to the rescue. Maybe "Get Off My Cloud" by the Rolling Stones or "Lightning Strikes" by Lou Christie. McKinney was no longer alive. We lay in silence, waiting and still pinned down by the VC machine gunner.

The helicopter airmada came in slow and high, staying out of machine gun range. It was a beautiful thing to hear their tidal roar. Sun beams glistened off whirling blades. One of the pilots, First Lieutenant Richard Moser, stared in amazement. The entire scene below was something out of a war movie or novel. That bare hill sticking up from the ridge saddle, chopped, cratered, and pulverized into raw red earth; a handful of Marines sprawled on top, holding it; all around the litter of enemy soldiers killed during the fight, motionless, grotesque, and twisted in death.

Lieutenant Moser hadn't caught the sergeant's name down there, only his call sign—Carnival Time—but Carnival Time seemed one impressive NCO. His concern was that no more Marines, his or anyone else's, die needlessly this late in the game. When the relief commander came on the air to express his willingness to land helicopters directly on the hill to kick out troops and pick up the exhausted and bloodied platoon, Sergeant Howard wouldn't hear of it until after all the snipers were eliminated. One helicopter had already been lost.

"Negative," he said. "There's no real place to land that's not covered by the enemy."

The circling helicopters pulled out of orbit and dropped from sight toward the bottom of the south slope where we were inserted three days ago. It seemed like three years ago. Full of Marines going down, they were empty when they hopped back into sight. Surely Charlie with the machine gun had to know his remaining hours on earth were limited.

Some of the H-34s went into a holding pattern, ready to airlift First Platoon off the hill and back to Recon headquarters and safety once Charlie Company of the 1/5 secured the objective. The company commander, First Lieutenant Marshall "Buck" Darling, went to work immediately doing just that. He detached machine gun sections from the main body to flank the steep sides of the hill to support the company's advance. The Big Rock that served as Sergeant Howard's command post was the most prominent feature on the peak and could easily be seen from below. The main column climbed straight toward it.

Enemy other than the sniper on the north propeller blade remained scattered about on the hill in isolated pockets. The Marine 60mm mortar team knocked out a VC mortar with the first round it fired. An enemy rifleman wearing camouflage and a camouflage net jumped out of a hole and ran. Sergeant Howard spotted him from the hilltop.

"Get that sonofabitch hauling down that finger!" he barked into his radio.

Charlie Company required no such encouragement. Sergeant Frank Riojas, weapons platoon leader, cut him down at 500 yards with his M-14. Roles had suddenly reversed. The North Viets became the hunted. Marines scrambled around the sides of the hill as well as up the slope in a maneuver to pinch off the enemy. They climbed fast and with purpose.

Lieutenant Darling's battalion CO raised him on the net. *"Is the landing zone secure, Buck?"*

"Well . . ." Darling hesitated. "Not spectacularly," he admitted.

Two NCOs safe at the battalion CP were eavesdropping. "What do you suppose he meant by that?" the junior of the two mused.

"You stupid shit," growled the other, a crusty veteran. "What do you think it means? He's getting shot at."

VC normally raked a battlefield clean afterwards, carrying off the bodies of their dead and securing any weapons they could find, theirs or otherwise. Marine fire from the hilltop had been so deadly overnight, however, that those soldiers who fell close to the perimeter had to be left un-claimed. Charlie Company's lead elements saw enemy bodies and equipment strewn about everywhere. Marines had to step over corpses to approach First Platoon's perimeter.

"My God!" someone murmured, horrified, "this must have been holy hell up here last night."

Machine gun rounds bounced shrieking off the Big Rock next to Binns and Bosley. I ducked automatically and caught the glimpse of a human form in the corner of my eye. I twisted desperately toward it, thinking my luck had finally run out.

"Hold it, Marine! It's us."

My rifle fell to the ground. I let out a sigh at the unbelievable sight of those fresh young troops scrambling up from the south. I choked out a warning to the rest of the platoon so no one took a scare shot. Relief and joy swept the perimeter, although we were too beat and too hurt to do much celebrating. We were glad to see these Marines; it was a good feeling to know someone had come to help us after all these hours, but we also *expected* them. Marines always came.

"Get down," were Sergeant Howard's first words of welcome. "There are snipers right in front of us."

The rest of us thought of other things.

"Hey, you got any cigarettes?"

"How about some water?"

"Any of you guys happen to have a candy bar?"

The relief force filtered onto the hilltop on their bellies. Some filled in positions on the perimeter while others began moving the wounded toward the rear. They seemed awed by what we had done, their expressions filled with pity, fascination, and admiration.

"I never thought I'd see the sun rise," Kosoglow admitted to the first man who crawled up to him, "but once it did, I knew you'd be coming."

Corpsman Billy D. Holmes was so stiff and sore from his wounds that he could hardly move. Shrapnel had shredded his hands and pierced both legs and buttocks, causing him considerable loss of blood. Dried blood on his face formed a hideous webbed mask.

"We're here to help you out," one of the relief point men said.

"Jesus Christ," Billy D sighed. "This is the greatest thing since peanut butter."

Bob Martinez knew the north finger sniper would open up with deadly accuracy if he or one of the relief men stuck his head up. He warned the new men and lay flat. He couldn't move anyhow; his legs were still paralyzed. One of the new arrivals, a Mexican-American, bellied forward.

"*Amigo, todo estaba bien ahora,*" he said in Spanish.

"I don't speak good Mex," Martinez apologized.

The rescuing Marine grinned. 'It's still all right, brother," he said. "We're getting your tough asses out of here."

He dragged Martinez away from the Big Rock by his feet, toward where the hill sloped back to the south away from the sniper.

Sergeant Howard refused to even consider evacuation until all his men, alive or dead, were removed. He sounded more relaxed, however, when he reported to Colonel Sullivan than he had all night.

"Skipper, we have friendly troops with us, but we're still pinned down by that machine gun in the hole. I'm not leaving yet."

I asked one of the point men if he had a fresh magazine for my rifle.

"Sure." He started forward, crouching.

"Get down!" I cautioned. "Stay low. Snipers have us pinned down."

He half-squatted when he handed me the magazine. The guy seemed excited and eager to get into the fray. He was just a kid, eighteen or nineteen at the most. The same age as me, but after last night I suddenly felt so much older and wiser. I felt ancient.

"Where are they at?" the young leatherneck asked.

"About twenty yards down the north slope."

He stood up unexpectedly, hunched over, to get a better look. "Where—?"

That was his last word. The machine clapped twice. His helmet clanged and spun off his head like a top, recoiling high into the air and landing downslope toward McKinney. The heavy bullet ripped into his forehead, splattering brains and blood and bone fragments. He was dead by the time he struck the ground. His fingers and feet continued to twitch.

I freaked out for a moment. "Damnit, damnit, *damnit!* I told him to keep his fucking head down."

58

First Platoon became spectators to the unfolding tragedy of the sniper and the new Marines. I watched with a combination of horror and fascination as the drama played itself out. I hadn't moved since the guy fell dead next to me with the top of his head blown off. I lay among the dead, in a graveyard of the still-unburied. And I watched, thinking: *Why can't we just give the gook this hill? We don't really want it.*

We wouldn't give it up though. Things had gone too far and assumed a momentum all their own. By God, Marines had fought for this damn hill and we were going to keep it. The sniper had to go, one way or another.

The platoon leader of the point platoon on the hill crawled up next to Sergeant Howard behind the Big Rock. Like most Marine officers, Second Lieutenant Ronald Meyer wore no rank in the field. Sergeant Howard assumed the short, muscular man to be another NCO like himself; Lieutenant Meyer didn't correct him.

Meyer had graduated from the Naval Academy the previous June and intended to make the Marine Corps his career. He married his sweetheart a month before he shipped out for Vietnam. Because of his build, officers and men alike called him "Stump."

Stump looked at the situation and talked it over with Howard. An impatient young officer, he called for members of his platoon to pass up grenades. He made a little pile of them within easy reach before nodding his readiness. Sergeant Howard pulled himself painfully to the edge of the boulder where he could peek around it downhill toward the sniper. Stump crouched behind the Big Rock, a grenade in each hand.

"Ready," he said.

Howard directed the throws while Stump pulled pins and lobbed grenades. "A little more to the right, buddy . . . About five yards farther . . . That's right . . . No, that one was a little strong. . ."

The VC down there was dug in deep. He had survived 250-pound bombs, miniguns and 20mm exploding shells. A few grenades weren't going to do anything but piss him off. Stump hurled everything within reach at him, except for the Big Rock, and the guy popped off a round as though to taunt us.

Move to Act Two. Lance Corporal Terry Redic, a tested sharpshooter with several previous kills to his credit, suggested he try a few shots with rifle grenades. He was a cool customer who disdained ducking during brief firefights while preferring to suppress hostile fire with rapid, accurate shooting. He made his way forward and went up on one knee behind the Big Rock, a grenade attached to the muzzle of his M-14.

Stay down, stay low, I breathed. It was like I knew what was going to happen before it did. This entire episode was becoming so predictable.

Redic eased up to aim over the top of the rock. I couldn't look. At the same time, I couldn't *not* look. The poor guy never found his target. The machine gun barked once.

Drilled through the head, Redic pitched backwards, dead even as his body flopped next to the still-unconscious Fitzpatrick.

Damn. That guy down there was good. I dropped my head into my arms and gave a weary sigh.

Stump swore with a vocabulary he had never heard at the Academy for Officers and Gentlemen. He pounded his fist on the ground. "I want air on that sonofabitch," he shouted.

Word went back to Lieutenant Phil Freed, the Forward Air Controller attached to Charlie Company for the day. Freed was still coming up the hill with the rest of the company and Lieutenant Darling's command element. He jogged uphill carrying his radio on his back.

Two of the Marines killed within a matter of a few minutes and Lieutenant Meyer still hadn't acquired patience. Now he was really pissed and unwilling to wait. He might not have been entirely rational. No gook was going to shoot his men and get away with it.

"That motherfucker has got to go," he raged. 'You coming with me, Sotello?"

Lance Corporal David Sotello turned to select some other men for a patrol. Stump thrust a Ka-bar knife between his teeth, grabbed a grenade with each hand, and started wriggling down the hill like a lizard in the grass before anyone could stop him.

"Keep your head down," Howard called after him. "They can shoot."

Again, I could have predicted the outcome. The guy was brave, but foolish as hell and too impulsive for his own good. I waited for the inevitable.

About ten feet down the hill from the Big Rock, the lieutenant lifted his head to orient himself. He looked back up the hill. An *Oh, shit* expression crossed his face. There was no cover at all between him and the enemy position. Most of the grass had even been burnt and chopped down from last night's bombing.

It was too late for second thoughts. The sniper shot Stump through the side and back. One shot—one kill. He didn't move again.

Another dead Marine dich'd up to the sniper's unerring aim.

"Corpsman! Corpsman!" somebody yelled. 'They've hit Stump."

Not again. Don't be a fool. Stay where you are. Would this shit never end? The act so far seemed to have been scripted for the sniper's benefit.

Hospitalman Third Class John Markillie hesitated only a second, as though for that brief instant he contemplated how it was suicide to go out there. But then, displaying his medic's devotion to duty, he went.

"For God's sake, keep your head down" Sergeant Howard anguished.

The corpsman reached his lieutenant. So far, so good. He rose up on one elbow to examine Stump's wound. That was all the target the sniper required; he shot Markillie through the chest. The corpsman collapsed on top of Lieutenant Meyer, moaning.

The sniper could have finished him off, but didn't. It was an old sniper's trick; I had learned it in Okinawa. A wounded enemy was better than a dead one under these conditions. Leave him out there crying for help until his buddies came to provide new targets.

Americans always came.

Another corpsman named Holloday and a squad leader named Melville were next. Sergeant Howard ordered the relieving Marines to provide covering fire. The air filled with crackling iron over their heads as Holloday and Melville slithered through the grass toward their buddies like a pair of fast snakes.

Stump's pulse was gone. Markillie still breathed, though he was unconscious. One pushing and the other pulling, the two Marines maneuvered Markillie back up the hill underneath the savage rattling of Marine M-14s.

The gook down there was one skillful, cunning little sonofabitch. Even with all that fire coming at him, he managed to squeeze off another shot. The bullet pierced Melville's helmet, going in one side and out the other. The helmet leapt off his head.

Melville must have been going to church regularly. The bullet only nicked his left ear. Stunned, his ears ringing, he lay for a moment to collect himself before he and Holloday dragged the wounded corpsman back into the perimeter behind the relative safety of the Big Rock.

Jesus God, would the carnage never end?

59

Marine First Lieutenants Richard Deilke and Edward Menzer flew their Crusader F-8s up the seacoast, returning to base from a mission in which they had not been utilized. They were still fully armed and had fuel. Menzer contacted DASC (Direct Air Support Center) and requested another assignment. DASC chopped him to Cottage 14, the FAC on the ground assigned to Marines engaged in a relief mission to Hill 488.

"*Blue One, this is Cottage One-Four,*" Lieutenant Freed radioed from the hill.

"Cottage One-Four, Blue, go."

"*We have a machine gun nest dug in right in front of us. Think you can help?*"

"You call, we haul."

"*Blue, this has to be real tight. Charlie is dug in right on our lines. Come on down in a dry run.*"

Menzer and Deilke had no idea how tight, nor how much their skills and nerves were going to be tested. They were about to fly one of the closest direct air support missions in the history of fixed wing aviation.

"How tight, Cottage?" Menzer asked.

"*I make it twenty meters, Blue.*"

Silence over the radio. Twenty meters was about twenty steps, the length of a large living room. Even the A-4s from last night and this morning hadn't attacked *that* close to Howard's perimeter.

"*You still hauling?*" Freed asked.

"Uh, roger that."

Freed appreciated the capabilities of the aircraft. He himself was a jet jock. He didn't know it at the time but, in fact, he and Menzer had flown jets together in another squadron a year previously. Pilots were often used as FACs on the ground because they understood air cover and could talk to pilots in a language they understood.

Freed deliberately called the jets in wide on the dry run so he could judge the pilots' technical skills and precision. They seemed rock steady. Satisfied, he called for them to attack in earnest.

In the air, Menzer was reluctant at first to fire so near friendlies. Still, he knew the Crusader to be a good shooting bird. He thought that as long as they flew parallel to the Marines, they could pull it off.

"Cottage One-Four, get your heads down. We're coming in."

The gunsight reflector plate in an F-8 Crusader resembled a bull's eye with the rings marked in ten-mil increments. At 3,000 feet altitude when the pilots lined up for a run and aligned their gunsights, the target lay inside the ten-mil ring while the Marine positions were at the edge of the ring. A Crusader flew at an airspeed in excess of 1,000 mph. One wobble, one minor error of judgment or calculation at that speed and with the target in such close proximity resulted in raking the Marine infantrymen with cannon fire.

The two jets approached from the northeast with the risen sun behind them. Two bright specks in a cloudless sky flying in tandem, one behind the other. They zoomed in silently in the blink of an eye, outrunning their sound, cutting across the ridgeline parallel to the Marine perimeter. There was no room for error.

I ducked my head and buried it underneath my arms.

Each aircraft made four strafing passes, skimming by ten to twenty feet above the ridge. I feared both would crash, so close did their wings dip to the crest of the hill. I saw the pilots so clearly I could have picked them out of a lineup afterward if they hadn't been wearing helmets and 02 masks. The impact of their 20mm cannon shells showered us with dirt.

In eight attacks, they fired 350 explosive shells into a grid sixty meters long and ten to twenty meters wide. The target area, gouged and torn, looked like bulldozers had churned back and forth across it. Nothing could have lived through that hell.

"How'd we do, Cottage One-Four?" Menzer asked as the Crusaders, depleted of ammo, circled the target.

"Good job, Blue. That should do it."

Lieutenant Freed cautiously lifted his head. A round cracked by.

"Can you believe that sonofabitch!" a Marine exclaimed in disbelief. "He's still there."

60

Every single enemy had been knocked off the hill except for the gook with the machine gun. He was one stubborn, hard-core SOB. I had to admire the poor bastard even as I wanted his ass waxed as quickly as possible. Except for the curiosity of *when* and *how* he would get it, I detached myself so completely from Charlie Company's efforts to get him that it was almost like I was watching a movie, anxious for it to reach the end so I could go home.

Lieutenant Stump's body lay a few yards downslope from the Big Rock, in the grass where he was shot with the knife in his mouth and the grenades clutched in his fists. A wide trail of mashed-down grass led to him. Beyond was the ploughed-up and gouged-up area the fast-movers worked over. I smelled the freshly turned-up earth even through the smoke and scorch. It reminded me of farm country around Bixby south of Tulsa when farmers began their spring ploughing and planting.

At the Big Rock, Lance Corporal James Brown went into a combat fury, emptying magazines and throwing grenades at the sniper. He wanted that SOB dead in the worst possible way. He and Stump and the medic Markillie were friends. No billboard Marine, he often exasperated superiors with his lack of military protocol and an offbeat sense of humor that conflicted with officers' ideals of duty and service. Once when the enemy caught his squad in a crossfire, he noticed that incoming rounds were zipping by high over their heads. Everyone else returned fire. Brown stood up and strolled over to a Vietnamese tombstone. He propped himself against it with one finger, nonchalantly crossed his legs, and shouted, "You pukes couldn't hit me if I was buried here."

Even though the Crusaders were out of ordnance, they came up on the net to ask if dummy runs over the sniper's position might be useful. That gave the company commander, Lieutenant Darling, an idea. He noticed that the sniper's firing paused when the jets made their low-level runs and the gook ducked into his hiding hole. He could use the planes as cover. He turned toward Lance Corporal Brown.

"I'm going after Stump," he declared. "You coming, Brown?"

Brown paused in his one-man fight when he heard the CO call his name. He ceased yelling blasphemies at the enemy, looked over at Darling, and calmly nodded his head. "Yeah, I'm coming."

I, for one, had been duly impressed by the vocabulary with which he blistered the gook.

Sergeant Howard would have said it wasn't worth getting more guys shot just to reclaim a corpse, but Lieutenant Darling called the shots now. Brown still hadn't run out of words when he crawled over the crest following the CO.

"Don't sweat it, Lieutenant," he quipped. "All they can do is kill us."

Darling didn't reply. The two Marines reached Stump without getting shot. Up on the hill, Sergeant Riojas set up an M60 machine gun and lay fire above their heads at the sniper. The two Marines, maneuvering on their bellies, hadn't the leverage to pull Stump back up the hill.

"All right. Let's carry him," Darling suggested.

Brown turned speechless for one of the few times in his life. Stand straight up? Any Marine who so much as raised his head got it zapped.

"We'll time our moves with the jets," the CO explained.

Brown calmly nodded. His voice returned. "I hope the gook has the same choreographer."

When the jets roared back around and came in low, the two Marines grabbed Stump and scrambled a few yards with their burden. They flattened themselves as the Crusaders pulled out. The sniper pinged in their direction, but his angle was wrong. Bullets dug into the ground. Riojas banged back at him.

It took a half-dozen such rushes to cover the few yards uphill. Finally, exhausted and panting, they rolled over the crest with Stump's body and lay there as though surprised at still being alive. I realized I had been holding my breath. I let it out in a burst.

0930 Hours

I still felt empty, detached. I simply lost interest in the fight. With no sense of involvement whatsoever, I watched as Lieutenant Darling attempted a different tactic by sending Corporal Samuel Roth and his eight-man squad on a flanking movement around the northwestern edge of the hill. I suppose he figured the only way to get rid of the sniper was to go in and take him out *mano a mano*.

Riojas, the machine gunner, fired cover for them, the Crusaders having run low on fuel and streaked back to base. A strange duel developed between him and Charlie in the sniper's hole. The sniper fired at Riojas, striking the bipod and sending the machine gun spinning. Riojas snatched it back and returned a burst of fire. It kept going like that, back and forth, at almost point-blank range. The Marine ducked when it was Charlie's turn; then he reached for the trigger and made the sniper duck.

That occupied the enemy gunner while Corporal Roth and his squad sneaked up on him from his right. They crawled into a line facing the sniper. On command, they stood up with fixed bayonets and began walking toward the sniper's lair. They saw no movement among the clumps of uprooted grass and torn earth.

Suddenly, the sniper popped up and unleashed a lightning blast of tracers directly at the line. Bullets whipped through Marine ranks. Roth's helmet spun off his head. He dropped. The rest of the squad flopped to the ground.

"Roth?" someone called out. "Sam, you all right?"

"Yeah. Why?"

In all the excitement, Roth wasn't even aware that his helmet had been shot off. It was the second time within an hour that a steel pot saved a Marine's life.

The sniper transferred his attention from the machine gun on the hill to the more immediate threat. A new face-off ensued.

"When I give the word, rise to a knee and fire on full auto," Roth instructed. He paused. "*Now!*"

The Marines snapped up, weapons blazing. Bullets kicked up dust and lumps of earth, driving the sniper underground.

"Marines, get down!"

Roth paused. "All right. Put in fresh magazines and lets do the same thing again . . . *now!*"

It worked. The sniper bobbed up like a duck in a shooting gallery just as the Marines rose and blasted away. A bullet caught him and knocked him backwards against the side of his trench.

Roth charged without hesitation. The rest of the squad sprinted behind him. Lunging with his bayonet, Roth leaped into the hole with the wounded enemy soldier. The long blade pierced the skinny little man and pinned him against the side of his hole.

Roth jerked out the bloodied bayonet and prepared to stab again. No other was needed. The VC's eyes rolled back in the head of this ballsy little man who had raised such havoc all morning and killed four more Marines and downed a helicopter, also killing the pilot. Defiant and full of fight to the last, he gurgled, slumped over his machine gun, and died as a grenade dropped from his left hand. The release pin remained intact. He hadn't been given a chance to take another Marine with him.

Hill 488 went quiet at last. Lieutenant Darling declared the objective secure. I stood for the first time since the attacks began last night. My legs buckled. They felt too weak to hold my weight. I staggered over to the Big Rock and leaned against it for support. Sergeant Howard looked up at me from the ground out of a face hollow and gaunt. His hair seemed to have turned white overnight.

I got my first full view of the battleground. I stared. Tears came to my eyes. Through the blur I continued to stare.

"My God," I murmured. "Oh, my God."

Aftermath

The end is where we start from.

T.S. Eliot

61

Daniel Mulvihill, Charles Bosley, and I were the walking
wounded of Hill 488, the only ones of the platoon's original
eighteen who did not have to be carried off on stretchers.
Fatigue and shock so numbed my senses that I actually forgot about the big hunk of flesh gouged out of my side. The
shakes would start later when I had time to think of what
happened and what could have happened.

We had fought as a unit during the long and terrible
night—but we had also fought alone. And died alone, each
of us witnessing private horrors that, for some of us, would
remain private for the rest of our lives. Some of us witnessed parts of the dying of others. The grenade exploding
on top of McKinney. I was also alone in seeing Adams die.
No one knew when or how Mascarenas got it. Only Binns
knew about Carlisi. Doc knew parts of Thompson's story,
but not what happened to him after he was dragged over
the crest of the hill. Everyone became aware of when
Sergeant Howard was wounded, and everyone at least
heard Powles's unearthly screams at the beginning of the
fight. Only conjecture explained how some of the rest of us
died and what happened before we died.

Eighteen-year-old Thomas Glawe took a round through

the head as he fought from across the Big Rock. He died immediately, or at least we assumed he died immediately. When the relief force found him propped up lying against the base of the boulder, a dead enemy soldier lay within his arm's reach, the muzzles of their respective weapons almost touching each other's chests.

Two more VC dead lay sprawled in front of Mascarenas, obviously waxed by the little Mexican-American before he himself was hit.

Corporal Thompson, his head and chest already bandaged from previous wounds, rested crumpled beneath an enemy body. Another dead VC lay face up next to him. The squad leader went down fighting. His stiffened hand still gripped the handle of the Ka-bar knife he borrowed from Sergeant Howard before the platoon inserted. The blade was sunk to the hilt in the back of the soldier dead on top of him. The only way Thompson could be identified was by his watch. His face was gone, shot off at point-blank range.

Rescuers recovered two Marine entrenching tools (collapsible shovels), both crusted with blood, flesh, and hair, near a group of mangled North Vietnamese. We never learned who they belonged to—or what happened.

Mulvihill and Bosley sat on the Big Rock staring down at their feet, waiting for evacuation. They looked filthy and torn, crusted with their own blood as well as blood from friends and foe. Their eyes appeared as caves, as hollow as mine felt. None of us would ever be nineteen years old again.

I couldn't sit still. At first, I simply stood on top of the hill, stunned, empty, looking around at the carnage and wreckage left behind. Throughout the recent night my world consisted of a few square yards of dirt on top of a hill no one had ever heard of. It was hard now to start expanding that world. I walked aimlessly about, like a man in a trance.

I spotted movement among a group of VC corpses. I

whirled and started shooting in a rage. Rounds popped flesh and geysers of blood from the offender. I kept on shooting, taking out my anger and frustration on that poor silly dying gook who had the audacity to *move* after killing my friends.

Somebody, one of the fresh Marines, placed a hand on my arm. "All right, all right. You got him, man. You got him."

I stared, breathing heavily. I fired once more. For good measure. Fuck him.

I went down and looked at the gooks I killed around the machine gun. They were the ones who killed Adams. I looked at them and felt nothing. I looked at others, and felt nothing. I didn't know if I would ever be able to feel again.

Our more seriously wounded were evacuated first, along with our dead, who were wrapped in ponchos and placed on the floors of the choppers. Mascarenas was among the first. He was still alive and gasping for breath when he left the hill. He died before he reached the hospital; somebody pulled a poncho over his face.

Sergeant Howard and Billy D still refused to be evacuated until they accounted for every Marine in the platoon, dead or alive. McKinney was still missing. They weren't going to leave without him. Only after Lieutenant Darling assured them that no one would be left behind did they consent to be carried off. I watched them go on the stretchers. Sergeant Howard's job was done.

Billy D could sit up in the chopper. Sergeant Howard lay on a stretcher next to one occupied by his friend, Richard Fitzpatrick. Fitz was so maimed and doped up on morphine that, even during fleeting moments of consciousness, he had no idea where he was. Three or four bodies wrapped in ponchos were stacked against the rear firewall. Elation, relief, sadness combined to overwhelm the medic and the platoon leader. They gripped hands and began sobbing as the chopper left the hilltop behind.

Dead were strewn everywhere on the hill. Some of the first killed started to bloat in the sun. Flies buzzed in busy swarms. Charlie One-Five started piling up gook bodies and collecting weapons. Mangled Asian bodies formed a huge mound of tortured flesh on top of the hill. Somebody counted forty-three for the dich board or whoever at higher-higher kept such stats. We were still winning, weren't we?

The score stood at forty-three to eleven. Six Marines died in First Platoon, four from Charlie One-Five, and one helicopter pilot. Not a good score ratio on the surface. However, drag marks and blood trails indicated many VC dead and wounded had been carted off during the night and the early-dawn withdrawal. A more accurate score might have been 100 to 11. Or even 200 to 11.

We *were* winning.

The pile of VC corpses were left stacked on the hill for relatives to claim, if any of them had the fortitude and grief to come up here after we were gone. Rot was already beginning.

I helped gather weapons. It kept me busy, kept me from thinking. Some relief Marines came down to McKinney and wrapped him in a poncho. I slung three AK rifles, a Chicom carbine, and my own M-14 over my shoulder and climbed onto an H-34 with Bosley, Mulvihill, and McKinney snugged into his poncho on the floor. The helicopter lifted into a sunny morning that contrasted obscenely with the picture of the hill below.

I watched the mound of human remains recede. I saw how almost no grass remained growing on the hill, except for that thin collar of it that separated our perimeter from the enemy during the night. Everything else had been blasted and torn into craters and raw earth. Tendrils of smoke oozed out of the ground here and there, like gasses leaking up through fissures from a volcano. This volcano had erupted, and now it was dormant again.

Wind whipping into the chopper through the open doors blew the corner of the poncho off McKinney's face. His face wasn't that bad, almost like he was sleeping with his eyes partly open. I bent over and covered my friend. There was still the wind. It was like McKinney didn't want his face covered. Bosley looked like he was about to be sick.

The chopper landed at Division Med. Medical people ran out and got Bosley and Mulvihill for treatment and took McKinney. I told them I was all right, leave me alone. The chopper lifted off again and dropped me off at the battalion helipad. Later, I would be summoned to positively identify some of the bodies. They were stored in big reefers. The graves registration people unzipped the bags.

"Is this . . .?" they asked.

I nodded. "Mascarenas."

"And this . . .?"

"McKinney."

I got off the helicopter in the battalion area and walked among the tents and dunes toward S-2 for debriefing. This was familiar ground, but now it was unfamiliar. Nothing for the rest of my life would be as familiar to me as the top of Nui Vu Hill with its Big Rock. S-2 expected me. A mighty-mite and driver pulled up and relieved me of my burden of enemy weapons. A staff NCO told me to go get some rest, that I would be debriefed later. I had hardly spoken since before I left the hill. I didn't know what to say when Moore came to meet me.

"I knew you'd be all right, Ray," he said. "But I was worried about McKinney."

Yeah. McKinney, our cajun brother whom we had always looked over. I nodded and walked off.

It was only after I got into the shower and the hot water and soap stung my open wound did I become once more aware of my own injury. I dressed again and walked to the battalion aid station to be treated. I went back to the platoon tent and sat on my cot, among all the empty cots of those who would never sleep here again. First Platoon had literally ceased to exist except on paper.

I sat there feeling empty and alone. I looked around after a while. Adams had left his swim trunks on the end of his cot to dry. Mascarenas hadn't finished a letter home. A book lay on McKinney's bed. . . .

I dropped my head into my hands. Alone in the tent, I didn't want to think about it anymore.

62

Of the twelve of us who survived Hill 488, HM1 Richard Fitzpatrick was the most seriously injured. He lost most of the frontal part of his brain and one eye. I saw him again at the White House on 21 August 1967 when President Lyndon B. Johnson presented Sergeant Howard the Congressional Medal of Honor. He had a glass eye and didn't seem completely aware of what was going on. Someone tended him constantly.

PFC James McKinney was the first of us to die in the battle. Lance Corporal Alcadio Mascarenas was the last, expiring in the medevac chopper on the way back to Chu Lai. Four others fell in between McKinney and Mascarenas: PFC Ignatius Carlisi, PFC Thomas Glawe, Lance Corporal John T. Adams, and Corporal Jerald R. Thompson.

The first thing Sergeant Howard wanted when he reached the hospital was a cigar. Lieutenant General Lewis W. Fields, First MarDiv Commander, pinned a Purple Heart to his hospital robe.

"They [the enemy] were well trained, well armed, well disciplined," Sergeant Howard said. "They were the best we'll ever run up against, but their best just ain't good enough, sir."

"Sergeant," General Fields said, "You've seen enough for one man. This is your fourth [Purple Heart], I believe, so I'm ordering you to knock it off and stop making a habit of getting wounded."

"Yes, sir. I hope this is my last one. The Man topside must have been watching over me."

Five of the original platoon members from the hill remained in-country to complete our Vietnam tours of duty: LCPL Daniel Mulvihill, LCPL William Norman, PFC Charles Bosley, LCPL Joseph Kosoglow, and me. The more seriously wounded—Sergeant Jimmie Howard, LCPL Robert Martinez, HM1 Richard Fitzpatrick, LCPL Billy D. Holmes, LCPL Thomas Powles, LCPL Ralph Victor, LCPL Ricardo Binns—were shipped first to the Naval Hospital at Subic Bay in the Philippines, then back to the United States. The next time we got together was at the White House more than a year later.

Because of Hollywood's portrayal of war and my naivety to combat, I actually thought battles like that of Hill 488 were commonplace. Norman had a big piece of shrapnel in his back, shrapnel in his legs, and a cut over his eye. He and the other four of us who remained behind fully expected to go back out on patrol as soon as we healed. Promoted to full corporal, I thought I was going to be a squad leader in a rehabilitated First Platoon.

Instead, Sergeant Major Turner talked to each of us.

"You want to be a Special Services NCO or an S&C [Secret & Confidential] file clerk?" he asked me.

"Sergeant Major, I thought I'd stay with the platoon."

"Son, you survived something that only happens once in a lifetime. We'll not take a chance of it happening again. None of you are going back into combat."

It happened twice to Sergeant Howard—once in Korea at Bunker Hill and again at Nui Vu. Still, I said nothing and became Special Services NCO and battalion mail orderly. I served out the rest of my tour issuing out swim trunks and volleyballs.

Norman became Colonel Sullivan's driver; Kosoglow went to supply; Bosley and Mulvihill worked at the motor pool. Norman and I were so enthralled by the work we saw Huey door gunners doing in the fight at Hill 488 that we contemplated extending in-country to become door gunners ourselves. Common sense eventually prevailed.

Every man on the hill received a Purple Heart for wounds, six of them issued posthumously. Howard, of course, received the Congressional Medal of Honor, the nation's highest award for valor. It was well deserved. Four of us were awarded the Navy Cross, the nation's second highest award for valor, also well deserved: Binns, Holmes, Adams, Thompson—posthumously for Adams and Thompson. The rest of us, thirteen, were awarded the nation's third highest award, the Silver Star for valor: Martinez, Mulvihill, Powles, Glawe, Mascarenas, McKinney, Fitzpatrick, Bosley, Carlisi, Victor, Norman, Kosoglow, and myself, Hildreth. Carlisi, Glawe, Mascarenas, and McKinney received it posthumously.

Howard, promoted to gunnery sergeant, eventually served a second tour in Vietnam with a military police company. Billy D made a lateral transfer to the U.S. Army's Helicopter Pilot Warrant Officer Program and returned to Vietnam as an army Cobra helicopter pilot. Nearly six years later—it was a long war—a mission brought Billy D near Hill 488. He gave his copilot a quick history on the significance of the hill and landed on its top.

Nothing remained on the ground except the Big Rock. Not even bones or cartridge brass. The VC bodies had been carried away and everything else policed up by locals for recycling. Grass grew in the bomb craters and once again looked like wheat blowing in a Kansas wind.

Warrant Officer Holmes stood on the hilltop by the Big Rock for about a quarter-hour, thinking about that night when we all fought there. He heard the screams, the din of battle, the shrieking singsong voices of the enemy: *"Marines, you die tonight!"* Smelled the blood and the cordite and dust caking in his nostrils. Saw Thompson being dragged off the hill, felt hands grabbing at him, and saw the VC face explode like a melon struck with a pickax.

It no longer resembled the same place. Not like he remembered it. Wind soughed through the saddleback and the grass rustled and there wasn't a cloud in the sky. He touched the Big Rock with his fingertips, touched the ground over which he crawled while lead flew inches above his head. Then he shook his head to clear it and climbed back in the helicopter.

The Vietnam war touched an entire generation in one way or another. It especially touched those of us who endured something like Hill 488 and saw our comrades killed. The Vietnam Veterans Memorial in Washington, D.C., is constructed of two rising black marble slabs that meet at a vertex of 125 degrees ten feet above the ground to form "The Wall." The shiny surface is intended to reflect the sun, the ground, and those who stand before the memorial. Names of those who died in Vietnam, 58,152 of them, are listed chronologically by date of death—from first to last. Near the first are the six names of the First Platoon members who died on Nui Vu.

Vietnam was a war of statistics, beginning with "body counts." Everything was catalogued, tabbed, folded, spindled, and kept for posterity. For example, we know that 2,100,000 men and women served in Vietnam during the period from 1964 to 1973. That was 24 percent of the 8,444,000 who were in the active armed forces during those years, but only eight percent of the 26,000,000 Americans eligible for military service.

The vast majority of Americans eligible for service were exempted by reason of physical, mental, psychiatric, or moral failure. Others gained deferments because they were college students, fathers, teachers, engineers, or conscientious objectors. Later, high lottery numbers made others ineligible.

A relatively small number refused to register for the draft. Some went to Canada or Sweden, while others found other means, legally or illegally, to evade, including a man who later became President of the United States. Few who evaded the draft were actually prosecuted, and most were eventually pardoned by President Jimmy Carter in 1977.

Contrary to popular opinion, most Vietnam casualties—70 percent—were volunteers, not draftees. The army suffered the most casualties—38,179, or 2.7 percent of its force. The Marine Corps, however, lost the largest percentage of its force—14,836, or 5 percent. Forty percent of all Marine enlisted casualties were teenagers.

Statistics are cold numbers. Names on a slab of marble tell little about the men or how they lived and died. It is my hope that this book brings to life the circumstances and drama of the men who defended Hill 488 that terrible night in 1966, of the six men, heroes all, whose names First Platoon contributed to "The Wall," and, by extension, of all the honorable men in all the various services who gave so much to the Vietnam war.

Eight of the twelve survivors of Hill 488 are still alive. HM1 Richard Fitzpatrick eventually died of his injuries; call him the platoon's seventh casualty of the hill. Sergeant Jimmie Howard passed away peacefully on 12 November 1993 and is buried at the Fort Rosecrans National Cemetery. Warrant Officer Billy D. Holmes was killed in an automobile accident in Kansas. Ralph Victor died of a drug overdose. Perhaps he might be called the hill's eighth casualty.

On 20 October 2001, the U.S. Navy commissioned a guided-missile destroyer, the U.S.S. *Howard*, in Sergeant Howard's honor.

"Gunny Howard represents the platoon," said Bob Martinez, who now lives in Tulsa, Oklahoma. "We're a part of the ship's history. By honoring him it's honoring us. And as a platoon, we represent the United States. So it's an honor to our country."

He paused.

"You don't have to wait until November to have Veterans Day," he said. "Every day of freedom we have is Veterans Day."

Citations

The President of the United States in the name of The Congress takes pleasure in presenting the MEDAL OF HONOR TO

Gunnery Sergeant Jimmie E. Howard
United States Marine Corps

For service as set forth in the following:

CITATION:

For conspicuous gallantry and intrepidity at the risk of his life above and beyond the call of duty while serving as a Platoon Leader with Company C, First Reconnaissance Battalion, First Marine Division, in the Republic of Vietnam. Gunnery Sergeant (then Staff Sergeant) Howard and his eighteen-man platoon were occupying an observation post deep within enemy-controlled territory. Shortly after midnight on 16 June 1966, a Viet Cong force of estimated battalion size approached the Marines' position and launched a vicious attack with small arms, automatic weapons, and mortar fire. Reacting swiftly and fearlessly in the face of the overwhelming odds, Gunnery Sergeant

Howard skillfully organized his small but determined force into a tight perimeter defense and calmly moved from position to position to direct his men's fire. Throughout the night, during assault after assault, his courageous example and firm leadership inspired and motivated his men to withstand the unrelenting fury of the hostile fire in the seemingly hopeless situation. He constantly shouted encouragement to his men and exhibited imagination and resourcefulness in directing their return fire. When fragments of an exploding enemy grenade wounded him severely and prevented him from moving his legs, he distributed his ammunition to the remaining members of his platoon and proceeded to maintain radio communications and direct air strikes on the enemy with uncanny accuracy. At dawn, despite the fact that five men were killed and all but one wounded, his beleaguered platoon was still in command of its position. When evacuation helicopters approached his position, Gunnery Sergeant Howard warned them away and called for additional air strikes and directed devastating small arms fire and air strikes against enemy automatic weapons positions in order to make the landing zone as secure as possible. Through his extraordinary courage and resolute fighting spirit, Gunnery Sergeant Howard was largely responsible for preventing the loss of his entire platoon. His valiant leadership and courageous fighting spirit served to inspire the men of his platoon to heroic endeavor in the face of overwhelming odds, and reflect the highest credit upon Gunnery Sergeant Howard, the Marine Corps and the United States Naval Service.

Lyndon B. Johnson
President of the United States

The President of the United States takes pleasure in presenting the NAVY CROSS to

Lance Corporal Ricardo C. Binns
United States Marine Corps

For service as set forth in the following

CITATION:

For extraordinary heroism as a Scout Team Leader, Company C, First Reconnaissance Battalion, First Marine Division (Reinforced), in Vietnam on the night of 15-16 June 1966. Corporal Binns's platoon established an observation post deep within communist-controlled territory to observe enemy movement. At 0100 a massive assault was launched against the Marine position by a determined and well trained North Vietnamese battalion. The murderous enemy fire was so intense that five of the eighteen-man platoon were killed and the remainder wounded. On two separate occasions, with complete disregard for his personal safety, Corporal Binns braved the withering enemy fire to forcibly pull to the ground several wounded Marines who had unconsciously exposed themselves to almost certain death. Realizing that his Platoon Leader was wounded and unable to move, and preoccupied with the direction of close support aircraft, Corporal Binns took it upon himself to direct the fire of the remaining seven Marines, redistribute the ammunition of those who could not use it, and care for the wounded. Although painfully wounded in both legs, Corporal Binns displayed magnificent courage throughout the night and long into the following morning. His selfless devotion to duty, superb professional skill, deep concern for his fellow Marines, and extraordinary heroism inspired all who observed him and were in keeping with the highest traditions of the Marine Corps and the United States Naval Service.

>For the President,
>Paul H. Nitze
>Secretary of the Navy

The President of the United States takes pleasure in presenting the NAVY CROSS to

Billie D. Holmes
Hospital Corpsman Third Class
United States Navy

For service as set forth in the following

CITATION:

For extraordinary heroism on the night of 15-16 June 1966 as a Medical Corpsman, Company C, 1st Reconnaissance Battalion in the Republic of Vietnam. Serving with a platoon which was attacked by a determined and well-trained North Vietnamese battalion after the platoon had established an observation post deep within Viet Cong-controlled territory, Petty Officer Holmes, in the face of intense enemy fire, left the meager cover of his position on the perimeter to render aid to the wounded. Oblivious to the shouted warnings of his Platoon Leader to take cover, he repeatedly exposed himself to the hostile fire by moving from one wounded man to the next, administering emergency treatment. On two separate occasions when there were enemy grenades exploding, he covered the body of his wounded companion with his own to prevent further injury. Although twice painfully wounded, he continued giving aid and comfort to the wounded throughout the night and morning. Petty Officer Holmes' outstanding professional skill, extraordinary heroism, and deep concern for his comrades were in keeping with the highest traditions of the United States Naval Service.

For the President
Paul H. Nitze
Secretary of the Navy

The President of the United States takes pride in presenting the NAVY CROSS posthumously to

Corporal Jerrald R. Thompson
United States Marine Corps

For service as set forth in the following

CITATION:

For extraordinary heroism as a squad leader serving with the First Platoon, Company C, First Reconnaissance Battalion, First Marine Division (Reinforced) in the Republic of Vietnam on 16 June 1966. While occupying an observation post at 0100 on Hill 488, Quang Tin Province, deep in enemy controlled territory, the platoon of 18 men were subjected to an intense assault by a North Vietnamese unit estimated at battalion size. Corporal Thompson immediately ordered his squad to withdraw to a predetermined defensive perimeter. Braving a hail of small arms fire, automatic weapons, and mortar fire, the small band of courageous Marines fought their way to the relative safety of the defensive position. In the course of this action, Corporal Thompson was painfully wounded by an enemy hand grenade and was unable to proceed. Armed with only a knife, he engaged the enemy in hand-to-hand combat and killed two before he fell, mortally wounded. By his indomitable fighting spirit in the face of seemingly insurmountable odds he was instrumental in the defense of his platoon's position. Corporal Thompson's courageous action under hostile fire reflected great credit upon himself and the Marine Corps and upheld the highest traditions of the United States Naval Service. He gallantly gave his life in the cause of freedom.

> For the President
> Paul H. Nitze
> Secretary of the Navy

The President of the United States takes pride in presenting the NAVY CROSS posthumously to

Lance Corporal John T. Adams
United States Marine Corps

For service as set forth in the following

CITATION:

For extraordinary heroism while serving with the First Platoon, Company C, First Reconnaissance Battalion in Vietnam on 16 June 1966. Corporal Adams was a member of a reconnaissance team occupying an observation post on Hill 488, Quang Tin Province, deep in enemy controlled territory. During the early morning hours the platoon of eighteen men was subjected to an intense assault by an estimated North Vietnamese unit of battalion size.

As the members of his team were withdrawing to a pre-designated defensive perimeter, Corporal Adams braved the withering small-arms fire and returned accurate rifle fire which momentarily slowed the enemy assault force and enabled his companions to reach the relative safety of the defensive position. Firing all his ammunition, Corporal Adams fearlessly charged directly into the assaulting horde and, using his rifle as a club, killed two of the enemy soldiers before he was struck down by automatic weapons fire. Severely wounded, he once again engaged an enemy soldier in hand-to-hand combat and, in a final effort, killed his foe. As a result of his courageous action and fighting spirit, his comrades were able to rally and withstand the onslaught of the numerically superior enemy. Corporal Adams upheld the highest traditions of the Marine Corps and the United States Naval Service. He gallantly gave his life in the cause of freedom.

For the President
Paul H. Nitze
Secretary of the Navy

The President of the United States takes pride in presenting the SILVER STAR MEDAL posthumously to

Lance Corporal Alcadio N. Mascarenas
United States Marines

For service as set forth in the following

CITATION:

For conspicuous gallantry and intrepidity in action while serving as a reconnaissance team leader with the First Platoon, Company C., First Reconnaissance Battalion on Hill 488 in Quang Tin Province, Republic of Vietnam, deep in enemy controlled territory on 16 June 1966. During the early morning hours the eighteen-man platoon was attacked by an estimated North Vietnamese battalion. Corporal Mascarenas, displaying great professional skill, covered the withdrawal of his men from an exposed area to a more advantageous defensive position by setting up a deadly base of fire. When he arrived at the position [he] skillfully directed the fire of his small band of gallant Marines and in so doing stopped the initial enemy assault in his sector. As the attack progressed, the enemy fire increased in volume and accuracy, but he continued to set an example of calmness and courage. Corporal Mascarenas inspired his men with dynamic leadership and courageous fighting spirit until he fell, mortally wounded by an enemy hand grenade. As a result of his professional abilities and stirring example the assaulting enemy force was repulsed. His bravery and devotion to duty were in keeping with the highest traditions of the Marine Corps and the United States Naval Service. He gallantly gave his life in the cause of freedom.

For the President,
Paul H. Nitze
Secretary of the Navy

The President of the United States takes pride in presenting the SILVER STAR MEDAL posthumously to

Private First Class Ignatius Carlisi
United States Marines

For service as set forth in the following

CITATION:

For conspicuous gallantry and intrepidity in action while serving with the First Platoon, Company C, First Reconnaissance Battalion in Quang Tin province, Republic of Vietnam on 16 June 1966. Private Carlisi was with seventeen other members of his platoon occupying an observation post on Hill 488 deep in enemy controlled territory. During the early morning hours a North Vietnamese force of battalion size, employing accurate mortar, automatic weapons, and small arms fire, unleashed a furious attack on their position. During the initial assault, Private Carlisi was painfully wounded in his legs by small arms fire, but, disregarding his wounds, he courageously remained in his position and continued firing upon the advancing enemy with deadly accuracy and thus assisted in repulsing the attack. When the unrelenting enemy force began another assault against the stalwart defenders of Hill 488, Private Carlisi was seriously injured by the blast of an exploding enemy hand grenade. After receiving emergency treatment he fearlessly returned to assume his position next to his gallant companions. With courage and skill he continued to inflict casualties on the enemy until he fell, mortally wounded by automatic weapons fire. Private Carlisi's courageous display of fighting spirit against seemingly insurmountable odds was instrumental in the defense of his platoon's position and was in keeping with the highest traditions of the Marine Corps and the United States

Naval Service. He gallantly gave his life in the cause of freedom.

> For the President
> Paul H. Nitze
> Secretary of the Navy

The President of the United States takes pride in presenting the SILVER STAR MEDAL posthumously to

Private First Class Thomas D. Glawe
United States Marine Corps

For service as set forth in the following

CITATION:

For conspicuous gallantry and intrepidity in action while on duty with Company C, First Reconnaissance Battalion in Quang Tin Province, Republic of Vietnam on 16 June 1966. Private Glawe, serving as a scout, and seventeen other members of the First Platoon were occupying an observation post on Hill 488, deep in enemy controlled territory. During the early morning hours a ferocious assault was launched against their position by an estimated North Vietnamese battalion. Courageously manning his assigned post, Private Glawe braved the intense enemy small arms and automatic weapons fire and returned accurate fire inflicting casualties on the advancing foe. The gallant members of the First Platoon stopped the assault of the enemy horde time after time. Carefully conserving his dwindling supply of ammunition, he repeatedly exposed himself to the withering hail of the enemy fire in order that he could better control the adjacent areas within the small defensive perimeter caused by rapidly mounting casualties. Private Glawe shouted encouragement to his beleaguered friends and staunchly refused to give up an inch of ground in the face of overwhelming odds until he fell, mortally wounded by enemy automatic weapons fire. His bravery and devotion to duty were in keeping with the traditions of the Marine Corps and the United States Naval Service. He gallantly gave his life in the cause of freedom.

> For the President
> Paul H. Nitze
> Secretary of the Navy

In the name of the President of the United States, the Commanding General, Fleet Marine Force, Pacific takes pleasure in presenting the SILVER STAR MEDAL to

Private First Class Charles William Bosley
United States Marine Corps

For service as set forth in the following

CITATION:

For conspicuous gallantry and intrepidity in action while serving as a Scout Team Member with Company C, First Reconnaissance Battalion in action against insurgent communist (Viet Cong) forces in the Republic of Vietnam. Shortly after midnight on 16 June 1966, Private First Class Bosley's eighteen man patrol was occupying an observation post deep within enemy controlled territory in the vicinity of Chi Tu, Quang Tin Province, when a Viet Cong force of estimated battalion size crept close to the Marines' position and, on a predetermined signal, launched a vicious attack with small arms, grenades, automatic weapons and mortar fire. While defending a sector of the perimeter which was subjected to extremely intense enemy fire, Private First Class Bosley noticed his team's grenadier had been wounded and was lying in a position of imminent danger. Without regard for his own safety, Private First Class Bosley unhesitatingly exposed himself to the murderous incoming fire to provide covering fire for the wounded man and the corpsman who was treating him. Later in the battle, he exhibited great presence of mind and unselfishness when he saw an enemy grenade land dangerously close to one of the casualties. Reacting instantly, he raced to the man and pulled him to safety before the grenade exploded. Although he sustained painful wounds in the course of the night's engagement, he valiantly continued to assist in the defense of the hill against the relentless enemy attack. The courage and professionalism he exhibited on this, his first encounter with the enemy, contributed in large measure to preventing the entire unit from being killed or captured. Private First Class Bosley's outstanding concern for others at great risk of his own life, daring initiative and loyal devotion to duty throughout were in keeping with the highest traditions of the United States Naval Service.

> For the President
> V. H. Krulak
> Lieutenant General,
> U.S. Marine Corps
> Commanding

In the name of the President of the United States, the Commanding General, Fleet Marine Force, Pacific takes pleasure in presenting the SILVER STAR MEDAL to

Corporal Robert Lewis Martinez
United States Marine Corps

For service as set forth in the following

CITATION:

For conspicuous gallantry and intrepidity in action while serving as a Radioman with Company C, First Reconnaissance Battalion in action against insurgent communist (Viet Cong) forces in the Republic of Vietnam. Shortly after midnight on 16 June 1966, Corporal Martinez's eighteen man patrol was occupying an observation post deep within enemy controlled territory in the vicinity of Chi Tu, Quang Tin Province, when a Viet Cong force of estimated battalion size crept close to the Marines' position and, on a predetermined signal, launched a vicious attack with small arms, grenades, automatic weapons and mortar fire. When the Viet Cong attempted to employ human wave tactics on an adjacent position, Corporal Martinez, with complete disregard for his own safety, quickly left the relative safety of his position and brought effective fire to bear on the attackers. His determined effort was instrumental in turning back the immediate threat. Although he was seriously wounded in the course of the battle, Corporal Martinez was of inestimable value in silencing a Viet Cong automatic weapon which the enemy successfully placed less than twenty meters from the Marines' defensive perimeter by taking advantage of the darkness and difficult terrain. His courageous action throughout the ordeal contributed in large measure to the successful defense of the hill, and helped to prevent his entire patrol from being killed or captured by the numerically superior enemy. Corporal Martinez's daring initiative, valor in the face of extreme danger and unfaltering dedication to duty were in keeping with the highest traditions of the United States Naval Service.

> For the President
> V. H. Krulak
> Lieutenant General,
> U.S. Marine Corps
> Commanding

In the name of the President of the United States, the Commanding General, Fleet Marine Force, Pacific takes pleasure in presenting the SILVER STAR MEDAL to

Lance Corporal Raymond Stanley Hildreth
United States Marine Corps

For service as set forth in the following

CITATION:

For conspicuous gallantry and intrepidity in action while serving as a Scout with Company C, First Reconnaissance Battalion in action against insurgent communist (Viet Cong) forces in the Republic of Vietnam. Shortly after midnight on 16 June 1966, Lance Corporal Hildreth's eighteen man patrol was occupying an observation post deep within enemy controlled territory in the vicinity of Chi Tu, Quang Tin Province, when a Viet Cong force of estimated battalion strength crept close to the Marines' position and, on a predetermined signal, launched a vicious attack with small arms, grenades, automatic weapons and mortar fire. Observing that an enemy machine gun positioned about fifty meters from the Marines' perimeter was bringing devastating fire on his unit, Lance Corporal Hildreth courageously exposed himself to the awesome firepower and, armed only with a rifle, literally fought a duel with its crew, killing the Viet Cong and temporarily silencing the gun. When other Viet Cong brought the gun back into action, Lance Corporal Hildreth repeated his valiant action and eliminated the relief crew. His determined effort at great risk of his own life contributed in large measure to the successful defense of the hill in the face of overwhelming odds. Lance Corporal Hildreth's resolute fighting spirit, bold initiative and unwavering dedication to duty throughout were in keeping with the highest traditions of the United States Naval Service.

> For the President
> V. H. Krulak
> Lieutenant General,
> U.S. Marine Corps
> Commanding

The President of the United States takes pleasure in presenting the SILVER STAR MEDAL to

Richard J. Fitzpatrick
Hospital Corpsman First Class
United States Navy

For service as set forth in the following

CITATION:

For conspicuous gallantry and intrepidity in action on the night of 15-16 June 1966 while serving as the senior corpsman with Company C, First Reconnaissance Battalion in connection with operations against insurgent communist (Viet Cong) forces in the Republic of Vietnam. During a patrol deep in enemy controlled territory, the eighteen-man reconnaissance unit, of which Petty Officer Fitzpatrick was a member, was viciously attacked by a Viet Cong force estimated at battalion strength and employing mortars, small-arms, automatic weapons and mortar fire. After determining that initial casualties were being treated by another corpsman, Petty Officer Fitzpatrick courageously moved through a hail of withering incoming fire to a position which had been left vacant by a fallen Marine. With keen marksmanship and composure, he skillfully employed an M-14 rifle and brought effective fire to bear on the advancing enemy. Constantly shouting words of encouragement to his comrades, he repeatedly hurled grenades into the ranks of the onrushing Viet Cong and successfully defended his area of responsibility. Later in the battle, although he was critically wounded when a grenade exploded near him, his timely warning to others in the immediate area undoubtedly prevented them from sustaining wounds from the blast. Inspiring all who observed him by his valiant efforts throughout, he contributed in large measure to the successful defense of the hill against an overwhelming enemy force. Petty Officer Fitzpatrick's daring initiative, exceptional courage in the face of extreme danger, and selfless devotion to duty were in keeping with the highest traditions of the United States Naval Service.

> For the President
> Paul H. Nitze
> Secretary of the Navy

In the name of the President of the United States, the Commanding General, Fleet Marine Force, Pacific takes pleasure in presenting the SILVER STAR MEDAL to

Lance Corporal Daniel Kenneth Mulvihill
United States Marine Corps

For service as set forth in the following

CITATION:

For conspicuous gallantry and intrepidity in action while serving as a Radioman with Company C, First Reconnaissance Battalion in action against insurgent communist (Viet Cong) forces in the Republic of Vietnam. Shortly after midnight on 16 June 1966, Lance Corporal Mulvihill's eighteen man patrol was occupying an observation post deep within enemy controlled territory in the vicinity of Chi Tu, Quang Tin Province, when a Viet Cong force of estimated battalion size crept close to the Marines' position and, on a predetermined signal, launched a vicious attack with small arms, automatic weapons and mortar fire. Displaying extraordinary courage and presence of mind in the midst of the relentless fury, Lance Corporal Mulvihill calmly stood up and fired into suspected hostile positions, deliberately drawing the Viet Cong fire in his direction and pinpointing the enemy positions for close support aircraft which were orbiting in the area. Although he was painfully wounded in his valiant effort, he continued to assist his comrades in their stubborn defense of the hill throughout the night. He contributed in large measure to inflicting heavy losses among the attackers and helped to prevent the surviving members of his platoon from death or capture at the hands of the enemy. Lance Corporal Mulvihill's exceptional courage in the face of almost certain death was in

keeping with the highest traditions of the United States
Naval Service.

> For the President
> V. H. Krulak
> Lieutenant General,
> U.S. Marine Corps
> Commanding

In the name of the President of the United States, the Commanding General, Fleet Marine Force, Pacific takes pleasure in presenting the SILVER STAR MEDAL to

Lance Corporal Ralph Glover Victor
United States Marine Corps

For service as set forth in the following

CITATION:

For conspicuous gallantry and intrepidity in action while serving as a Scout with Company C, First Reconnaissance Battalion in action against insurgent communist (Viet Cong) forces in the Republic of Vietnam. Shortly after midnight on 16 June 1966, Lance Corporal Victor's eighteen man patrol was occupying an observation post deep within enemy controlled territory in the vicinity of Chi Tu, Quang Tin Province, when a Viet Cong force of estimated battalion size crept close to the Marines' position and, on a predetermined signal, launched a vicious attack with small arms, automatic weapons and mortar fire. Although knocked to the ground and painfully wounded in both legs by an exploding enemy hand grenade, Lance Corporal Victor reacted swiftly and rapidly fired his rifle into the advancing Viet Cong force, helping to stop the initial assault. Persistently refusing medical treatment until the more seriously wounded had been cared for, he continued to inflict casualties among the attackers. While gallantly holding his position as the Viet Cong attack gained momentum, he sustained additional wounds in his back from another hand grenade. No longer able to stand alone, he leaned against a rock and, in full view of the enemy, continued to fire with keen marksmanship. After submitting temporarily to emergency medical treatment, he bravely dragged himself back to his fighting position. Throughout the night, he ignored his own suffering and assisted in defending his sector of the perimeter against the savage enemy onslaught. His heroism and determination were instrumental in the successful defense of the position, and undoubtedly helped prevent the surviving platoon members from being killed or captured by the numerically superior enemy. Lance Corporal Victor's extraordinary courage, resolute fighting spirit and selfless dedication to duty throughout were in keeping with the highest traditions of the United States Naval Service.

> For the President
> V. H. Krulak
> Lieutenant General,
> U.S. Marine Corps
> Commanding

In the name of the President of the United States, the Commanding general, Fleet Marine Force, Pacific takes pleasure in presenting the SILVER STAR MEDAL to

Lance Corporal William Charles Norman
United States Marine Corps

For service as set forth in the following

CITATION:

For conspicuous gallantry and intrepidity in action while serving as a sniper with Company C, First Reconnaissance Battalion in action against insurgent communist (Viet Cong) forces in the Republic of Vietnam. Shortly after midnight on 16 June 1966, Lance Corporal Norman's eighteen man patrol was occupying an observation post deep within enemy controlled territory in the vicinity of Chi Tu, Quang Tin Province, when a Viet Cong force of estimated battalion strength crept close to the Marines' position and, on a predetermined signal, launched a vicious attack with small arms, grenades, automatic weapons and mortar fire. Throughout the savage nine hour battle, Lance Corporal Norman repeatedly exposed himself to the withering enemy fire to fire at Viet Cong who were attempting human wave assaults. As the Marines' supplies of ammunition were depleted, he courageously braved the hostile fire to gather and redistribute the ammunition and hand grenades of the incapacitated casualties. As the battle continued and the Marine force dwindled in size, Lance Corporal Norman demonstrated outstanding marksmanship and fighting spirit in defending an entire sector of the perimeter, forcing the enemy to withdraw from that area. Although painfully wounded, he fought valiantly throughout the night, contributing in large measure to the successful defense of the hill and helping to prevent the remainder of his patrol from meeting death or capture at the hands of the Viet Cong. Lance Corporal Norman's resolute fighting spirit, daring initiative and selfless dedication to duty throughout were in keeping with the highest traditions of the United States Naval Service.

> For the President
> V. H. Krulak
> Lieutenant General,
> U.S. Marine Corps
> Commanding

In the name of the President of the United States, the Commanding General, Fleet Marine Force, Pacific takes pleasure in presenting the SILVER STAR MEDAL to

Private First Class Joseph John Kosoglow
United States Marine Corps

For service as set forth in the following

CITATION:

For conspicuous gallantry and intrepidity in action while serving as a sniper with Company C, First Reconnaissance Battalion in action against insurgent communist (Viet Cong) forces in the Republic of Vietnam. Shortly after midnight on 16 June 1966, Private First Class Kosoglow's eighteen man patrol was occupying an observation post deep within enemy controlled territory in the vicinity of Chi Tu, Quang Tin Province, when a Viet Cong force of estimated battalion strength crept close to the Marines' position and, on a predetermined signal, launched a vicious attack with small arms, grenades, automatic weapons and mortar fire. In the course of the relentless enemy attack, Private First Class Kosoglow exhibited exceptional courage and presence of mind when he saw a hand grenade fall next to his wounded platoon leader, who was engaged in directing close air support on the platoon's only radio. Without hesitation or regard for his own safety, Private First Class Kosoglow leaped toward the grenade and kicked it away before it exploded. His unselfish act not only saved the life of his comrade, but also preserved the unit's only means of communications. Although he was painfully wounded by the murderous enemy fire, he courageously and successfully defended an entire sector of the defensive perimeter. His determined effort throughout the encounter were an inspiration to all who observed him and contributed in large measure to the successful defense of the hill. Private First Class Kosoglow's exceptional composure in the face of danger, daring initiative and unswerving dedication to duty throughout were in keeping with the highest traditions of the United States Naval Service.

> For the President
> V. H. Krulak
> Lieutenant General,
> U.S. Marine Corps
> Commanding

The President of the United States takes pride in presenting the SILVER STAR MEDAL posthumously to

Private First Class James O. McKinney
United States Marine Corps

For service as set forth in the following

CITATION:

For conspicuous gallantry and intrepidity in action with Company C, First Reconnaissance Battalion in the Republic of Vietnam on 16 June 1966. As a scout with the First Platoon, Private McKinney and the other seventeen members of his platoon were occupying an observation post on Hill 488 near the village of Chi Tu, Quang Tin Province, deep in enemy controlled territory. During the early morning hours a North Vietnamese force of battalion size launched an extremely vicious assault on their position. Because of the difficult terrain the enemy troops were able to creep close to the Marine forward elements and suddenly charged from their concealed location, employing intense small arms fire, automatic weapons, and accurate mortar fire. Private McKinney and his valiant companions withdrew under the hail of fire to nearby predesignated defensive positions and immediately engaged the determined enemy with accurate rifle fire and hand-to-hand combat. Aggressively and instantaneously, Private McKinney reacted to the desperate situation and courageously fired into the advancing horde until he was mortally wounded by an enemy hand grenade. By his heroic action and fighting spirit, he assisted in repulsing the first and most ferocious wave of the assault and thus enabled the beleaguered platoon to continue to withstand the onslaught of the enemy throughout the night. Private McKinney's initiative and fearless devotion to duty were in keeping with the highest traditions of the Marine Corps and the United States Naval Service. He gallantly gave his life in the cause of freedom.

> For the President
> Paul H. Nitze
> Secretary of the Navy

In the name of the President of the United States, the Commanding General, Fleet Marine Force, Pacific takes pleasure in presenting the SILVER STAR MEDAL to

Private First Class Thomas Glen Powles
United States Marine Corps

For service as set forth in the following

CITATION:

For conspicuous gallantry and intrepidity in action while serving as a grenadier with Company C, First Reconnaissance Battalion in action against insurgent communist (Viet Cong) forces in the Republic of Vietnam. Shortly after midnight on 16 June 1966, Private First Class Powles' eighteen man patrol was occupying an observation post deep within enemy controlled territory in the vicinity of Chi Tu, Quang Tin Province, when a Viet Cong force of estimated battalion size crept close to the Marines' position and, on a predetermined signal, launched a vicious attack with small arms, automatic weapons and mortar fire. Positioned at the time with a scout team which received the brunt of the attack, Private First Class Powles courageously stood up in the midst of the withering incoming fire to obtain a clear field of fire. Again and again, he fired his grenade launcher with devastating effect until he fell, seriously wounded in the abdomen. His determined and heroic effort contributed in large measure to the successfully defense of the hill against a numerically superior enemy force. Private First Class Powles' extraordinary valor in the face of extreme danger, relentless fighting spirit and unfaltering devotion to duty throughout were in keeping with the highest traditions of the United States Naval Service.

> For the President
> V. H. Krulak
> Lieutenant General,
> U.S. Marine Corps
> Commanding

Not sure what to read next?

Visit Pocket Books online at
www.simonsays.com

Reading suggestions for
you and your reading group
New release news
Author appearances
Online chats with your favorite writers
Special offers
Order books online
And much, much more!